Recreational
Witchcraft

Thank you to:
N for showing me the wonder of magic,
R for going down this journey with me,
E for seeing the potential in this story,
A for supporting me as I finished this book,
and R for all of your incredible feedback.

First published in 2022 by Liminal 11

Graphic Designer: Jing Lau
Editor: Eleanor Tremeer
Editorial Director: Darren Shill
Artistic Director: Kay Medaglia

Fleuron Font © 2022 MICKAËL EMILE
areminiscentsmile Font © 2022 Yoo Ji Hun

Printed in China

978-1-912634-45-3

10 9 8 7 6 5 4 3 2 1

www.liminal11.com

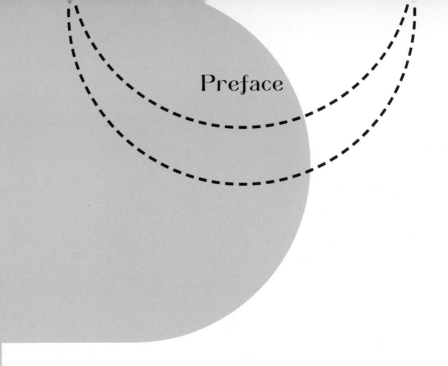

Preface

We've all been told stories about magic – about evil witches who cast curses on innocent princesses, or schools for precocious wizard children, or the corrupting influence of beautiful priestesses with long red hair and ruby necklaces. Perhaps your place of worship told you that witchcraft is an abomination, or maybe your spiritual leader explained that there's a difference between "good" magic and "black" magic.

Mostly we see witches who are old, ugly, female, and wicked. Witches are in the shadows, and on the margins. That's what makes them so terrifying – you barely even know they're there, and yet they're casting their spells anyway.

Outside the realm of pop culture, most people still have ideas about who among them practices witchcraft. You think back to the self-described Wiccan from your high school, or the man you met once who railed against the "Christianization" of pagan holidays.

Even the witches reading this come with your own prejudices and beliefs. *Moral witches don't curse. Natural is better. Love spells are wrong.*

But magic isn't just one thing, and a witch isn't just one type of person, archetype, gender, belief, ethnic background, or even set of abilities.

No. Witchcraft is for everyone.

In my opinion, there's nothing more off-putting than picking up a spellbook and reading in the first three pages that the author grew up doing magic as a child. Or that they come from an "ancient lineage" of witches. Or that witchcraft means following a particular religion with a series of precise steps and rituals.

When writers do this, they immediately cast the reader in the role of an outsider coming to the witch for guidance. These books frame magic as something elusive that can only be learned through decades of practice, or some genetic predisposition, or by spending lots of time with closed communities that probably don't even want you there.

But all of these stories about magic are false. They're about as true as the idea that witches live in gingerbread houses or go to hidden castle schools with other wizard children.

So instead, I'm going to tell a story about magic that is real – one that's filled with all of the mundane and shockingly normal aspects of witchcraft, and one that could give those fairy tales a run for their money.

Anecdotes about successful rituals, disastrous spells, and hair-raising scenarios were why I got into magic in the first place. They made me curious about what I was missing out on and made me wonder what my life could be like if I harnessed this secret knowledge. After I became a witch, these trusted first-hand accounts gave me insight that available magic books could not – or perhaps *would* not – give me.

I also want to inspire more people to become witches, and so I've written a guide that isn't so much about what you should *do*, but how you should *think*. I never found paint-by-numbers witchcraft guides particularly useful when I was getting started. I learned more from books and blogs that spoke to me at eye level. They were honest.

So instead, I've written the spell book I would have wanted when I started out. *Recreational Witchcraft* is focused on my favorite spells, interwoven with anecdotes and stories from my practice. For better or worse, all of these stories are true, and hopefully you can learn from my successes as well as my tremendous failures.

Unlike your typical witchcraft book, I'm not going to cover the whole spectrum of magical practices, and I'm not going to include spells on topics I never found useful. I'm not going to tell you *how* to practice, because witchcraft isn't about switching one set of rules for a slightly more alternative set of rules. Instead of droning on about the Threefold Law and how to pray to the Lord and Lady, I'm going to tell you about the glamours that made me look like a supermodel, how I wove my magic with mind-altering drugs, and the biggest curse I ever cast – which also turned into an accidental foray into blood magic.

Because the thing about recreational witchcraft is that there are no defined paths, and there aren't many limits. Witches were outcasts because they were people in charge of their own destinies, and they didn't need an institution to tell them how to shape their lives or the world around them. I believe that recreational witchcraft takes that spirit of wicked women doing what they want and makes it applicable today. You get to decide what's relevant and what's irrelevant. Whether you want to stage a full ritual or cast a simple spell over your morning coffee is your choice. And if you're missing an ingredient, or some tool is too rare or expensive, you have the power to change the spell as you see fit.

In this book, magic
is for everyone.
Especially you.

Contents

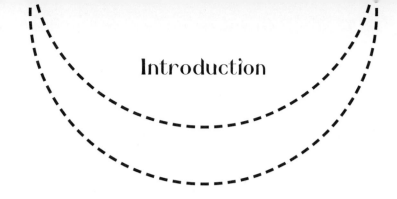

Introduction

I doubt many people picking up witchcraft books ask themselves "on whose authority" the author is writing, but it does beg the question – why listen to me?

I had an ordinary introduction to magic. I didn't discover any special psychic gifts when I was a child, nor did I turn 16 and have my grandmother teach me everything she knew about the occult. I'm not a high priestess of a prominent coven (or any coven, for that matter), and most people who know me have no idea I practice magic at all.

Instead, I became a witch as a young adult, with my best friend. We plunged into magic soon after starting university and so, with all the naive, unearned confidence of college freshmen, we naturally decided to run a blog together.

We lovingly named it *Recreational Witchcraft*.

For us, recreational witchcraft stood for choosing which rules did and did not apply to us and deciding how to integrate magic into our lives, while also serving as a not-so-subtle nod to our running dalliance with marijuana. We wrote in our About page that "witchcraft should be personal, sensitive, and accessible," and these are the tenets I still stand by today.

We started *Recreational Witchcraft* as a hobby to prove that we could create beautiful and entertaining spells. We knew the magic space online was missing something that so many other interests, pastimes, and subgenres already had – a readable, enjoyable, and aesthetically pleasing place to feel connected to another person (or in our case, two people).

Luckily for us, we were right about our gamble. Our efforts quickly evolved into the most popular witchcraft blog on our platform of choice. We had over 90,000 followers, post engagement in the tens of thousands, and we saw our spells spread to different social networking sites and across the internet. We received quite a bit of pushback for the way that we went about our magical practices, but we also received a ton of love and support. People were realizing that the way magic was being taught and talked about during the last 50 years was completely counterintuitive to the foundational beliefs of witchcraft – and we were lucky enough to ride that wave.

But nothing can last forever. Like many other digital phenomena before us, we burned hot and bright, made a noticeable impact on the community around us, and then faded out as quickly as we had begun.

For a long time, I was proud of our tiny legacy, but I also knew that I wanted to articulate more about witchcraft than I could in a 300-word post or one-minute video. The best stories and knowledge don't come from bite-sized pieces of content that can be consumed anywhere. Instead, they should transform the way you think, so you can apply their insights to other aspects of your life. This is what I've set out to do with this book.

Whereas *Recreational Witchcraft* the blog was about entertainment, community, consumption, and a bit of practical information sprinkled throughout, *Recreational Witchcraft* the book is a true guide to magic, with humor and stories woven in.

A Note on Structure and Terminology

Because many different individuals with varying levels of familiarity with witchcraft (and with me) may come across this book, it's important for me to give a couple of notes about how I've structured it and how I'll be using certain words over the next couple-of-hundred pages.

First off, I've written this book so that it can be understood by absolute beginners while still being entertaining and useful to more practiced witches. If you want to skip the introduction to magic and the theoretical foundations that I'll be referring back to, I recommend starting at Chapter Two.

In general, I recommend that you read what you want and leave the rest behind. (The stories in this book aren't told in chronological order, so you can read them as individual experiences about how I practiced during a period of my life.)

If something doesn't work for you, change it. If you don't like my recommendation, disregard it. You won't hurt my feelings by not following my advice (even if I've often written things that are in your own best interests to follow). Your practice is yours. Shape it how you see fit. Make it what you want it to be.

Pivoting to terminology, I'll continue to use the spelling of "magic" over "magick" – mostly because I think the spelling with a "k" looks ridiculous. And while I hinted at it in the preface, let me say explicitly that this is not a book about Wicca. Wicca is a religion where one prays to a God and Goddess, and these religious beliefs are imbued into all of the rituals and spells within the practice. If you are Wiccan, all the power to you. However, many spells and ideas in this book are not in line with Wiccan doctrine, so don't come to me and say that *xyz* spell doesn't follow the Rede – I know it doesn't. Consider yourself warned.

Finally, I want to add a note about gender and witchcraft. While I'll occasionally write about witches as "women" or use "she" as a stand-in pronoun, I strongly believe that magic is for everyone, regardless of gender.[11] I most regularly write "you" or "they" for this reason. In cases where I'm emphasizing the connection between women and witchcraft, it's because women were historically the objects of so much societal hatred and paranoia.

So now, with all of this out of the way, let's go all the way back to the beginning – to where this story really begins.

---

11   There is a deeply uninteresting debate that bubbles up now and then about whether men should use the terms "warlock" or "wizard," but this isn't something I'm at all compelled to weigh in on, and all the non-female people I've known in the occult referred to themselves as "witches" or "magical practitioners," anyway.

Chapter One: The Fundamentals of Magic

Meeting Rhea

y first interaction with magic was when I was fifteen. Normally I'd prefer not to write about the choices I was making when I was fifteen, but unfortunately for me, they're important for the purpose of this book.

It was the fall of my sophomore year of high school, and I was head-over-heels for a completely average guy named Luca. We shared a few classes, texted all the time, had precisely "okay" chemistry and a couple of common interests – the only issue was that he was in a three-year-long relationship with another girl in our year: Rhea.

Rhea was in a similar orbit to me. We both took advanced classes and were in the performing arts department, so although we went to a school with over 2,000 students, I saw her around campus regularly and had a pretty decent idea of who she was. She was also hard to miss, as she wore black clothing head-to-toe and had an especially sophisticated goth aesthetic for a teenager in the pre-Instagram era. And while I would've been loath to admit it at the time, she was also witty, captivating, likable, and beautiful.

To say that I was jealous of her was an understatement.

When I passed her in the hallways, my stomach would drop, and I'd brace myself like I was entering an arena. I'd try not to look at her – instead, I would don a wide smile and laugh extra loud at whatever the person next to me was saying – but inevitably, I'd always try to catch a glimpse of her face. I liked to believe that she was also trying not to look at me. Like my presence had caught her off-guard.

In the classes we shared together, I took note of what she was wearing and what she said. Her style seemed effortless, authentic, and cohesive in a way that I could only aspire to. When she started carrying her school supplies in a black leather satchel, it seemed so cool and yet so obvious. *Why hadn't I thought of doing that?* Whenever she made a thoughtful comment about a passage in our English class, it felt like a judgment on my own abilities. *She's right. Why hadn't I made that connection?* The longer I held this crush on Luca, the more my life was morphing into a zero-sum game where everything that Rhea possessed was something I personally lacked.

For months, I subtly hinted to Luca that I could be a better girlfriend than her – I'd be more fun, more understanding, more sexually available – and I even tried to sow some seeds of discord between them by flirting with him in front of their mutual friends. But nothing happened. It didn't seem to impact their relationship at all.

Right before the Christmas break, Rhea asked me if I would model for some pictures. She was an aspiring photographer and had taken photos of some of our other classmates to build out her portfolio, but I was surprised that she asked me at all. We weren't even friendly in our shared classes, let alone outside of school. Plus, I was sure that news of my overt flirting with her boyfriend must have reached her by then. It seemed like a trap.

That said, Rhea also mentioned that Luca would be there to assist on set – so I agreed.

Once I got to Rhea's house that weekend, she explained the set-up of the photoshoot she wanted to execute: Ideally, she wanted to capture me outside – in the middle of winter – while I was wearing a white nylon nightgown. On top of that, she had been to the Asian supermarket earlier in the day and she wanted to cover me in dead octopi.

The set-up felt like payback. Like well-deserved payback.

On the one hand, I'd certainly earned it considering how I had disrespected her relationship; on the other, I wanted to prove that I was game for her avant-garde ideas. *Go ahead, put dead octopi all over me. I'm cool, I can handle it.*

I tried to put on my least-forced smile and asked what we needed to do.

Surprisingly, the shoot itself went quite well. Rhea and I laughed about the different white nightgown options she owned: some were too sexy, others too matronly. It was uncomfortably cold (by Arizona standards), but I still felt glamorous. And having Luca carefully place tiny, dead cephalopods all over my exposed skin was just the right mixture of erotic and completely repulsive.

There was something disarming about how natural the flow was between the three of us. Most of all, I was shocked by how much I liked Rhea now that I was seeing her outside of class. Spending time with her felt *good*, even putting aside the fact that she was dating the guy I was interested in.

I left Rhea's house with the uneasy feeling that the photoshoot wasn't going to be the last time I hung out with her. So, the question was how I was going to reconcile that with my crush on Luca.

A potential solution came to me a few weeks later.

One of the nice things about winter when you live in a desert environment is that outdoor activities finally come around to your small corner of the world. For me specifically, this meant the return of the annual Renaissance Festival.

This was one of the only acceptable places to publicly mingle with the occult and not have anyone bat an eye. After all, we were all just pretending, weren't we?

I had passed by the Renaissance Festival's palmistry tents and stalls for tarot readers many times before. In those early years, I hadn't thought anything of them. For me, divination was something that eccentric people did to try and make a buck off the naive. Sure, there was always a slight pull to having these mystics read *my* future, but what would I say to them? I wouldn't know what to ask or where to begin.

And then there were the enchanted objects. If I looked down on the fortune tellers, then I held peddlers of supposedly magical objects in particular contempt. They reminded me of a time when I was younger: when I was curious about the world and desperately wanted it to be filled with magic as a fix for all the things I didn't like about my life. Thinking back to that time and that grand optimism made me wince.

That being said, desperate times called for desperate measures.

Rhea and Luca continued to date, and my crush was getting worse. My strategy to drive them apart had failed, and the photoshoot with Rhea had added another issue: I could no longer hate her, and I didn't want to do anything that would upset her (or at least, do anything that would make her upset with *me*).

So, there I was, at the stall of a vendor selling necklaces with funny symbols carved on them, trying to find something to finally end Rhea's relationship.

"What are these?" I asked, grazing the various pewter pendants with my fingers.

"They're called *talismans*," the salesman said with a big, overconfident smile. "They're magical necklaces, and each design holds a unique magical power." He went on to point out the placards next to each talisman that explained what it did.

I tried to look like I was nonchalantly browsing the different options until I stumbled upon what I was really looking for: a small, circular talisman that could purportedly break up couples. It had several abstract shapes on the front of it, and I could only make out the symbol of a hammer menacingly striking a nail. I bought it without a second thought and put it on immediately.

I wore the talisman every day for about two months. Then Rhea and Luca split up.

With the hindsight of someone who's successfully sent an evil spirit after her ex-boyfriend, waiting two months for a simple spell to kick in is pretty underwhelming. But at the time, it felt like the most amazing feat I could imagine. After exhausting all my practical options, magic had pulled off in a handful of weeks what I had failed to accomplish in six months.

This is certainly not the most empowering or flattering story, but I knew in that moment that magic was real. This one charm planted the seed for the magical journey I would later take.

So, what about me and Luca? (You are almost certainly *not* asking.)

Needless to say, the long-term outcome of this spell wasn't romantic bliss. I did date Luca for a couple of months after his breakup, but we weren't compatible, and he ended up getting back together with Rhea for a while – all of which was completely predictable from the type of charm I'd used.

But there is one more crucial outcome of this story: by the time our senior year of high school rolled around, our progressive, feminist politics pulled Rhea and me together as friends, and subsequently, best friends.

Perhaps most importantly, she also had an interest in magic, witchcraft, and the occult – and I wouldn't be writing this story if she hadn't come into my life.

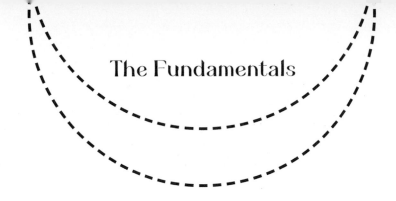

The Fundamentals

n a perfect world, your first spell is not a talisman to break up the relationship between your crush and your future best friend. At the same time, I refuse to believe that beginners are relegated to boring, rote spellwork until they can "level up."

When I was first starting out in magic, it felt like every blog post and book would state emphatically that the first three things to learn *before anything else* were grounding, cleansing, and protecting.

At face value, this is not bad advice. These three aspects of magic can give you a solid foundation for what comes next. Still, I found this advice condescending and completely ignorant of the reasons why most people get into magic. For instance, if I just wanted to feel more grounded, I could get into meditation. If I wanted to feel clean from the inside out, I could go to the sauna. If I wanted to feel protected, I could buy a gun (at least when I still lived in America). No, I wanted the guy I had a crush on to break up with his spectacular girlfriend and date me instead. And then, several years later, I wanted to unleash my wrath on someone who betrayed me and lived 1500 miles away. No amount of centering myself was going to actualize either of those desires.

And on some level, I just have a bone to pick with people who think that beginners can't accomplish any other magic before they've learned these basics. I'm much more in favor of an approach that takes beginners' limitations into consideration, but also gives them a wide variety of spells to test the waters with. Otherwise, you end up with bitter fledgling witches blood-bonding themselves together as their first spell.

This is all to say that I've structured this introduction to magic differently.

First, I want to start with a little exploration of the mechanics of magic. We need to know *what* we're doing and *why* in order to be confident spellcasters and magical rule-breakers. This will also give you a strong foundation in magical theory so that you're not dependent on spellbooks forever. Think about it like cooking: you could be reliant on cookbooks and recipes for the rest of your life, *or* you could take time to understand the basics of heating foods thoroughly, mastering salt and seasonings, and some of the basic chemical reactions needed for baking. Then, you can go back and break all the rules. Both options work – but this book is for the second type of person.

Next, I'll move on to an explanation of why I think grounding as a specific type of magical action is overrated. And finally, I'll close out with an overview of cleansing and protecting, and some common ways to cleanse and protect different items in your practice.

The Mechanics of a Spell

When you're just starting out, reading spells can feel like you're just looking at a list of nonsensical items paired with a series of ultra-specific steps to complete. (And after you look up the cost of the ingredients, it seems like an especially *expensive* list of nonsense items and specific steps.)

That's why I believe the first step of any decent magical practice is to understand *what* you're doing and *why*, rather than simply following easy spells others have written. Once you understand the basics, you can easily substitute and omit ingredients, change steps, or come up with your own spells on the fly.

Simply put: *The recreational witch knows how a spell works, and so she knows where she can cut corners.*

To help get you to that point, I'm going to break from my usual do-whatever-the-hell-you-want attitude for a few pages and wade into some magical theory.

The Philosophical Set-up

To understand what a spell is doing, first we need to think of what it means to change the environment around us.

I like to imagine the universe as a river, where there is a current of energy and events that slowly moves things forward. If you move *with* the direction of the flow, it is exceedingly easy to give the course of events a tiny push, and accelerate your preferred outcome. If you move *perpendicular* to the flow – changing things that might have stayed the same otherwise – you will feel some resistance, but it's not so challenging. And then if you want to move *against* the current, bringing about events that would not otherwise have occurred at all, it is technically feasible, but will require significantly more power.

If you follow this analogy, it's easy to see that magic is really all about *energy*. And the more energy a spell requires to be successful, the more complex it will be.

Magical Energy

Once you strip away the ceremony, lore, and ingredients, all magic boils down to energy. Really, these ritual elements and items are just there to help you summon and move that energy.

The most common types of energy used for spells are:

- Intention
- Ingredients (herbs, crystals, minerals, etc.)
- Entities (people, spirits, celestial bodies, etc.)
- Actions (ceremonies, incantations, etc.)

Many of these sources of energy positively influence the others, so it can be hard to say where one stops and another begins. Still, let's briefly go through each of these types.

Intention

Intention is easily the most important aspect of any spell – in fact, it's so important that it's the only component listed here that you can't do magic without.

In the most basic sense, your intention is just what you want the spell to do. However, when I speak in this book about "setting your intention" or "visualizing your intention," what I really mean is imagining what it would be like if your spell came to fruition. And yes, that absolutely includes conjuring an image in your mind of what it would look like, but it's not just about the visuals. Ideally, it should be rich with detail and involve as many senses as possible.

Let's take the example of casting a love spell (we can get into the ethics of love spells later, on page 161). You want to imagine that the object of your affection is also in love with you. What scene comes to mind? Are you in bed together? Maybe taking a walk somewhere? Are they smiling at you? What about their scent? Are they wearing fragrance? Can you smell the soft notes of their body odor? When it comes to sound: Can you hear their voice saying, "I love you"? And regarding touch, is their skin smooth under the gentle brush of your fingertips? Or are they covered in a thin layer of sweat from your activities together? (As for taste, I'll let you ask yourself those questions.)

When you fill your intention with this specificity, it carries a lot of momentum and energy. Even outside of witchcraft, there's a strong belief in intention in popular culture, and you're probably already familiar with it as the "law of attraction," manifestation, or even in certain types of prayer. If you were raised Christian, you might be familiar with the Bible verse Matthew 21:22: "If you believe, you will receive whatever you ask for in prayer." Meanwhile, if you were raised Hindu, you might be more familiar with the mantra 3.1.10 from the Mundaka Upanishad: "Whatever destinations and objects of pleasures, the man, whose mind is free from impurities, he obtains those destinations and those objects of pleasures."

And while I believe theoretically that you could pull off a spell with intention alone, let's look at some of intention's best helpers.

Ingredients

Besides incantations, ingredients are probably the top thing that comes to mind as essential components of a spell. When you think of traditional witches' concoctions, you probably think of something along the lines of the witches in Macbeth with their "eye of newt and toe of frog" ingredients.

Real magic is kind of like that, except I don't think I've ever used any animal body parts in my practice, and the specific ingredients in a spell are less prescriptive than people make them out to be.

Contrary to what you might have read before, I don't think that there's a specific vibration to rose quartz that makes it particularly suited to love spells, nor do I think there's something essential about lavender that ties it to relaxation and peace. Rather, I'd say that rose quartz's appealing pink color reminds many of us of love and beauty; therefore, it's easy to tap into this object's energy and send it towards the intention of love. Likewise, lavender has a known calming effect for most humans (and other mammals, for that matter), so it makes sense that most of us use it to represent these qualities in our spells. However, if you are allergic to lavender, I would strongly dissuade you from using it in your spells, not only for your own health and safety, but because I doubt you would be able to tap into this mental association and direct that energy into your magic.

This isn't to say that I don't use herb or crystal association lists – I actually use them all the time. (See my incredibly abridged association lists on page 69.)

So why would I choose to use them, and even provide them for my readers, if I don't think they're essential?

For one, I am extremely lazy. I'm not sure about you, but I don't have time to sit down and meditate on my true feelings about every plant's meaning to me. Sometimes I'm also looking to craft a spell on a more niche topic, and I don't want to wrack my brain for everything that I think would be good for that theme. I'd rather just pull up an association list and *command+F* my way through different key words until I find something reasonable.

Secondly, there *is* a power in sharing a belief about something with others. For example, if you were raised in North America or Western Europe, you probably subconsciously associate rabbits with springtime, fertility, and new beginnings. Not only is it easy for you to tap into this, but since millions of people would agree with you on this association, their shared belief adds weight and momentum when you do your spell. Now, if you were born in East Asia, you might associate rabbits more strongly with the moon, likely because you were exposed to different cultural folklore. Again, millions of people would agree with you. Neither association is right or wrong, but one will probably be easier for you to tap into than the other.

Entities

"Entities" is a broad term that I'm using to encompass anything that can project its own strong *energy + intention* combination. This includes (but is not limited to) people, spirits, deities, celestial bodies, ancestors, and demons.

What makes entities distinct from objects and ingredients is that they have their own willpower which can positively (and occasionally negatively) affect your magic. Casting a spell with someone else will almost always be stronger than casting one by yourself. Then, if you really want to up the ante, you can call in a non-human entity like a spirit, ancestor, or deity.

You might have also noticed that I included *celestial bodies* on this list, by which I mean the sun, moon, planets, comets, and so on. This would seemingly fly in the face of my earlier statement that objects don't have a specific energy charge, but I have two primary reasons why I put these in a different category: 1) So many religions throughout time have equated celestial bodies with gods that the line between them is now incredibly blurred, and 2) planets and stars are on a totally different scale to the piece of amethyst on your nightstand. A single solar flare from our sun gives off energy roughly equivalent to 2.5 million nuclear bombs exploding. The surface temperature of Venus can melt lead. Jupiter's cute red spot is actually a high-pressure storm that's twice as big as the planet you're on right now. That piece of amethyst is pretty, but it's not in the same league.

Celestial bodies also work slightly differently to other entities on this list. While you typically summon or invoke spirits and deities and then interact with them as you'd interact with a person, here you'll charge objects under the light of the sun or moon or conduct certain spellwork during a favorable planetary transit.

Just as a note from my side, I typically choose only to work with people and celestial bodies in the entity category. Why? Because the other types of entities are not really *recreational*.

Deities are usually high maintenance. Spirits can be good, bad, chaotic, or just weird, and therefore need to be verified before you work with them. Demons are *demons*, and as for ancestors, I don't have the time to talk to the spirit of my great-great-grandmother about my queer identity before getting down to business.

Still, you will probably end up encountering other entities during your practice, especially if you practice cursing (see Chapter Seven), so don't be surprised if you come across one.

Actions

Finally, we get to actions.

Some would (rightly) argue that my grouping of "actions" is woefully inadequate and should be broken down into a variety of subcategories. I would not disagree with these people, because this is a catch-all category for the energy sources that don't fall under the previous types.

When I say "actions," I mean anything you *do*, like a verb. If you *say* an incantation, that is an action. If you *bless* a piece of food and then *eat* it, those are actions. If you *draw* a warm bath and *enter* it, those are also actions. To make things a little sloppier, I'm also going to group in *burning* things, such as incense or dried herbs. Of course, the ingredient you're burning has its own association, but burning it and releasing the smoke unleashes additional energy.

So, why would actions add energy to a spell? It's not as if our current, mundane, daily actions are imbuing the world with magic.

In general, I believe that an action *plus* a clearly articulated intention is fundamentally different from doing something mindlessly. But each action also has its own unique properties related to creating energy or how we can direct it.

There are actions that physically relate to energy: For instance, burning something is a chemical reaction that literally releases energy. Likewise, eating something is an energy transfer from the food to you. Then there are actions that are more psychological or metaphysical: Saying something aloud – especially in a ritualized way, like swearing on a religious text, exchanging marriage vows, or clambering into a wooden box to confess your sins to a man who doesn't have sex – is significant to most of us. We consider a major action to have taken place, even though all we've done is said something aloud.

The Energy Equation

Now that we have a shared understanding of each of these types of energy, we can understand the mechanics behind a spell.

As stated before, every spell needs an intention. This is your foundation, and your magic will misfire if this aspect is not clear. But because your intention is probably not clear enough on its own, you will need to add ingredients, entities, and actions together until you have enough energy to change an outcome. (To use mathematical framing, your total energy needs to be *greater than* the momentum of the current trajectory.) Many of the spells in this book have multiple ingredients and several moving parts, because the more elements you combine, the more energy you typically add.

If I were to visualize this, it would look something like:

intention + **ingredients** + **entities** + **actions** > **current trajectory**

Unfortunately, rarely do we know at the outset what the current trajectory looks like, and therefore how much energy we'll need to change it. You could do some divination before crafting a spell to get an idea of how difficult something will be, but typically, I just wait until I cast the spell and see if I feel any resistance. From there, you can either add additional elements to your spell, recast, or simply shrug and say it's not meant to be.

Everything Can Be Substituted

At last, we should have an OK understanding of why we're doing what we're doing, which brings me to probably the most important mantra of the recreational witch:

Everything can be substituted.

Yes, everything! Don't have any sweet orange essential oil lying around? Try orange zest or orange juice instead. Run out of rose buds? Jasmine flowers can work in a pinch. Are you traveling and don't have access to your ingredients, but you'd still like to curse someone horrible on the airplane? No worries – just make a sigil (see page 81), which functions like a super-charged version of your intention.

The most important thing is that your intention is clear, and you have other sources of energy to tap into. If one part of a spell really isn't working for you, just try to understand what role it's playing and then figure out another way to get there. It will seem tricky at first, but once you have more confidence in yourself and your craft, it will become second nature.

Now, with all this background information out of the way, let's get to the basics of spellcasting.

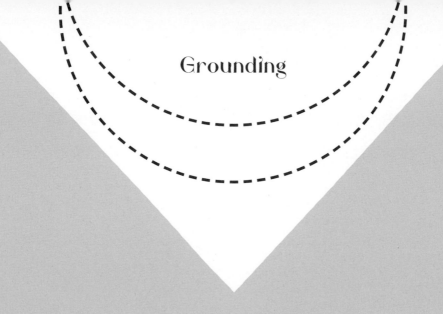

Grounding

ots of magical resources will espouse the benefits of grounding before engaging in spellwork, and as noted in the introduction, it's a fundamental piece of magic that needs to be mastered before moving on to other things. I'm not in complete disagreement, but I also think it's something that benefits some individuals more than others and shouldn't be written about as essential.

But first, we need to take a step back, because you might be asking yourself what grounding *even is*.

Unfortunately, it's not a straightforward answer. Why? Because there are two competing definitions of grounding: one which describes grounding yourself as a solely individual act (also known as *centering* yourself), and the other, which describes attuning yourself to the Earth's energy. My unpopular opinion is that these different actions are basically getting at the same thing – to feel calm, collected, and in the right frame of mind to do magic. Both definitions are also similar in practice, because they call for visualizing both the energy in your body and the process of moving it to different places.

As a refresher of the last section, casting a spell is more than gathering the right ingredients and saying the right words. It's about your intention, your confidence in yourself, and being in the right mindset to send this energy out into the world. That last part is where grounding comes in.

If you're getting ready to cast your spell but can't stop thinking about your horrible boss, or a late paper, or the fact that you keep putting off calling your mom, you won't be able to direct energy to the best of your ability. You need to be present in the moment, concentrating on your intention and believing whole-heartedly that your spell will work in order to pull off any type of magic.

Now, you *could* say "Yes, exactly," and then proceed to tell me that's why you envision your energy concentrating in your chest and do deep-breathing before starting spellwork. That's all fine, and I'm not here to convince you to stop.

However, I would counter that, and say there are a whole variety of ways in which someone can feel calm and collected. For me personally, that's the whole point of creating ritual spaces.

There's nothing inherently special about sitting in the dark with a bunch of lit candles and incense, but this type of space is often conducive to giving all of your energy and concentration to the matter at hand. I'm not thinking about my breakup when I am calling on the different elements to come to my circle. I'm not thinking about my late report when I sit in a hot bath filled with herbs and surrounded by crystals. These types of spells already take us out of the ordinary and into a different space, and so, in my opinion, it's not necessary to do extra grounding work.

More than anything, I'd just encourage you to check in with yourself. If you're feeling like your mind and mental energy are all over the place when trying to cast spells, then research some different grounding methods and see if one of them helps you. Otherwise, I'd recommend seeing how your brain reacts once you create a ritual space – you might not need this extra step after all.

Cleansing

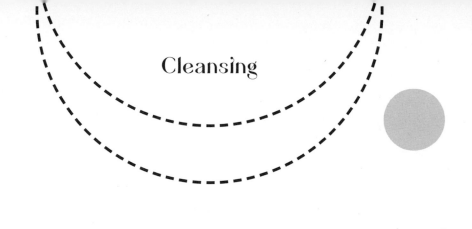

nlike grounding, you really do need to learn how to cleanse things. I'm not saying you have to learn it *first* (because I don't want to sound like a killjoy), but you probably should add it to your repertoire early on. It'll come in handy almost immediately, so it's better to get into the habit sooner rather than later.

While it's probably obvious what cleansing is, I'm going to spell it out and go into the background of cleansing so we're all on the same page. Cleansing is just the magical version of cleaning. As with mundane cleaning, cleansing can and should be performed on lots of different things, including (but not limited to) your space, your ritual items, magical ingredients you repurpose, new stuff you buy, and of course, yourself. Why? Because energy and associations build up on things over time, and it's good to periodically wipe the slate clean – just in case.

It's akin to germs on your hands. Sure, if you go out in public one day and touch knobs, handles, buttons, railings, your phone, strangers' hands, testers in stores, etc. and then come back home without washing your hands, statistically speaking… you will probably be fine. On any given day, you surely have something disgusting on your hands, but your immune system does a good job and you'll likely live to see another day. And yet, there's a reason why we're supposed to wash our hands after coming home: because one day, you might bring back something that is horrible and debilitating – and comparatively speaking, washing your hands is low-effort prevention. Cleansing works the same way.

For any given magical item that you're using or new tool you bring home, the energy attached to it is probably fine. More often than not, any lingering energy is neutral or even positive. But every now and then, something will end up in your space that has some seriously gross energy, and it's better to cleanse it right away than wait for something seemingly benign to fester into something toxic.

Plus, like showering and tidying up, cleansing yourself and your space often is just considered good magical hygiene.

With that brief intro in mind, let's take a look at some easy ways to cleanse your space, your things, and yourself.

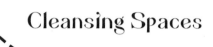

Cleansing Spaces

et's start with cleansing our spaces, because if you're just wandering into witchcraft, this is probably the section you might already be somewhat familiar with. This will also introduce a few methods that we can return to later for cleansing our objects and ourselves.

A Brief Word on Smudging

If you've encountered anything about cleansing your space, you're probably most familiar with smoke cleansing, or *smudging*.

The term and practice of smudging gets ethically convoluted pretty quickly, as it's an English term (duh) that was picked up by white guys to describe a variety of North American Indigenous smoke cleansing rituals and ceremonies. Then, they took that term, flattened it, threw it in New Age books, used it in their "Shaman" retreats, and made a ton of money off it.

Still, people really like cleansing their spaces (and things) with smoke, so let's break down a couple of the issues at hand and see what's salvageable and what's not.

First, the term *smudging* in New Age books is often discussed as being a "Native American practice," as if there were only one Native American culture and religion. That is patently false, as there are hundreds of Indigenous peoples from the Americas, each with their own unique cultural, linguistic, and religious practices. Rolling them all into one is reductionist and lazy.

Of course, the bigger issue is whether this is a closed practice that reopens historical wounds and continues harming people. Many people who casually cleanse with smoke do think the legitimacy of the practice lies in Indigenous people having some kind of special magical knowledge – and are totally fine with plucking out this one element from a myriad of Indigenous cultures. That is also deeply reductionist and lazy.

But that doesn't necessarily mean that you should stop wafting smoke throughout your home. As far back as we can tell, people from all around the globe, from Siberia to Scotland to Australia, have been burning herbs, woods, and spices in spiritual cleansing practices. These could be for religious purposes; to get high; to get in the mood for sex; to cure illnesses; or just to make rooms smell nice. There seems to be something in our little Homo brains that just loves the smell of pleasantly scented smoke.

In my mind, therefore, the issue with smudging can be broken down into four issues: 1) a general lack of respect for American Indigenous cultures and their unique differences; 2) assuming that Native individuals possess some kind of special magical powers rather than viewing them as real people; 3) feeling entitled to repurpose these Indigenous customs; and most crucially, 4) being ignorant of the real-world impact of the previous three points.

The popularization of white sage and palo santo really does have a negative impact on the people who've used it for centuries. Driving up demand means that price increases inevitably follow, incentivizing poor farming practices and even illegal harvesting. So, even if we put aside the cultural arguments, it's probably best to avoid using either white sage or palo santo in your practice (unless you're Native and that's part of ritual practices you grew up with, of course). If you want to try growing white sage in your own garden, I'll leave that ethical question up to you. Luckily, there are plenty of other herbs that are widely available and excellent for smoke cleansing.

Finally, let's loop back to the term *smudging*. As noted, the word itself is English, but at this point, it's commonly used to describe a variety of North American Indigenous smoke cleansing practices in academic literature and journalism. Meanwhile, in the magic community, it's recently become rather scorched earth because of its ties to the aforementioned white "shamans." For that reason, I'll be referring to this action as *smoke cleansing* for the rest of the book.

Cleansing with Smoke

Just because white sage and palo santo are off the table, it doesn't mean we don't have other great alternatives for smoke cleansing. The only thing you're really limited to is what you can buy or use in a stick format, for practicality's sake. When cleansing objects, you have more freedom in terms of technique, because you can also produce smoke from burning objects on top of self-igniting charcoal in a heatproof bowl. For cleansing a room, however, it's not very practical because the bowl will almost certainly become too hot to safely handle.

Popular alternatives include, but aren't limited to:

- Garden/common sage
- Mugwort
- Lavender sprigs
- Rose petals
- Rosemary
- Cedar

You can either buy pre-bound cleansing sticks (my preference) or, if you're more talented than I am, you can harvest, bind, and dry your own.

If either of these options feels daunting, but you still want to use smoke as part of your cleansing ritual, you can always fall back on using a stick incense with ingredients that align with your associations for cleansing. Copal, frankincense, and benzoin varieties are particularly well suited to this, but you can use whichever incense has a cleansing energy for you.

But *how* do you smoke cleanse your space? Take either your herbal bundle or incense stick and hold it to a flame until it starts to catch fire. Let it burn for a few seconds, then gently blow on it, watching to see if some initial embers are forming. If you can see some glowing red embers, blow out the flame – you should be left with a continual stream of smoke.

From there, take some small, lightweight object – such as a fan, palm frond, feather, postcard, or whatever you have lying around – and waft the smoke into the nooks and crannies of your space. (You might want to bring a small bowl with you to catch any falling bits of ash.) Walk around wafting the smoke until you've cleansed the whole space. How in-depth you are with your cleansing is up to you, but I typically cleanse until the space feels lighter and easier.

Cleansing with Steam

An underrated (albeit less practical) alternative to cleansing with smoke is cleansing with steam. Yes, it is difficult to transport steam around a room, and yes, I did just strike a method from the previous section for a similar reason – but hear me out. You simply don't know the joy of cutting up some herbs, throwing them in a deep pan of water, and letting them simmer for hours while making your home smell delicious and oh-so-rejuvenated until you actually try it.

Steam cleansing is just one variety of what we used to write about as "Stovetop Incense" on the blog. The basic premise is that, instead of drying out your botanical items and then burning them to create smoke, you use them fresh and simmer them in water to release their energies. I really enjoy this method because, while I enjoy smoke, steam is much more sensorily related in my mind to becoming clean – like taking a long shower or enjoying a sauna.

Here are a couple of easy steam cleansing combinations to try:

- Lemon slices, sprigs of rosemary, sprig of lavender
- Grapefruit slices, sprigs of rosemary, handful of fresh mint
- Lime slices, orange slices, sprigs of thyme

To cleanse with steam, simply slice up any fruit you might be using and briefly crush your fresh herbs in your hands to release their aromas. Set them in a deep pan and add a couple of inches of water. Bring to a simmer. Then, sit back, relax, and enjoy the pleasant steam in your home. Just be sure to top up the water in the pan if you want it running for several hours.

Obviously, this method is best suited to kitchen witches, those with open-floor-plan homes, and those with smaller homes, but it's also a nice cleansing option to run in the background if you're doing prepwork in your kitchen for other spells.

Cleansing with Oil Diffusers

The lazier but more portable option of steam cleansing is to use an oil diffuser with essential oils. This is also a great option if you're not feeling very open about your craft with others, because having a cute oil diffuser running in the background is going to raise precisely zero eyebrows.

Without getting into the technical details, there are actually several different types of diffuser, from ultrasonic vibrational ones to nebulizers to good old heat diffusers. Whichever type you decide to use, you can make it work for magic. The only thing to keep in mind is that some types have broader dispersal than others, so you might have to move your diffuser more or less depending on which type you have.

To cleanse with an oil diffuser, all you need to do is pick a few essential oils that align with your cleansing goal, and then use your diffuser according to its instructions. Once you feel that one room has been thoroughly cleansed, pick up your diffuser and move it to another room until the whole space is purified.

As always, you should feel free to experiment with what works best for you, but here are a few cleansing oil blends to try:

- ⌀ Thyme, lemon, eucalyptus
- ⌀ Peppermint, frankincense, lemon
- ⌀ Eucalyptus, peppermint, rosemary
- ⌀ Lavender, rosemary, cedar wood

Cleansing with a Spray Bottle

A popular way to cleanse that's popped up in the last decade or so is cleansing with a spray bottle. This method really blew up because of the number of witches on university campuses who couldn't have an open flame in their dorm room (and similar fire-banned residences), but it's stuck around because it's incredibly customizable. It's also another great option for the smoke-averse.

Essentially, you'd take ingredients that you'd use in other cleansing methods and add them to one spray bottle, fill the bottle with water, and spritz the mixture around the room. People often add fresh herbs, crystals, salt, and essential oils, but theoretically you can add lots of other items, too. That said, cleansing using the spray bottle method isn't as simple as throwing some herbs in an old plastic bottle, filling it up with tap water, and calling it a day. There are actually a couple of key factors to keep in mind in terms of materials, ingredients, and shelf life.

First, I strongly recommend using a glass bottle over a plastic bottle, because 1) most witches believe energy flows better through glass than plastic (see page 67), and 2) if you use essential oils in your mixture, they can be quite corrosive to many types of plastic.

Secondly, the liquid you use is important if you want the mixture to last more than a few days. Using tap water and fresh ingredients is a pretty fast way to start growing mold in less than a week, so ideally you should be using half distilled water and half witch hazel. You can also use a high ABV clear alcohol like vodka in lieu of witch hazel, but it'll be significantly less pleasant as an olfactory experience. To be safe, you should still store your mixture in the fridge to extend its shelf life.

Finally, be careful if you're using crystals that they won't dissolve, or worse, break down into toxic chemicals in your spray bottle. Crystals like selenite can dissolve completely in water, while the rare but beautiful stibnite can release a mineral called antimony, which is chemically similar to arsenic and lead, and is toxic to humans (this is also your daily reminder that "natural" does not equal "safe!").

Once you keep those things in mind, feel free to add sea salt, crystals, fresh herbs, essential oils, and other items to your mixture. Then, go around your space and spritz your solution until you feel the atmosphere is cleansed.

Cleansing with Herbal Infusions

The traditional counterpart to the spray bottle method is to make an herbal infusion. For this, simply take herbs associated with cleansing, steep them in boiling water for 15-20 minutes, and strain the herbs out. Now, you can walk through your space, sprinkling the mixture throughout, or you can add it to your mop water and use it to physically clean your floors.

Other Cleansing Methods

Of course, this is not an exhaustive list of methods, but merely the methods that I like and recommend to others. You could have other methods that work far better for you.

For instance, some witches will take their besom (a ceremonial broom) and go through their space "sweeping" the negative energy out. Others will use sound – with bells, drums, singing, a sound bowl, playing loud music, saying an incantation, etc. – to clear their space. Some individuals are partial to crystal grids, while others simply visualize the energy changing.

If you find that none of the methods that I've listed above really work for you, that's completely fine. Just search and tinker around until you find something that resonates.

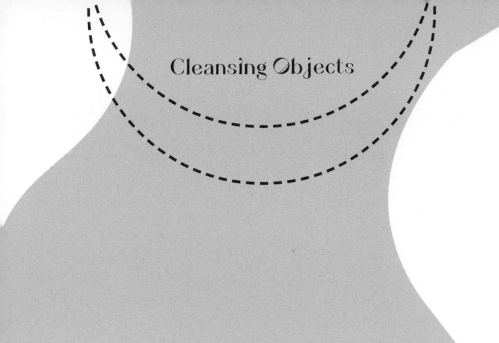

Cleansing Objects

 leansing objects is just as essential as cleansing your entire space. Especially when bringing new items home that you'll use for magic (and doubly true for anything used), you'll want to give them at least a quick energy cleanse.

The good news about cleansing objects is that you have all of the previously listed options for cleansing spaces, plus a whole new slate of methods to choose from at your disposal. Here's a quick overview of the most popular techniques.

Smoke Cleansing

Yes, our favorite but complicated cleansing method is back – but with an additional technique, if you're looking for more options. Of course, you can simply take a smoke cleansing or incense stick, light it, and pass your item through the resulting smoke – that is a totally valid and easy option for cleansing something.

If, however, this doesn't work for you, there's another option that works well for stationary cleansing. You can take a heatproof bowl, fill the bottom with sand and then place a piece of self-igniting charcoal in the middle. After lighting it[12], you can place a teaspoon of dried herbs, spices, bits of wood, and/ or resins on top to create smoke, then pass your items through it as normal.

This method is very customizable and easy, which is why I've included it, but there are a couple things to watch out for: 1) The bowl will probably be very hot afterwards, so plan on handling it with an oven mitt or something similar; 2) this option can produce a lot smoke depending on the ingredients you use, so when in doubt, do this outside or in a very well-ventilated space; and 3) some dried herbs can catch fire with this method, so have some extra sand on hand in case you need to quickly extinguish an open flame.

Submerge in Salt

A popular cleansing method that we haven't encountered yet is to submerge an item in salt. Salt is highly regarded in witchcraft as a robust cleansing and protection ingredient, and this method is as straightforward as it gets.

To cleanse using this method, just take out a bowl (or other container) and fill with salt. Then, take the object you want to cleanse and submerge it. Leave for somewhere between a day and a full moon cycle, then remove. You should probably discard the salt after use, as it will have "absorbed" any negative energy and shouldn't be reused (unless you purposely want to give someone a negative energy hex, in which case, you do you).

If you think this method is kind of boring and want to add more elements, feel free to experiment with different types of salt (e.g. black lava salt), adding in dried herbs and flowers, or even mixing in some baking soda, which some witches also use as a cleansing agent.

Obviously, this method works best for small items, otherwise it gets pretty pricey. Additionally, be careful which objects you submerge in salt, because not all of them will react well. For instance, porous crystals (like hematite and pyrite) can get damaged in salt, as well as many items made out of wood.

---

12   Using self-lighting charcoal has a bit of a learning curve. Essentially, you need to hold it with a pair of tongs, and then hold a flame to it for several seconds until it starts to crackle and burn. You might want to watch a tutorial online before you do it for the first time.

Saltwater Bath

Love the idea of submerging your items in salt, but not the idea of budgeting 10% of your income to cleansing? Then saltwater cleansing is the method for you.

In this method, simply dissolve salt into water and then use this water to bathe your tools. Easy-peasy. Practically speaking, there are a couple of things to keep in mind: 1) Salt dissolves better into warm water than cold, so I recommend heating your water slightly on the stove and then adding in your salt; 2) I don't use a fixed ratio of water to salt, but a couple of tablespoons for a medium-sized pot of water should be fine.

As with the previous method of salt cleansing, you have a wide array of options for personalization and increasing its potency. For instance, you can use different types of water, such as storm water (for an explanation of different types of water, see page 71), different types of salt, or add in additional ingredients.

Finally, you need to watch out for objects that this might not be suitable for. Several types of crystals react really poorly to water, and some to salt water specifically, so be sure to research the properties of your stone before using this method. Wood is another substance that will be both damaged by salt *and* water, and when in doubt, plan on also giving any metal objects an extra rinse in normal water after a saltwater bath.

Herbal Infusion

A close cousin of the saltwater bath is the herbal infusion. Here, instead of primarily relying on salt to do the heavy lifting, you use herbs to do the hard work for you.

To make an herbal infusion, gather herbs associated with cleansing (think basil, rosemary, marjoram, hyssop, mesquite), then bring a large pot of water to the boil. Remove the pot from the heat, and add the herbs to the boiling water. Let sit for at least 20 minutes, then strain out the herbs. You can optionally add a squeeze of citrus juice to increase the potency of the infusion.

Use the herbal water to wash your objects. As always, be careful not to use this method on items that are easily damaged by water, or citric acid (if adding citrus juice).

Other Popular Methods

Of course, this is not an exhaustive list – this is just a list of things I have personally used and recommended firsthand to others. Just to give you an idea of the other possibilities out there, here are some alternative methods you might regularly hear about:

- *Ø* **Cleansing with crystals.** Use specific types of crystals, either on their own or in grid patterns, to remove negative energy from items.
- *Ø* **Burying items.** It might seem a bit strange at first, but for this method, you take an item and bury it in the ground for two weeks to a month to remove its energy.
- *Ø* **Sound cleansing.** Use music, high frequency vibrations, chimes, singing, or other type of sounds to neutralize an object.
- *Ø* **Using moon phases.** Starting the day after the full moon, place your item outside where it can get moonlight on it. Keep it outside until the new moon, then consider it cleansed.

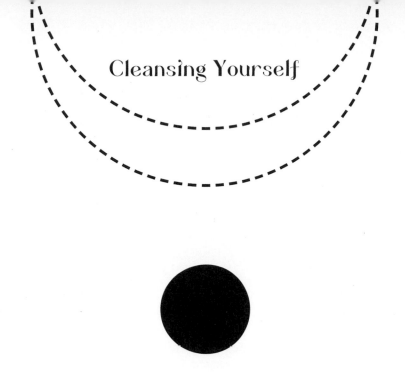

Cleansing Yourself

ast but certainly not least, it's also important to know how to cleanse yourself. At any time, you could be picking up lingering negative energy from your environment, but especially because you practice magic, it's essential to cleanse now and then. Spells can misfire, backfire, attract spirits or other entities, and on rare occasions, you can have negative energy purposely sent your way. Plus, to go back to the handwashing analogy from earlier, sometimes you just accidentally pick things up while going about your business. (Like finding a strange, headless doll in your AirBnB rental – how would you ever know if that's cursed?)

Luckily, I think cleansing yourself is actually one of the more enjoyable aspects of cleansing, and that's because you can easily wrap it into the normal self-care that you already do.

Cleansing baths are probably the best form of self-cleansing you can do, if for no other reason than you're submerging yourself in the mixture and combining it with something that makes you feel physically clean. I highly recommend the Cleansing Bath on page 216, but if you're in a pinch, throwing in a handful of salt and/or a cleansing herb can also work wonders. Need something more heavy-duty? Try bathing in an infusion of angelica instead.

And if you don't have a bathtub? Try making a salt scrub, such as either of the Purification Scrubs on page 150. You could also make an infusion and wash yourself with the water or pour it over your head. I also have suggestions on page 138 for taking pre-made bath products and charging them for your intended purpose.

Of course, cleansing baths and showers aren't the only option (even if they are the most enjoyable). I highly recommend making teas (from peppermint, sage, marjoram, and so on) or drinking crystal elixirs to cleanse you "from the inside out." For crystal elixirs, you're essentially just putting crystals in water and drinking said water, but it is crucial to pick the right crystals so that you don't accidentally poison yourself. Research every stone before putting it in water, and also be mindful that putting crystals in your water is a potential choking hazard.

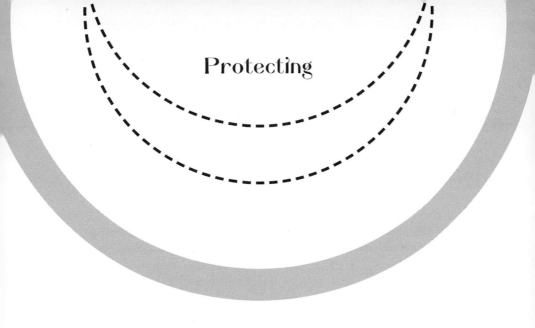

Protecting

ow that we've covered grounding and cleansing, we finally make our way to protecting. The purpose of protection spells is also probably a bit obvious, but let's go over it anyway.

Protection is an essential part of magic because once you've gone through the hard work of wiping the slate clean, you want to ensure that it stays clean for as long as possible. Again, this is generally good practice (think of it like maintaining energy boundaries, in addition to your physical and emotional ones). But especially when you're practicing magic, you have a higher risk of attracting unwanted wayward energy. Best to keep yourself protected – just in case.

In my mind, there are two ways to think about protection: 1) the cold, hard, spiky, and traditional view of protecting something, like a heavy suit of armor or a thick wall of stone, or 2) a soft, supple, more balanced view of protection, such as how oiling wood keeps it from being damaged by water, or how moisturizing the skin prevents it from cracking and developing infections. Typically, I prefer protection spells along the lines of the second sort, but occasionally, I'll lean on the first if I need to pull out the big guns. Therefore, most of the spells here are more in line with the second type of protection, but whichever option you gravitate toward is fine.

As with my previous suggestions for cleansing, you shouldn't take this as an exhaustive list of every possible way to protect something. The options for protection are nearly limitless – this is just an overview of the most popular methods with some of my favorites mixed in. You should interpret it only as a starting place for your own journey.

Protecting with Oils

Ideal for both people and things, oil is a great option for protection spells. Charge some coconut or flaxseed oil under the light of the full moon, then use it post-cleansing bath to protect yourself, massage it into tools, or dab a drop of it into each of the corners of your house to form a protective barrier to the outside world.

Protecting with Crystals

Even as a witch who's not particularly into crystals, I do love to protect my space with them. A variety of crystals are very well suited to protection, including (but not limited to) black tourmaline, black obsidian, pyrite, and jack-of-all-trades clear quartz.

To use, make a sigil (page 81) with your intention and set the stones on top of it for at least 24 hours, then place one in each of the corners of your home. You can use the same method and carry a stone with you to protect you when you're out and about.

Protecting with Plants

For the green thumbs among us, growing plants indoors or on your property is a great way to protect yourself (and is a very incognito option to boot). Great options for indoor varieties include aloe, basil, ivy, cilantro, and parsley.

Meanwhile, some outdoor choices include ivy, cacti, mint, lavender, rhubarb, sunflower, and moss. And for those lucky enough to have space to plant trees on their property, adding birch, juniper, elm, or lime all offer strong protection to your household and other nearby items.

Can't keep even the most basic of plants alive? You can also take dried varieties of any of the plants listed above and sprinkle a pinch in each corner of your home instead. In the same vein, you can carry dried herbs with you in a pouch to protect you outside the home.

Protecting with Witch Jars

Witch jars are a wonderful, magical option for the laziest among us – kind of like the witchy version of a one-pot pasta. The premise of a witch jar is that you take a glass jar (any shape or size will do) and fill it with various ingredients matching your intent, add a sigil for good measure, and then call it a day.

To make your witch jar geared towards protection specifically, I'd recommend starting with salt, then adding sand, a few dried herbs of your choice that you associate with protection (basil, cilantro, and lavender are all good options), and then finish with a large chunk of a protection crystal.

Other Methods

Of course, almost all of the methods for cleansing also work for protection with a couple of ingredient tweaks. For instance:

- **Smoke.** Follow burning garden sage and lavender with cedar or juniper, and your space will be cleansed *and* sealed.
- **Oil diffuser.** Swap your eucalyptus and citrus varieties for warmer scents like frankincense, cinnamon, and sandalwood to spread protecting energy throughout your space.
- **Stovetop incense.** Add cinnamon sticks, anise seeds, cloves, fresh ginger, and oranges to a pan and cover with water. Bring to a simmer and let the steam protect your space.
- **Floor wash / herbal infusion.** Take any herbs that you associate with protection and steep them in almost-boiling water for 15-20 minutes. Then add the mixture to your mop water or sprinkle throughout your home.

Chapter Two: The Lazy Witch's Toolkit

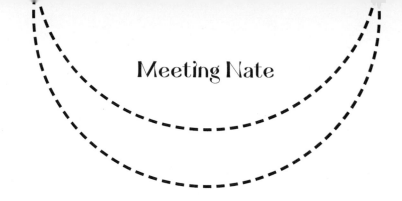

Meeting Nate

remember almost nothing about the first time I met Nate. I know which coffee shop we went to, and I vaguely remember where we were seated. But I don't remember what I was wearing, or whether we split the bill for our overpriced coffees or just one of us picked it up. I don't have a clue what we talked about, and I don't even think that I was particularly attracted to him during our short date. (I was actually worried I had misinterpreted our conversations because he seemed like he could have been gay.)

It was August, only a few weeks before my freshman year of college, and I had connected with Nate on social media after some nudging from one of my friends, Kaia. We had been in my childhood bedroom a few days prior, scrolling through our feeds and complaining about the prospects of finding partners that shared our progressive political beliefs.

"Ooh, you should date Nate," she said, coming across a post from him that was either an image of stark, modernist architecture or a frail white woman in lingerie. "I know him from Speech and Debate competitions, and now he goes to a liberal arts school out of state. I'd date him if I weren't already taken." She proceeded to show me some blurry pictures of him on his profile where he was surrounded by other young people who looked drunk and effortlessly happy. There was something about the setting of the pictures that signaled to me that these individuals were the children of rich, successful people – or otherwise raised to live a more privileged life than I was supposed to. At the time, it looked glamorous.

I started following him, and an hour or so later he followed me back. Soon after, he messaged me something about politics. Two days later, he gave me his phone number, and we made plans to briefly meet up at this coffee shop before he flew back to Portland, Oregon to start his sophomore year.

In hindsight, meeting Nate was surprisingly nondescript and common-place considering the number of events it put in motion. If you had told me then that less than a year later I'd be casting a curse against him that included accidental blood magic, I would have told you that you were out of your goddamn mind.

Despite the unspectacular first encounter, our romance started quickly picking up steam. We'd text every day and Skype once per week. He asked if I'd learn German with him and I happily obliged. We'd share our dreams with each other, and he'd affirm my aspirations to take over the world. I sent him lots of nude photos and he'd tell me how much he wanted me. We'd mail each other small care packages with things we thought the other would like. I thought about the future we could share if only we could be together in the same location.

He would also tell me about his friends and the interesting things they were up to while I spent my first semester alone in my dorm room. One of his friends in particular stood out to me: Tommy Bishop (we often spoke about him using his first and last name) was a year older than Nate and he featured in a lot of Nate's more interesting stories. Supposedly, Tommy came from a very wealthy family that also had a long history of practicing witchcraft. I didn't fully buy the story, but whenever Tommy popped up in Nate's texts, I knew I'd get an interesting account the following day about how they'd stayed up all night reading tarot by candlelight or ingesting strange, hallucinogenic herbs.

I thought about Nate all the time. With the long distance, I idealized him in my mind. I couldn't possibly imagine anyone more perfect: so intelligent, good-looking, sensitive, talented, knowledgeable, mysterious, funny, unique. Thinking about having sex with him triggered a desire inside me that felt like setting myself on fire. And perhaps most importantly, it seemed like he felt the same way about me. He told me he adored me, and in the moment, that felt like it was enough.

We finally saw each other again at the end of November – the weekend of Thanksgiving. He came and picked me up from my childhood home and we shared a kiss in the driveway that was (unlike our first encounter) very memorable. Whatever worries I had that our connection wouldn't pan out in real life quickly dissipated. We drove back to his parents' house, all the way on the other side of Phoenix, then went down to his bedroom in the basement and finally had sex.

This is where my informal education in magic really began.

Over pillow talk, Nate would brag about the wild things he'd done and theorize about how he thought the universe worked. He would tell me about how he and Tommy would stay up late into the night and read massive tarot spreads over the course of hours. He told me about how Tommy had taught him to make sigils, and how they'd take drugs and talk to deities.

The more I heard about it, the more intrigued I was with Nate and Tommy's adventures with magic. Nate never shared anything practical with me – it was always a brag about how scary or enlightening or unexplainable something was – but it piqued my interest. In those moments, magic seemed a boys' club that these two privileged people could engage in because they held secret knowledge, and I was just someone lucky enough to be in their orbit. Nate always talked to me like I understood what he meant, which I found frustrating because I didn't know what *The Hermetic Tarot* was or what it meant when he'd talk about being a "Cancer Sun," but I appreciated that he allowed me to save face.

I didn't pry too much because I wouldn't even have known what the right questions were to ask without exposing that I was totally clueless about esotericism. I don't even think that I shared my experience with the talisman – I just kissed him and let him keep telling me more stories.

Early in December, after Nate had flown back to Portland to finish the semester and I was back in Tucson, I received a text message from a woman who said that she was Nate's girlfriend. At first, I felt devastated, but Nate assured me that she was not really his girlfriend, but rather a jealous former friend seeking retribution for something else. The story barely held water, and his communication was sporadic over the following days, but I believed him because I wanted to believe him.

He came back to Arizona a few weeks later, after his semester ended, and we reunited. The rest of my family went to Washington to visit my stepsiblings the day after Christmas, so I invited Nate to spend the suspended time from the 26th of December to New Year's Eve with me at my parents' place.

We played house for a couple of days: having more sex, sharing more hours of pillow talk, going to dinner, and pretending to be a real couple. He'd wake me up in the morning with corny gestures, like tickling me and telling me: "You have a cuterus!" He spent hours telling me in painstaking detail about the story arcs in the *Halo* game trilogy, and we talked about the deeper meaning underpinning Don Draper's infidelity in *Mad Men*. He also shared even more details about his beliefs on magic, including his own history with Christian spiritualism growing up, and how he thought that the Archangel Michael protected him personally (he had apparently spoken with Michael while with Tommy on several occasions). Nate told me how his mother had taken him to see a mystic when he was younger, to tell him about his past lives and that he'd meet his soul mate in his mid-twenties. How in past incarnations, he thought he was likely a great spiritual healer, and perhaps his mother had previously been his lover.

All of the strange details and sporadic interests made Nate feel like a real person to me. He felt like an individual, like I was, and all of the peculiar stories just made me fall in love with him more. As we spent more time together in person, I felt increasingly sure that this was the person I wanted to be with, and I wanted the hollow security of a mutual agreement. We didn't even have to be exclusive – I just wanted to be recognized officially as a special person in his life.

Unfortunately, our label-less connection unraveled quickly the night of New Year's Eve. I went with him to a party at his friend's house, and between being introduced as a "friend" of his and feeling uncomfortable that everyone there was wealthier than I was, it clicked that our bond wasn't going to pan out. I asked him to take me home.

The drive back to my place was awkward as I ruminated over all the different things I wanted to say to him.

"You're never going to really date me, are you?" I blurted out.

At first, he said nothing, just glanced away and looked sad with his big Cancer eyes. Then, he gently shook his head. "No."

I pressed him for answers, but none of his answers felt satisfying. He said he couldn't do long distance, but things just didn't quite add up. We were two people who spent every day texting each other for hours and Skyping every weekend. We confided in each other, and we told each other we'd never felt like this with anyone else. Why not slap a label on it and call it a day?

Still, he held his ground, and I couldn't convince him to change his mind. We parted ways.

He went more easily than I did.

I didn't hear a thing from him, and he looked just as content as ever on social media. Meanwhile, I felt like a mess. I kept running our last difficult conversation in my mind, looking for some clue about what I was missing.

I went through his social media, painstakingly reviewing the accounts of everyone he followed and interacted with. That's when I stumbled on the account of the woman who reached out to me claiming to be his girlfriend. The first thing that stood out was how similar she looked to me. We had similar features, similar haircuts, similar style and a similar way in which we did our makeup. As I scrolled through her pictures, a cold, uneasy feeling spread from my shoulders down into the rest of my body.

The second thing that caught my eye was that even though she was supposed to be a spurned friend, he liked all the pictures she posted of herself. My stomach felt oily and like it was twisting itself into tight knots, so I dug deep into her archives until I could find proof of what my body was telling me. Two months previously, she posted something that confirmed my fears – a quote attributed to her boyfriend: "You have a cuterus! You have a cuterus!" Then I knew she had been telling the truth.

I called Nate, twice, in a rage, but he didn't pick up. Then, I went back into my phone and called the woman in question with the number she had originally texted me from.

When she first picked up, she was silent. Then she quietly asked: "Hello?" Her voice shook slightly.

I answered, "I'm not sure if you remember me, but you texted me a while ago because you found text messages between me and Nate. I just wanted to let you know that while he's been in Arizona, he's been seeing me for the last several weeks."

I don't remember the rest of the call or how long it lasted, I just remember that she sounded nice and very sad. And I remember feeling relieved that someone else was going to feel just as awful as I did for the foreseeable future.

Right after I got off the phone with her, Nate called me back. The only thing I distinctly remember was that when I answered, I greeted him with disdain: "You stupid son-of-a-bitch."

The Essentials

The thing about modern witchcraft is that, like most other things in our consumer-based society, the underlying message pushed out is that *more is more*. In some ways, this is true: Having a wide variety of herbs and spices (and a few jars of specialty dried flowers from your cousin's last trip to Japan) gives you more possibilities with your magic than if you have a bottle of Italian herbs and a plastic shaker of table salt. At the same time, this message is misleading and disheartening for those trying to get into witchcraft.

Before I get to work on taking apart this sentiment, I want to take a second to say that I don't think the whole witchcraft community is full of blood-sucking consumer capitalists. No, I think the space is largely comprised of pleasant and well-meaning individuals, but the incentives are wrong. I can speak from experience when I say that the online witchcraft space subtly nudges you to publish spells with rarer, specialty ingredients because it helps you stand out. Even if people are just publicly asking you where they can source a particular ingredient, that is typically helping you with Google's algorithm (or the algorithm of whatever social network you're using). Beautiful photographs filled to the brim with crystals, tarot cards, animal skulls, and other items are more eye-catching and shareable than realistic portrayals of your kitchen herb cabinet or candle wax-covered workstation. Even in witchcraft, everyone is competing in the attention economy.

Still, you don't need hundreds of different ingredients to be a real witch. In fact, I think it's quite the opposite.

Witches – at least in the last thousand or so years of the European tradition – have traditionally been those who didn't have much to work with and were some of the most marginalized people in a community. If you don't have a lot of material possessions or money, you'll fit right in with other witches throughout time.

I found witchcraft when I was in my first year of college, when I had essentially zero discretionary money, my home was a small room I shared with a stranger, and I wasn't allowed to burn candles or incense in said room. Trust me when I say that you can still do magic with all of these restrictions and more – you just need to think strategically about it.

To help you get started on that, I've laid out this chapter as an overview of different spell components, and in sections that are heavy on things you'd buy (e.g. botanicals and crystals), I've highlighted the most popular varieties within that category. You're not obliged to buy everything on those lists (gods know I only have approximately three types of crystals in my whole apartment), but it should give you a good idea of where to start so that you're not totally overwhelmed the first time you walk into your local herb shop or gem show.

I've also written a section about what you do and don't need to make an altar – if that's of interest to you – and a guide for how to make a lazy witch's best friend: sigils. And lastly, I'm going to end this chapter with how to substitute ingredients, because thinking on your feet is key to understanding the recreational witch's ethos.

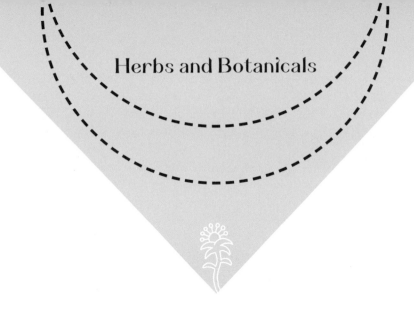

Herbs and Botanicals

ou might have already noticed the prominent position that natural botanicals take in witchcraft. They're one of the main components that I use in almost every spell, and – while I'm sure it's not impossible – I have a hard time imagining someone doing witchcraft without them.

At the same time, I am not a green witch (I can kill just about any plant) and this is not a book on botanicals or herbalism. The world is filled with hundreds of thousands of plant species, and we use a couple of hundred regularly in witchcraft. Associations differ from culture to culture and person to person. I personally believe I have more interesting ideas to convey to you than what people used a particular herb for 300 years ago – so I'm not going to do that.

Instead, for the purposes of this book, I'm going to share my top herbs, flowers, woods, and fruits that come up again and again, along with my associations for them. After that, I encourage you to find an association list, either online or in a book, that you like and resonates well with you. This will save you a bunch of mental work, and you're no less of a witch for using an association list. (I strongly believe that my brain has better things to keep track of than all the different magical associations for comfrey or ragwort.)

I also encourage you to develop your intuition if you haven't already. If you're gravitating towards using some flower in a spell, there's probably a good reason why. Most of the time, it works out well. Plus, most association lists are based on European herbs, and I think it's worth trying to use as much of your natural environment as possible. If you don't live in Europe or a place where European herbs grow well, you can do your own research and follow your intuition to make the most of your local environment.

With this preamble out of the way, let's go through some of the most popular botanical ingredients and their associations, so you have an idea of where to start.

Herbs & Spices

- **Basil**. Ideal for protection, purification, and luck. In a pinch, basil can stand in for almost any herb in a spell.
- **Cayenne**. For witches who like to obey the rules, cayenne is good for "repelling negativity," but for the witch who makes her own path, it's even better for banishing and cursing.
- **Cinnamon**. Like basil, cinnamon is another multi-purpose positive ingredient. It's well suited for luck, success, protection, love, and strength.
- **Cloves**. Best used for protection and banishing but can also be used for lust and general "positive energy."
- **Mugwort**. This is the only "specialty herb" I've added to this list, and that's because it's perfect for divination and astral travel, which are key subject areas for most witches.
- **Peppermint**. Well suited for cleansing and healing spells, but also works well for sleep and dream magic.
- **Rosemary**. Another great herb for purification and healing, but also aids mental abilities, such as memory and intellectual pursuits.

Flowers & Fruits

- **Chamomile**. Best suited for relaxation and reducing stress but can also work as a gentle cleansing ingredient. Brings luck.
- **Bergamot**. This is an ingredient I almost exclusively use in essential oil form, but it's a very strong luck and money stimulator.

- **Jasmine.** Very powerful both for drawing deep love and aiding in divination.
- **Lavender.** Like basil and cinnamon, lavender wears many magical hats. It's well suited for protection, peace, relaxation, love, and aiding in the healing of mental issues.
- **Lemon.** A very strong ingredient for cleansing and purification but can also work well in some love spells, too.
- **Orange.** A good choice for love spells, but especially those of the long-term (read: marriage) variety. Specifically, good for bringing happy partnerships.
- **Rose.** Unsurprisingly, this is yet another good floral addition to love spells. That said, roses can also work well for close friendships and healing spells.
- **Ylang ylang.** This is another ingredient I use exclusively as an essential oil, but it's perfect for glamours to increase your attractiveness and your sexual persuasiveness.

Woods

- **Cedar.** Traditionally seen as a more "masculine" spell ingredient, and thus often used to increase strength, success, and confidence. Also works well for cleansing and purification.
- **Juniper.** Well suited for healing, as well as generally attracting positive energies. Historically also used for spells to increase male potency.
- **Pine.** Very powerful ingredient for cleansing and grounding. Can also be used for success, growth, and new beginnings.

Depending on the item, its availability in your location, and the type of spell, you can use these botanicals fresh, dried, ground, as essential oils, as incense, or in any other medium you come across. Throughout this book, I've specified which form a botanical ingredient should be in for each spell, but you often have the flexibility to change things as you see fit.

I also need to take a brief break from my laid-back, recreational witch attitude because I have another axe to grind with parts of the modern witch community. I implore you to do your research when using any plants or herbs that aren't regularly used in cooking (and even some that are, in cases where you're using them in particularly large quantities). For those who are pregnant, nursing, have blood sugar issues, a history of seizures, are allergic to other plants, or have another acute medical condition, herbs have the potential to be *just as physically impactful as they are magically powerful*. Again, just because something is natural does **not** mean it is inherently safe.

Throughout the course of this book, I've tried to note when an herb has a common risk or side-effect, but to be safe, you should always do your own research to verify that you personally won't experience any adverse reactions.

As a separate but related note, you also need to be careful when using essential oils. Even though your aunt or high school best friend might sell them through an MLM, essential oils are ultra-concentrated forms of herbs, flowers, and other botanical ingredients. One medical article explains that although essential oils are pure in a chemical sense, they are volatile even when used normally. They can cause serious skin irritation if not dosed correctly or if you use them topically without a carrier oil. To be on the safe side, you should always dilute essential oils in a neutral oil, like coconut, grape seed, or almond oil.

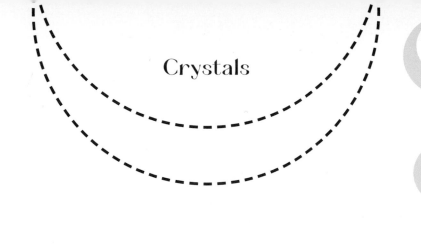

Crystals

To be totally honest, I'm not really that into crystals and I only use them occasionally in my practice. That said, I'm writing a book on witchcraft geared towards Millennials and Gen Z, so it would be a bit strange not to write anything about them here, as crystals are a key aspect of the modern witch aesthetic.

Of course, crystals are very pretty, and they look absolutely stunning on an altar. But for those who incorporate crystals more regularly in their practice, they can be used to charge other items, cleanse or protect spaces, bring a certain vibrational energy to a space, and of course, for their impact on people if they're carried or worn.

For the purposes of this book, I've included them as optional items to improve the potency of particular spells, or otherwise kept them as decorative additions. Still, in case you're more into the idea of crystals than I am, here's a brief overview of the most popular varieties:

- **Amethyst**. This crystal is well suited to calming your nerves and helping to regulate your emotions. It also helps with opening yourself up to psychic visions and improving divination.
- **Black tourmaline**. Well regarded for its ability to protect spaces and people, black tourmaline is also often sought out to absorb negative energy.

- **Clear quartz.** The jack-of-all-trades of crystals, clear quartz is most often used for cleansing, protection, and charging other crystals, but can act as a substitute for many other crystals in a pinch.
- **Citrine.** This crystal is ideal for bringing positive energy to yourself and others, such as confidence, happiness, motivation, and creativity.
- **Hematite.** A powerful crystal for grounding, hematite is also sometimes used for concentration, stress relief, and other types of mental regulation.
- **Jade.** A gentler crystal, jade is a calming healer and a stone that subtly brings out good fortune and happy friendships.
- **Moonstone.** This is a crystal for enhancing intuition and psychic abilities but can also stand for new beginnings and romantic love.
- **Obsidian.** This is another strong protection stone but is also well suited for grounding and giving someone confidence in dark times.
- **Rose quartz.** As the crystal for all things love, it's ideal for romantic love, close friendships, self-love, and increasing empathy for other people.
- **Selenite.** Promotes clarity, harmony, finding one's purpose, and attracting divine energies (if that's part of your path).
- **Smokey quartz.** The mysterious cousin of clear quartz, this crystal is said to diminish negative thoughts, depressive feelings, and help dispel general negativity.

As I wrote at the end of the section on herbs, it's important to note here that just because crystals are natural does not mean that they are inherently safe. Do your research before putting any of your crystals in water, both for the long-term integrity of the crystal and for your own safety. You should assume that all crystals ending in -*ite* are not safe to add to water or put anywhere in your body – many of them can seep lead, arsenic, lithium, asbestos, and other toxic substances.

Even crystals that are part of the quartz family (which also includes amethyst and citrine) can be toxic if you're cutting them, smashing them, or handling them in a way that causes them to break and send tiny bits into the air. They're rich in silica which, if inhaled, can cause silicosis or permanent lung scarring.

In short, always double-check how to handle your crystals, and never assume that what you're about to do is perfectly safe.

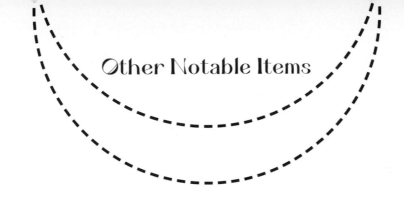

Other Notable Items

Although nothing in witchcraft is strictly necessary, there are some types of items that come up again and again. Personally, I think it's worth considering having these items on hand, just because it'll make your life easier in the long run.

Candles

Witches love candles. The stereotype is true – for better or worse – and we just can't help ourselves. Besides their dreamy, dancing flames, atmosphere-enhancing glow, and extremely flattering light, they are regular supporting characters in spells.

Many of the spells in this book are recommended to be done by candlelight. It's not that anything will break if you cast a spell in daylight or with artificial lighting, but it's certainly easier to get into the right mood with candlelight, and the energy from the candle will add extra *oomph* to the spell. Plus, you can get bonus energy for your spell by matching the color of the candle to your intention. You can also do things like carve symbols, sigils, or words into candles and then let them burn to activate the spell's intent.

I personally try to keep a variety of candle shapes, sizes, and colors around my home at all times, just in case I need to whip a few out for an impromptu spell. If you can't burn candles where you currently live, that's also fine. You can invest in electric candles to set the right mood for spells or skip them altogether.

Incense

Incense is slightly more contentious than candles (because smoke is polarizing), but most witches also love incense casually burning in the background and during spellwork. Incense is doing for the olfactory sense what candlelight does for the visual: it's creating an atmosphere that is conducive to ritual work and is adding energy to your practice.

In many of the spells in this book, I recommend a particular type of incense that goes well with the spell's intent, but in reality, it's just a suggestion. I recommend keeping a couple of incense types that you really love around your home; only if you're doing something really important and/or energy-intense should you go and buy something more specific.

Like candles, if you can't burn incense in your current home, there are alternatives. You can use an oil diffuser to replace the scent, or stovetop incense to replace the scent and foggy atmosphere (from the resulting steam).

Mortar & Pestle

If you're regularly working with herbs, spices, salts, or are into making powder spells (see Chapter Three), it can be really handy to have a mortar and pestle in your arsenal. For one, they're just practical – there are times when you'll want to grind your ingredients down into smaller pieces or a fine powder, and mortar and pestles are perfect for that. Secondly, they are great for magic as well, because you can visualize your intent while you grind it down, imbuing the mixture with this extra energy.

I bought my mortar and pestle from a culinary store a few months after I started practicing witchcraft, and I've never looked back.

Divination Tools

While I'll talk more extensively about this in Chapter Ten (which is entirely dedicated to divination), I recommend to anyone practicing magic that they find a divination tool that they like and trust. If you've never heard of divination before, it's essentially just a fancy term for fortune telling or foretelling the future.

In real-life magic, people typically use tarot decks, oracle decks, or a pendulum over the more pop culture-famous crystal ball scrying (although crystal balls are a real thing), and there are many other options available (see page 319). Whatever you use, the purpose of having a reliable divination method is that it's often prudent to check for further information before or after casting spells. Sometimes, there are roadblocks that we can't anticipate, or we've cast a spell on someone else and can't watch it materialize, so we can use our divination tools to check on the spell's progress.

On top of the practical considerations, most people who do magic just find divination fun to do. I highly recommend tarot: it's a great party trick to pull out and running your hands over a beautiful tarot deck will almost always make you feel better.

Glass Containers

At least since the New Age movement came to prominence in the 1970s, the recommendation for those who practice witchcraft has been that you should store everything in glass and stay away from plastic. I'm going to mostly recommend the same, with a few caveats.

The traditional logic is that glass allows energy to "pass through," while plastic forms a hard (and artificial) barrier that stops energy flow. Without diving deep into the physical makeup of plastics and what that would mean for our metaphysical theory of magic, I think that this paradigm has held up pretty well in my experience. I do mostly store herbs and other small items in glass jars and bottles, but that's also because it looks cute as hell. I use plastic, meanwhile, for a couple of odd reasons. For one, sometimes you actually want to "lock" the energy into an object, as I did when my ex was sending back items from our relationship and I wanted to preserve his energy on them for the curse I was planning. I also use plastic when glass wouldn't be practical due to size considerations, e.g. when storing rain water, or when I'm just feeling lazy and there aren't any clean glass containers on hand.

In order to save money (and cultivate that eclectic look, if that's your thing), I recommend going to thrift stores, charity shops, and flea markets to find your glass containers. There are all kinds of very cute glass jars, bottles, and other storage options available on the cheap. If you're extra short on cash, I recommend going to flea markets or yard sales, where you can haggle with vendors and practice your negotiation skills. (Asserting yourself and stating clearly what you will and won't accept is a skill that will come in handy both in magic and in your daily life.)

Other Common Associations

You might have picked up by now that associations are an incredibly important aspect of magic – we're essentially building patterns and complex symbolism to form spells, and these associations make up the constituent parts. We've already covered some of the most popular types of spell ingredients and tools, but here are some other fairly common associations that will pop up in spells again and again.

Moon Phases

In the current societal paradigm, we typically see witches operating by night and casting their spells in darkness. Of course, this is quite a limited view of witches, but it does also hold some truth: Most spells I've cast have been performed during the night, and this holds true for lots of other magical practitioners. One related aspect of this is that most witches I've known have felt some sort of reverence for or kinship with the moon.

Of course, celestial bodies of all sorts can be important to witches depending on their cultural background and interests, but the moon is probably the frontrunner for community favorite. Besides being the dominant body in the night sky, the moon is also thought to represent the unseen, unconscious, and emotional desires, and traditionally is the more "feminine" counterpart to the sun. Even putting weird gender essentialism aside, it's pretty cool that the moon operates on a 28-day cycle, just like the menstruation cycle.

Now, besides being cool as hell, witches often like to use this cycle to time their spells and charge objects with specific intents. Here's an overview of the best way to maximize each stage of the moon cycle.

Full Moon

Obviously, this is the stage of the cycle when the moon is at its biggest, most-revealed stage and is fully round.

This is generally the most powerful stage of the cycle, and if possible, it's best to execute your biggest spellcasting undertakings on this night. It's also good for healing, protection, and strength. If you're trying to work with prophecies or do any major divination, this is another ideal type of spellwork to do at this stage.

Waning Moon

The waning moon is the period of time between the full moon and the new moon, a.k.a. the days during the cycle when the moon is becoming smaller and smaller.

This stage is perfect for spellwork where you're trying to *decrease* things, such as slowly banishing a toxic person from your life or doing cleansing work. It's also a good stage for using divination to examine a set of circumstances, like a post-mortem on a spell or understanding a set of recent events.

New Moon

The new moon is also known as the dark moon, and this is the stage where the moon is not visible (or is hardly visible) to the naked eye.

The new moon can be a great time to set intentions and for new beginnings. It can also be an ideal time to engage in "darker" aspects of spellwork, like curses, bindings, and banishings. It can also be a good time to explore the hidden parts of ourselves and our unconscious desires.

Waxing Moon

Finally, there's the waxing moon, or the period of time after the new moon up until the full moon.

This is the perfect time to conduct spellwork where you want to *increase* things, like money, success, love, confidence, strength, and so on. It's also a good time to continue manifesting intentions that you set at the new moon, so that hopefully they come to fruition at the full moon.

Charged Waters

One spell ingredient that gets less attention than the others I've touched on so far is charged waters. These are either waters charged by specific celestial bodies, or different types of precipitation that we collect for magical uses.

You can then take these waters and add them to your spells to increase particular types of energy. Not only is this ingredient often strongly magically charged, but it's also essentially free, which makes it a great option for witches without a lot of financial resources.

Moon Water

In the simplest sense, moon water is just water put outside on a clear night and charged by the light of the moon. Moon water is good for generally increasing the power of a spell, and more specifically for spells requiring intuition, subconscious desires, and hidden truths.

That said, you can also dive deeper and create moon water for each of the phases; then that water would pick up qualities related to its specific phase. For example, full moon water would be ideal for increasing abundance, while waning moon water would be a great addition to a cleansing bath.

Witch tip:

If you love the idea of timing your spells to the moon's phases, but don't love waiting up to a month to cast a particular spell, invest in making a large batch of moon water for each of the four phases when you have spare time. You can then use this water in the future to tap into a specific phase's energy.

To make moon water, take either an open container (like a bowl) or a clear glass bottle and leave it out during a clear night, so the moon can imbue the water with its energy. In the morning, take the water inside and ideally store it in a glass container until you need to use it.

Solar Water

The magical "opposite" of moon water is solar water (or sun water), and just like its counterpart, this is simply water that has been charged outside in the sun. Not only is it a nice addition to generally increase the power of spells, it's also especially good for adding warmth to relationships, increasing abundance, and cultivating success.

On the surface, it might seem that solar water has fewer options for customization and refinement than moon water, but you'd be surprised. One thing I always do is charge solar water during the solstices and equinoxes in order to extract extra significance from those holidays (see Chapter Eight on Sabbats to read a longer explanation of those days and their associations). You could also charge solar water according to the time of day, so that you'd end up with dawn water, day water, dusk water, and so on.

To make solar water, follow the same steps above that you'd use for moon water. If you live in a hot place, I'd recommend using a closed, clear glass bottle instead of an open bowl to minimize evaporation.

Rain Water

Unlike moon and solar water, the next varieties of charged waters are actually collected from your environment. Rain water is the simplest form of these waters, as you just put a bowl outside when it's raining and collect what falls inside.

Rain water is best for spells about growth and cleansing, or for anything that is tied to your personal associations with rain. For instance, as someone from the desert, rain is a special and happy occurrence, so I'd use it in spells for healing and emotional regulation. If you hate rainy days, you might use it in banishings.

Storm Water

Storm water is just another variety of rain water (you probably saw that coming) – except in this case, it's water collected from a storm. In my experience as a self-proclaimed storm witch, I find that this water is a bit trickier to collect than rain water. For one, many places rarely experience thunderstorms, and if they do happen, it's only during one time of year. Secondly, the increased wind makes it physically more difficult to collect the water.

Regarding the first issue, if you're serious about collecting storm water, you need to put in a bit of work. If your area sporadically experiences thunderstorms, you should figure out the time of year when it's most likely to happen. During that time, have a receptacle (or several) ready to set outside on short notice, and plan to set it out whenever there's a decent chance of rain. (Do not wait until it's already raining to set your bowls outside, otherwise you will spend at least a couple of storms when you're away from home irritated and disappointed to have missed your window of opportunity.)

As to the second issue, I recommend using a heavy bowl and setting it on the ground or in another location where it can't get knocked over or fall. It can be pretty disappointing to go outside after a massive storm, excited to see how much water you've collected, only to stumble on an upturned, empty bowl.

In terms of its uses in spells, storm water is an excellent power enhancer, and is perfect for anything related to strength, courage, banishing, or protecting.

Snow Water

The fluffier, more seasonal cousin of rain water and storm water is snow water. Unlike the first two, this one is much easier to collect. As long as it sticks, you can simply go outside after it's been snowing and scoop up the snow from the ground. Once you've done this, you can either let the snow melt and then store it at room temperature, or you can keep the snow in your freezer until you want to use it.

Snow water is well suited to glamour spells, purification, and bindings.

Stream/River Water

As common sense would dictate, this type of spell water is just water collected from a river or stream. Ideally, this should be from a place that you find soothing – perhaps a place where you go regularly to relax or go on hikes – and you should store it in a glass bottle until you use it.

This last type of water is best for cleansing, as well as any spell that is action-oriented or needs to be sped along.

And of course, there are other waters that you can collect as well, like dew water or ocean water, which each have their own associations. Just keep in mind that you should be careful about which waters to ingest (depending on pollution levels in your area), and which ones should be used right away. You don't want to keep ocean or river water sitting around your home for too long, as it could have organisms living in it that might want to grow.

M y unpopular opinion for this section is that having set color associations is short-sighted and culturally naive. How two different cultures view any one color is influenced by a multitude of factors, and there is no "one true association" for any given color. For instance, in the United States, where I'm originally from, green is commonly associated with money because our paper currency is green. In Europe, where I live now, green is much more wrapped up with climate change, the environment, and leftist politics. Neither is right or wrong – they're just different.

Still, colors are an easy way to shove more energy into a spell. I would encourage you to tap into your own associations for each color, but if you're really feeling uninspired, here are some popular connotations:

- ⊘ **Red**. Power, anger, caution, passion, love, heat, and negativity in financial and business matters.

- ⊘ **Orange**. Warmth, happiness, fun, energy, autumn, originality, and creativity.

- ⊘ **Yellow**. Solar events, fun, joy, happiness, youthfulness, and abundance.

Colors

- 🍃 **Green**. Nature, the Earth, growth, calm, and good luck.
- 🍃 **Blue**. Calm, peace, tranquility, communication, intelligence, water, cold, and professionalism.
- 🍃 **Purple**. Wealth, nobility, intuition, and psychic abilities.
- 🍃 **Pink**. Love, romance, self-love, healing, nurturing, understanding, queerness, and acceptance.
- 🍃 **Black**. Protection, night, justice, death, sophistication, positivity in financial and business matters.
- 🍃 **Brown**. Earth, practicality, hard work, stability, honesty, and tradition.
- 🍃 **White**. Peace, cleansing, purifying, sterility, innocence, and blank slates.
- 🍃 **Gold**. Success, wealth, abundance, decadence, and luxury.
- 🍃 **Silver**. Technology, modernism, wealth, success, and new ideas.

Do You Need
an Altar?

t doesn't take long when reading a traditional book on Wicca before the author typically mentions that you'll need to start building an altar. In their defense, having an altar can be incredibly useful when doing certain types of rituals, but how necessary is it for the recreational witch to have a standing altar set up?

In my humble opinion, not very necessary.

Just to reiterate, Wicca is a *religion* that includes modes of worship; this is separate from witchcraft, which is simply a *practice* without a defined belief system behind it. If you're Wiccan (or another type of pagan) and are actively giving offerings or performing rituals in the service of deities, it might be useful to have a standing place in your home dedicated to this. For everyone else, I would suggest understanding the tenets of an altar so that you can build one on short notice if you need one for a ritual. Otherwise, you can take it or leave it.

Most traditional Wiccan books will list the following as necessary items for an altar:

- God and Goddess statues
- God and Goddess candles
- Pentacle
- Bowl of salt and/or other earth element
- Bowl for water
- Chalice
- Cauldron
- Incense
- Athame
- Candle (separate from God and Goddess candles)
- Wand
- Candle snuffer
- Optional: an offering of food

Let's go through these one by one to touch on what their purpose is in Wicca and whether you'd need them. And if having an altar seems a bit much for you, then don't worry about it. It's totally feasible to spend time casting spells that don't require an altar and never feel like you're missing out.

God and Goddess statues: In Wicca, these objects help you dedicate your altar to these two deities, who are the primary source of power within the religion. They essentially represent the duality of divine masculine and feminine, but unless you're a practicing Wiccan, you don't need them. In fact, it would be weird and probably inappropriate to have them if you weren't worshiping them.

God and Goddess candles: Same as above.

Pentacle / Pentagram: This symbol has a surprisingly complex and convoluted religious history for something that is essentially a star that a five-year-old could draw. Depending on your particular magical philosophy, each point on the pentagram can represent an aspect of spirituality, or the entire symbol can represent protection. But without getting into the weeds, many pagans and Wiccans use the pentacle similarly to how modern Christians use the cross – as a sign of affiliation. If this object has some meaning to you, by all means use it. If not, don't worry about it.

Bowl of salt and/or earth element: If you aren't worshiping a deity, the easiest things to dedicate your altar are to the elements. (And, as Wicca shows, you can dedicate your altar to the elements *in addition* to deities. It's not an "either/or" scenario.) Using salt is the simplest way to do this, but you could also use soil, crystals, stones or numerous other alternatives. I would say this particular item, along with the other elemental representations, should be considered necessary unless you'll be dedicating your altar to something else. But don't fret: Simply go into your kitchen, grab a cute bowl and dump some salt in it.

Chalice: A chalice is essentially a glorified wine glass. If you want to drink something during your ritual, you should have some kind of receptacle on your altar to make that happen. Some people also use the chalice to represent the water element here, but you can easily substitute with a bowl filled with water.

Cauldron: If you want to burn something in the course of your ritual, you'll need to have a fire-safe dish in which to do that. It could be a cast iron cauldron if that's your thing, but you can also use another fire-safe dish you have lying around in your kitchen. If you're not burning anything, it's not necessary.

Incense: As mentioned earlier in this chapter, *witches love incense*, but there are alternatives to incense if you can't use it. In rituals that involve an altar, incense is playing two roles: 1) to represent the element of air, and 2) to add energy to the spell through whatever you're burning. If you just want to substitute the air element, grab a feather, or pick an herb associated with air. For adding energy, you could likewise burn a candle or use an oil diffuser.

Athame: An athame is essentially just a fancy, ceremonial knife that you don't actually use to cut anything. Instead, you use it to direct energy, as with a wand. Never once have I felt that I needed one in my practice, so you probably won't either.

Candle: As with incense, witches love candles. It just kind of comes with the territory. That said, these can also be substituted with herbs, crystals, or other items to represent the element of fire.

Wand: This can also represent fire (especially if you're doing tarot work), but I've also never used a wand in my practice. I still associate them with my days as a child playing with a fake Harry Potter wand, and now I can't ever take them seriously. If they help you direct energy better, though, more power to you.

Candle snuffer: There are two ongoing debates about candle snuffers. The first is about magic: Long-running tradition holds that blowing out a candle with your breath scatters the energy everywhere, which some people like, and others consider heresy. Customarily, people use snuffers to calmly diffuse the energy in place. As to the second debate: Some people like the smell of smoke to proliferate throughout a room, and others prefer a more confined smoke trail post-candle. I am pro-snuffer (for both energy and smoke reasons), but it's honestly not that important and certainly not a hill I'm willing to die on.

Offering or other food: If you're not worshiping any deities, then you certainly don't need an offering. That said, eating or drinking small amounts of food during magic is a blast, especially if you're going to the full effort of casting a circle or doing a full ritual – you'll be surprised by just how tired you can get afterwards. Magic is draining! Meanwhile, some of the most fun you can have is setting up your space like you're about to do some serious magic, getting half-naked, casting a full circle, invoking the elements, and then just chilling in said circle eating bread and drinking wine. The space feels very charged, and it's nice to take a couple of minutes just to hang out and snack.

All About Sigils

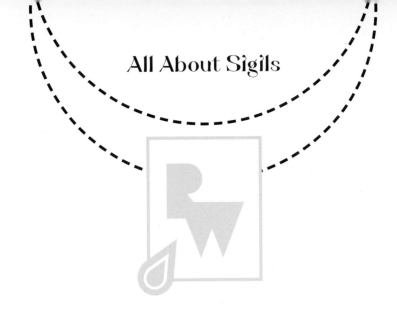

Sigils are truly a recreational witch's best friend, so if you walk away with only one piece of knowledge from this book, I would want it to be how to make a sigil. All the other spells in this book are certainly interesting, fun, and make for excellent party stories – but you could basically do away with all of them in favor of a really good sigil.

What is a sigil?

When talking about modern magic, a sigil is simply a symbol that represents our intention. We then charge this symbol to manifest what we desire.

If you think back to my section on the mechanics of a spell (page 22), I wrote briefly about how intention is the one part of a spell that is not optional. Sigils are essentially a distilled version of that intent, plus a quick burst of energy to send it in the right direction. And because they're so adaptable and comparatively low energy, you can use them on their own as well as add them to other spells, keeping your intent on track and all the moving parts in sync.

What types of magic are sigils good for?

Sigils are good for almost any type of spellwork you can imagine, from simple luck charms to little hexes you'd like to send to your hellish neighbors. If you write your intention clearly and charge it well, you can use it for more complicated spells too, but most of the people I know use sigils for easy magic. It can take less than 10 minutes to create a sigil, charge it, and get rid of the remnants, so it's perfect for something you want to execute quickly and then forget about again.

The other primary way in which witches use sigils is to support more complicated spells and rituals. Have a love attraction jar but want to give it a little extra *oomph*? Set a sigil with a love attraction intent in the bottom of the jar. Casting a curse and want to make sure it hits the right person? Turn your target's name into a sigil and use it to dedicate a poppet. Baking a magical pie for your partner's parents so they warm up to you more? Create a sigil and inscribe it in the pie crust before baking to ensure your intent is crystal clear. I could suggest a hundred more ideas, but you probably get it by now.

Sigils are small and relatively inconspicuous, so they're easy to add and adapt to your needs. If you're asking yourself, "Could I use a sigil for this?" the answer is almost always "yes."

How do you make a sigil?

There are undoubtedly dozens of ways to make sigils – each with their own benefits and drawbacks. That said, I learned precisely one method for making sigils and it never led me astray:

1. Write out your intention on a piece of paper. It should be present tense and positively formulated. For example, *"My home has a calm and relaxing atmosphere,"* or *"The woman sitting in 28A experiences continued travel delays and irritations this week."*

2. Now, go through and cross out all of the vowels in the sentence. Using the first example from the previous point, you'd be left with: M Y H M H S C L M N D R L X N G T M S P H R

3. Pass over the sentence again, this time crossing out any letters that repeat. Using the same example, you'd be left with: M Y H S C L N D R X G T P

4. Take these letters and form them into one shape together. In my experience, it can take a few attempts to create a shape that you're happy with, so don't be afraid to start over until the sigil feels right to you.

At this point, the sigil is technically done, but you'll still need to charge it for it to accomplish anything magical. Sigils have a long history of use, but they became particularly popular thanks to the Chaos Magic movement of the '70s-'90s. In Chaos Magic lore, sigils must be charged and then destroyed, and preferably forgotten about completely. Other magical practices (and some particularly argumentative Chaos mages) take an alternative approach to sigils, with some practitioners opting to keep them in full view on a daily basis, so your intention can keep charging them.

Honestly, there's no hard-and-fast rule, but charging a sigil is definitely the most important takeaway. And there are lots of ways you can do that.

How do you charge a sigil?

Probably the best-known (and my personal favorite) way to charge a sigil is to burn it, but luckily there are many other ways to charge a sigil if burning isn't possible. Here are a few other alternatives:

- Write the sigil in water-soluble ink and let it dissolve in water, vinegar, wine, or another liquid.
- Leave it outside for the sun or moon to charge.
- Charge it with a crystal matching your intent.
- Carve it on a candle and let it burn down or melt away in the wax.
- Write it in oil on a cooking pan and then heat it up.
- Look at the sigil and focus your energy on it until it blurs in your field of vision.
- Trace the lines of the sigil with your sweat after an intense workout (you can do the same with sexual fluids post-orgasm).
- Anoint it with an oil you've charged to be sacred or powerful.
- Write it on biodegradable material and bury it when you're planting seeds.
- You can even place it under your phone while it's charging. (This works even better if you can set it on top of a wireless charger.)

These are just a few ideas that I like and recommend, but there are dozens of other options if none of these suit your needs. Just keep in mind that some of these methods destroy the original copy of your sigil, so you might want to make two copies, depending on how you're planning on using it.

Everything Can Be Substituted

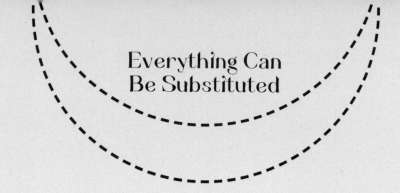

ow, before I send you out into the rest of the book, I want to add one last caveat.

Over the course of the following chapter, I'm going to share with you a series of spells that each call for a variety of ingredients. The ingredients required for the spells you want to do can be incredibly overwhelming, especially when you're starting out. You might ask yourself how someone can afford to keep 15 different types of essential oils and an assortment of crystals on hand at all times. Over the course of a couple of years, you'll naturally build up an impressive toolkit, but I want to reiterate here that none of these ingredients are necessary in order to do magic.

For this reason, I want to double back to one of my assertions from earlier: *Everything in magic can be substituted.*

Think of magic as more akin to cooking than baking. Baking is *chemistry* and things will quickly go awry if you make too many substitutions and don't follow the directions. Cooking, meanwhile, is about trying to reach an end goal (i.e. getting energy into your body) and making it tasty along the way. Sure, swapping dill pickles for sweet pickles will definitely change the flavor of your dish, but it'll still give your body energy and satiate your hunger.

When I'm explaining a spell in this book, I'm detailing the best version that I can think of to set you up for success – but if you're allergic to roses or don't feel like going to the store to pick up more basil, you can always swap out the ingredients for something you have on hand.

Now, let's take a look at how this works in practice.

How to Substitute Ingredients

If we revisit the "equation" in Mechanics of a Spell that I wrote on page 27, you'll recall that for every spell, we're combining our intention with ingredients, energy from other entities, and ritual actions to create enough momentum to budge things from their current trajectory towards our end goal. This is how I visualized it:

intention + **ingredients** + **entities** + **actions** > **current trajectory**

(Obviously, we're just looking at this second section here, but the premise also applies to substituting energy from entities and ritual actions.)

If you think back to that same chapter, I talked about how most ingredients get their power from your belief in them and the connotations large groups of people give them. If you follow this simple concept, it's easy to find substitutes.

Let's take my Goddess Glamour Bath spell on page 194 for example. I originally wanted to use ylang ylang essential oil for this spell, because I knew it would make me more sexually persuasive and attractive. Unfortunately, I didn't have ylang ylang on hand, so I went with jasmine absolute instead. I could have just as easily used lemon verbena essential oil or a pinch of powdered ginger, or anything else that stuck out to me as something that could work to boost my attractiveness. So long as you know what this ingredient is supposed to be doing, you can find a similar ingredient and swap it in.

The only big things to watch out for here are times when it might change the physical composition of the spell. For instance, if I wanted to use orange juice instead of orange essential oil, I would want to add at least a teaspoon of juice to make up for the lost potency of an essential oil. And because that could have a spillover effect, I would also need to see if that changes the consistency of the spell and adjust accordingly. It seems difficult at first, but if you try it a few times, your intuition will often take over and send you in the right direction.

Chapter Three: Limited Witchcraft

Finding Witchcraft

n the days and weeks after I stopped talking to Nate, I felt slow, heavy and weak. I didn't understand how I could feel so empty and yet weighted down at the same time – like my blood sugar was low and I was desperate for anything that would take away the shakiness. I probably would have taken his affection and shoved it down my throat like a sugary granola bar if he had offered it to me.

It would've only been a short-term fix, but a fix nonetheless.

Instead, he offered that fix to his girlfriend in Portland. It made sense: She lived in the same city as him, she interacted with his whole social group, she was even a resident in the dorm where he was a Residents' Assistant. Meanwhile, our relationship was isolated, conducted primarily through a phone. I didn't live where any of his other friends lived, but rather in a decaying town 30 miles from the US-Mexico border. Objectively, there was a lot more to be gained from reconciling with her than from reconciling with me.

Still, it felt personal. For one, she and I had promised that neither of us would take him back, and the two of us sharing our pain was the one brief silver lining to the whole horrible experience. It didn't matter that I also would've accepted him with open arms if he came groveling back to me – the fact that she did was a personal failing on her part. I refused to see it any other way.

And so, the heaviness and the emptiness compounded.

I would lie on Kaia's bed in her childhood room while I cycled first through feeling sad, then indignant, then furious, then the quiet stillness of nothingness. And then the cycle would start all over again.

There was nothing to keep me busy – I didn't have classes, or a job, or any purpose at all – and so the days melted into each other, one after the next. It didn't help that Kaia, Rhea and I would stay up late, smoke weed, get donuts in the middle of the night, watch the sun rise, and fall asleep only after our adolescent bodies finally gave out from exhaustion.

It was my lowest, saddest point in a decade – but I had to fall this far to find my craft.

I was in Kaia's clawfoot bathtub late one night, soaking in the warm water and telling her and Rhea about some of the ridiculous-sounding pillow talk I'd had with Nate.

"Can you believe that he went to this psychic woman and she told him in a past life that his mother might have been his lover? I don't know what's worse: that he actually believed her, or that he told *me* about it."

The two of them laughed. Then Rhea asked, "Do you think any of it's true?"

I paused. "I don't know. He told me about these tarot sessions that he and Tommy would do, and the crazy things that would happen. I believed him when he was telling me."

"You know," Kaia started, "my mom used to have a tarot deck around the house. I bet I could find it."

We all lit up with the possibility of a mini adventure – something to do that wasn't listening to me cry or go on about Nate. After I got out of the tub, we helped Kaia search the house, but unfortunately, we couldn't find the deck anywhere. We pledged to go out looking for one the following day.

The search the next day set us off on a course through several local establishments. First, Kaia insisted we try the local hippy smoke shop, but they just sold incense, pipes, and overpriced ugly clothing. We all bought some incense and left.

Next, we walked down the street to a small herbal apothecary, which seemed thematically closer, but again, no tarot deck. Still, we bought some divinely scented rosemary bath salts on our way out.

"What about the used bookshop?" Rhea suggested. "They sell all kinds of weird things."

So, we drove across town to the used bookshop. It was there that we stumbled upon several large shelves filled with books on magic, the occult, and New Age religion. Each of us picked up a different book and started thumbing through it, reading aloud when we came across something particularly funny or interesting.

And that's when it hit me. As I read about the same themes and practices that Nate had told me about, the idea finally materialized. "I think *we* could do this," I announced.

Kaia and Rhea both stared back at me, blankly.

"I mean, I think we could do magic. I think we could actually do it *better* than Nate and Tommy ever did. We have all of this information right here, in addition to what Nate told me."

We all smiled.

At the end of that day, we did not end up finding a reasonably priced tarot deck, but we did walk away with several used books on witchcraft, a bunch of incense, and some lovely bath salts that we were determined to use in a ritual. More importantly, we finally found a purpose in those last long, excruciating days during the winter break.

From that point on, our descent into magic quickly started picking up momentum.

A few days later, we were back at the used bookstore and devouring its section dedicated to witchcraft, magic, and the occult. Sometimes, if we could afford them, we'd buy these books, but mostly, we spent our time in corners of the shop reading as much as we could over the course of a couple hours before leaving empty handed. We'd make it a habit to go into any strange herb shop or alternative medicine shop we'd pass on the street, and strike up a conversation with the salesperson. Sometimes, we'd learn something useful or interesting; sometimes, we'd run into someone who believed the spirit of Walt Disney lived in the crystal grid in her shop.

Looking back, it felt like this period lasted months, but the majority of our initial research only lasted (at most) a couple of weeks. Mere days previously, our overabundance of time had been a curse, but now it was a blessing: no jobs, no classes, no children or family obligations – just time to read, share ideas, laugh, and smoke weed.

During this time, we also started visiting a rundown mall on the other side of town. At one point, it had been a bustling shopping center with an IMAX theater and several popular department stores, but since the Great Recession, it had mostly been taken over by outlets. Conveniently for us, many of the boutiques had also been replaced by dinky New Age shops selling cheap crystals, white sage, and other trinkets that were within our price range.

It was at just such a shop that one of us had come up with the idea for our very first spell: We'd purchase three matching crystal pendants and then *blood-bond ourselves to them and to each other* so we could officially be in a coven together.

While I'm sure others have done stupider first spells than this, I haven't met any of them yet.

Even though we had read that blood-bonding should only be used sparingly (and I'm *sure* there were warnings not to do this type of magic as a beginner), we felt convinced that our friendship would last forever. There was something deceptive about the intensity of our friendship – we conflated the depth of our emotions with how resilient they would be in the long run. Plus, we were about to start classes again soon, so we wanted to do something special to kick off our new lifestyle and keep our connection strong across the 100-mile distance.

We held the ritual at Rhea's place since she had the most space (and a bathtub). We started by drawing a hot, cleansing bath with the bath salts purchased from the local herbal apothecary and then bathing, one by one. Then, we sealed the energy with sweet almond oil and lay on Rhea's bed naked until we had all cleansed ourselves. Following this, we poured out a full salt circle on Rhea's bedroom floor; cast a circle with the four elements; carved our name into three matching black candles; drew blood; and used said blood to bond ourselves to each of the three crystals. Then, whenever we'd wear the crystals, we'd keep a piece of each other with us at all times.

Despite being a rather complex and totally reckless first foray into magic, the spell itself actually went off without a hitch. We basked in the happy glow of our ability to pull off something of this magnitude, and then split off the following day to go back to our respective universities and separate social circles.

Unfortunately, it didn't take long for the first signs of our magical naiveté to start manifesting.

With the benefit of hindsight, I'm a firm believer that blood magic has a funny way of working – and it's more complicated than simply intensifying a spell or tying yourself to something forever[13]. I've found that, much like receiving a blood transfusion from someone with a different blood type, blood-bonding with someone you're not meant to be with long term can result in a very adverse reaction.

Less than a month later, it became obvious that Kaia was not as into magic as Rhea and I were.

Rhea and I would send different spell ideas in our group chat, exchanging mood boards, sharing blog posts from the online witch community, and suggesting ways to modify their ideas for our personal use. Kaia, meanwhile, stayed mostly silent. While Rhea and I tried to pin down a date for our next in-person magical gathering, Kaia started dating a cute new girl and couldn't carve out the time to see us. As time passed, it became clear that Kaia was less interested in witchcraft than what it could do for her "dangerous woman" personal brand.

Writing about this with the distance of many years, I should have been more understanding of Kaia and her standpoint, but at the time, it felt like just one more betrayal in a series of betrayals. Nate had led a complete double life, his girlfriend couldn't keep a simple promise, and my best friend would rather see her new flame than find a few hours to do something with me.

Rhea and I talked about it over the course of a couple of weeks, then resolved that the best way forward was to quietly dissolve our blood bond to Kaia and thereby remove her from our three-person coven.

We tried twice to secretly get the crystal back from Kaia – including one instance of rifling through her jewelry display when she was in the other room – but both attempts were completely unsuccessful (and extremely stressful). After it was clear that that option wasn't going to pan out, we settled for burning down the rest of her black candle from the blood magic rite and carrying out the strongest cleansing ritual we could find at the time.

---

13   As an aside, I'm not even convinced that blood magic lasts forever. I'm more persuaded by the argument that blood magic lasts approximately seven years, or the length of time that it takes for every cell in your body to turn over and be replaced with a new cell.

We conducted the ritual without any major issues, after which we drove to her house in the middle of the night, to bury the remnants of the spell in a large flowerpot in her front yard. We jittered with nervous excitement as we dug into the soil and dropped in the bits of wax, ash, and other pieces.

As we jumped back in the car, we were exhausted from the energy expended in our ritual, and yet awake from the adrenaline and the high from the spell. We both laughed as we drove down the deserted streets.

"This has already been one wild ride we've gotten ourselves on," I said to Rhea.

"Well, I can't imagine it getting any less exciting from here," she added, smiling.

And it didn't. Although we were down one member in terms of manpower, it was clear that the two of us worked quickly and creatively together. We pushed each other to do crazy things in the name of our magical adventure, and at the time, we didn't even know where it would go.

Minimalist Magic for the Maximalist Witch

As I noted in my section on the Fundamentals of Magic, I'm a strong believer that beginner witches are not limited to boring spells until they acquire more advanced magical abilities. I also believe, however, that more experienced witches do themselves a disservice by only engaging in big rituals. Of course, these rituals are fun and impressive, but they also require a significant amount of time and effort (and speaking from personal experience, it's much easier to let magic fall by the wayside if you think of it as an all-or-nothing, expensive lifestyle).

There's also a big upside to simplicity: In many cases, easier spells can be *more* successful if you're just starting out or don't have very much energy to invest. That's because, with fewer moving parts, there are fewer ways to royally screw up.

So, with that in mind, here are some of my favorite simple-but-not-boring spells.

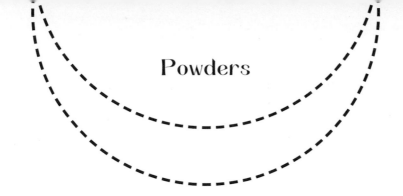

Powders

agical powders are something of a daily bread for recreational witches. For one, you only have to assemble and charge a batch once and then it's ready whenever you need it (like meal prepping, except you're not embarrassed to tell other people about it). It's also very transportable, and – in the larger scheme of enchanted items – more inconspicuous. Lastly, if you charge them correctly, these powders can really pack a punch.

The simplest way to make a magical powder is to assemble your ingredients and then visualize your intent while you grind them together in a mortar and pestle. If you want to add a little something extra, store your powder in a jar with a crystal matching your intent, or draw a sigil on the bottom of the jar for an additional charge.

Just as a practical note: Because powders can be made in varying batch sizes based on how much of an ingredient you have, the size of your mortar and pestle, and your available storage space, I haven't listed the quantities for any spell ingredients (for the most part). You can use your own judgement as to what ratio "feels right" to you, or – worst case scenario – combine everything in equal parts.

Luck and Money Powder

f all the spells we ever created, this one and the Goddess Glamour Bath are tied for the positions of Most Beloved and Most Relied Upon. I'll speak about GGB later, but the advantages of our Luck and Money Powder are clear: 1) When wouldn't you be better off with more luck or money? 2) It was wildly effective.

The origins of this spell were also quite illustrative of the dynamic of Rhea's and my two-woman coven. When we were practicing our craft together, Rhea lived in a decent-sized house with plenty of storage space, and I lived in a small apartment for college students about 100 miles away. Whenever we'd find new ingredients for spells, we'd pool them together in a cabinet at Rhea's house for us both to use, and then I would take finished powders, salves, and some emergency ingredients back to my apartment. One notable example was when I had been bringing naturally pastel green eggshells from my parents' chickens over to Rhea's place for a couple of months, and we were storing them away for weeks because we didn't know what to do with them.

Then, one hot summer day, I went over to Rhea's house. Immediately upon opening the door, she brought me over to a jar filled with white and green-speckled powder.

"I have to show you what I've made," she told me. "I used the green eggshells with some simple herbs to create a luck and money powder. It works like a charm." She was beaming with a proud and knowing witch's smile.

She went on to tell me about how she sprinkled it in her shoes before her recent job interview and received an offer a couple hours later. Earlier that day, she had even sprinkled it over some old clothes that she wanted to sell, and the consignment shop had bought practically all of them off her.

Needless to say, I used the powder myself as soon as I could. I trialed it for a job I was applying for – and promptly received an offer. It was another magical success story.

From there, we used it for big tests when we were worried that we wouldn't get good grades and carried it with us in small vials when we were feeling particularly cash strapped, so that we could find $20 bills on the ground and have drunk men buy us extra drinks at bars. It was a tiny miracle-worker in a vial.

Ingredients

- 🌿 **Eggshells** (green if possible)
- 🌿 Dried **basil**
- 🌿 Dried green **mint**
- 🌿 **Fennel** seeds
- 🌿 Dried **thyme**

Grind all the ingredients together with a mortar and pestle while visualizing your intent. Continue grinding until you've achieved a powder-like consistency (small pieces are fine, just keep in mind that a true powder is easier to use). Decant into a small glass container. To use, sprinkle into shoes, into a candle flame, or onto an object that represents your intention.

Harmony Powder

There are times in your life when you know you'll be seeing someone you dislike, facing conflict with a loved one, or thrust into a tense interpersonal situation. You really ought to have an adult conversation to work through your differences, but at the same time, you really *don't* want to have said conversation. You'd rather have the uncomfortable atmosphere magically dissipate.

This is where this Harmony Powder comes in. Make it beforehand, sprinkle it on the ground or in your hands, to take the edge off any stressful scenario.

Now, I can't say I really recommend this approach, as this powder won't resolve any major issues – it will merely cover them up for a short period of time. But it's your life, and if there's someone in your life you really can't have that hard, frank conversation with (or if you just prefer sweeping things under the rug), this spell is for you.

Ingredients

- Dried **lavender buds**
- Whole/ground **coriander**
- **Pink Himalayan salt** or **sea salt**
- 1 stick of **lily of the valley incense**
- Optional: dried **gardenia flowers**

To prepare, start by lighting your lily of the valley incense. As the smoke slowly fills your space, think of peaceful memories of times that you enjoyed with others, ideally ones where the atmosphere felt easy and harmonious. Set the ashes from the burned-down incense stick aside.

Then, add your lavender buds, coriander, salt, and gardenia flowers (if using) to your mortar and pestle. Grind as much as you can until you've achieved a powder-like consistency, then stir in the ashes from the incense stick. For best results, store in a glass container with a small piece of amethyst.

Confidence Powder

or better or worse (mostly for worse), you can get pretty far in life by just seeming confident and self-assured. People like you more in job interviews, you're more appealing on dates, you're considered better qualified at your job, and other individuals will find themselves strangely drawn to you – all because of how you deliver your speech and hold your body.

It is a deeply unfair setup (and all the more unjust considering society does it best to tear down those in the minority). It is also hard to avoid. This powder helps level the playing field.

Now, maybe you don't feel like playing society's game (and who could blame you) but let me counter and say that this is actually the perfect type of spell for those who are worried about leveraging too much influence on the world around them. Yes, technically people will interact with you differently based on your behavior, but magically speaking, the only thing you're changing is *yourself*.

Plus, why shouldn't you feel confident? You're a badass witch.

Ingredients

- 🌿 **Tobacco** from 1 cigarette
- 🌿 Ground **ginger**
- 🌿 1 fresh **tangerine**
- 🌿 **Sea salt**
- 🌿 **Neroli essential oil**

Before getting into the process of actually creating your powder, take your fresh tangerine and finely grate off all the peel. Spread this zest out thinly on a clean surface to dry. Wait for it to be completely hard and brittle before proceeding to the next step.

To prepare the powder, start by adding your salt to your mortar and pestle, then add one to two drops of the neroli essential oil. Combine with the tobacco, a few dashes of ground ginger, and the tangerine zest, and grind together until you've achieved a powder-like consistency. For best results, store in a glass container with a small piece of citrine.

Energy Powder

Sometimes, caffeine is really not the solution to your tiredness – and I don't just write this as a lover of decaf coffee. Caffeine blocks the effects of adenosine, which makes you feel less tired, but it also increases your adrenaline, which can make you feel anxious and on-edge.

This simple energy powder, meanwhile, can help you feel alert but also calm and in control. While you can use it as a standard powder spell, I actually recommend it more in the form of smelling salts, or chemical compounds that help you feel more awake. Traditionally, smelling salts use ammonium carbonate to make you feel alert, but this mixture is just magic and essential oils.

Ingredients

- *Ø* A few **fennel seeds**
- *Ø* A pinch of dried **spearmint**
- *Ø* **Sea salt**
- *Ø* **Peppermint essential oil**
- *Ø* **Eucalyptus essential oil**
- *Ø* Small **glass vial** with a screw top

Take your fennel seeds, sea salt, and a pinch of dried spearmint and add them to your mortar and pestle. Lightly grind them together so that the fennel and spearmint start to break down, but don't grind fully into a powder consistency. Visualize energy flowing from your body into the salt mixture as you do this. Then, take your essential oils and add them in equal amounts (at least three drops of each oil). Funnel the mixture into your glass vial.

To use, unscrew the top from the vial and inhale the scent from the mixture. If the strength of the fragrance wears down after a couple of months, you can top up the mixture by adding one drop of each essential oil to the vial.

Other Powders

here are also other powders listed in this book on pages 178 and 224. Especially if you're looking for powders that cause negative effects, I highly recommend the hexing powders located on page 224.

Charms

echnically speaking, a charm is any item you've charged with a magical intent. You could charge your earrings to make yourself a better listener, or your socks to bring you good luck, or your pen to increase your productivity. The sky's the limit when it comes to this type of magic – you just have to find ways of imbuing an object with your intent.

This section isn't going to be about how to charge mundane objects to make them magical (I trust that you can use the information outlined in the opening chapters, along with your own creativity, to make that happen), but rather, it will cover how to make dedicated charms. These items are typically mixtures of botanicals, crystals, and other raw materials that you can combine into a new object. And while I haven't covered the whole spectrum of desired outcomes in this section, you'll quickly see that they are often formulaic in their setup and therefore easy to adapt to any intent.

With that in mind, let's get into it.

Motivation Charm

There are, unfortunately, dozens of tasks that one must attend to regularly as a person living in a modern society, and most of them are not pleasant. The majority of us need to file taxes, call our health insurance provider, pay our bills, schedule appointments, buy gifts for our in-laws, finish our homework, prepare presentations, and so on. It's exhausting, and it can feel borderline impossible to get it all done.

That's where this charm comes in. While you'll still have to do all the aforementioned tasks (sorry), this little guy will at least help you get them all done so they don't pile up.

Ingredients

- 3 whole **allspice berries**
- 1 piece of **amber**
- 1 whole **vanilla bean**
- 1 old **envelope**
- 1 **sachet**

Start by taking your old envelope and tearing it into small pieces, until the entire envelope is broken down. As you do this, imagine that you are breaking down your tasks and slowly lightening your burden. Next, take all the small bits of paper and add them to your sachet. Follow by adding in the allspice berries and piece of amber. Finally, take your vanilla bean and break it in half, then add it to the mixture.

To charge, leave it out in the sun for one day. Afterwards, leave it at your workstation.

Just as a practical piece of advice: Don't feel guilty if you can't do it all by yourself. Sometimes, you really can't "do it all," and that's okay.

Self-love Charm

Self-love is something we talk about a lot as a society, but rarely do we speak of practical ways in which to achieve it. We often read social media posts that talk about loving yourself like you'd love somebody else, but I don't think this is actually prudent advice: when I start dating someone, I don't know all the worst things they've ever done, or how they smell after coming out of a three-week-long mid-grade depressive episode. I *do* know these things about me, and therefore "taking myself out on a date" isn't going to cut it.

Of course, this charm isn't a substitute for therapy or a healthy, supportive group of loved ones. But it does move things in the right direction, so that you're better equipped to keep caring for yourself.

Ingredients

- 1 pretty **glass container**[14] that you like
- 1 piece of **rose quartz**
- Dried **chamomile flowers**
- Dried **lavender buds**
- Dried **marjoram**
- 1 **pen**
- 1 piece of **paper**

---

14   Since I'm going to recommend this charm be left in your bathroom, you can use a small container that you'd use for cotton pads or swabs if you want your magic to fit in with the rest of your decor.

Start by taking your pen and paper and writing a list of things that you like about yourself or that you're proud you've accomplished. You should aim for at least 10 items, but more is better. After you finish that list, draw a line and write down any reminders that you know to be true intellectually, but which are difficult for you to embody. Depending on what you personally struggle with, these could be statements like: "I am human, and all humans make mistakes," or, "It is normal to change as I age," or, "It's okay to need help from those around me."

After you're done, fold the paper and place it in the bottom of the glass container. Add the piece of rose quartz on top of it, and then fill the rest of the container with equal parts chamomile flowers, lavender buds, and marjoram. For best results, charge under the light of a waxing moon.

Finally, I recommend placing this charm in a location where you interact with yourself often, such as your bathroom counter. (For an additional self-love spell, see the Self-Love Bath on page 130.)

Creativity Charm

t first, it seems like a blessing – you're a creative person, you love to write, design, draw, film, etc. for fun, and now, you finally get paid to do what you love. It's like a dream come true. Unfortunately, many people then realize that constantly being asked to "be creative" for your livelihood is as much a curse as it is a blessing. Especially if you've only experienced the arts as a hobby or a stress-reliever before, pivoting to produce creative works on demand can be quite the rude awakening.

This creativity charm helps take some of the pressure off by increasing your ideas and regulating the flow of inspiration. (For a longer-term strategy, however, I recommend finding ways to limit distractions, increase your self-confidence, and let go of perfectionism.)

Ingredients

- 1 dried **carnation flower**
- 1 tablespoon of dried **jasmine blossoms**
- 1 **citrine** or **tiger's eye crystal**
- 1 small **piece of cloth** you like[15]
- 1 small **piece of ribbon** or **twine**

---

15   This is a great opportunity to reuse fabric that you no longer have a practical use for, like a piece of your old favorite blouse that's too small, or an embroidered handkerchief from your grandmother.

Start by taking the piece of cloth and placing it over the open palm of your non-dominant hand. Next, place the piece of citrine in the center, followed by the single carnation and the jasmine blossoms. Pull the corners of the fabric together so nothing falls out, then hold the bundle in both hands as you think of your favorite past creative works. Remember how the ideas came to you, and how it felt to produce them.

Finally, take the piece of ribbon and tie the bundle closed. Let it charge for one full day in the sun (you can make a sigil if this isn't possible where you live), then keep it on your desk or on your person when you work on creative tasks.

Simple Shielding Charm

f you're sensitive to people's feelings[16], you know how challenging it can be to do even basic tasks when others' emotions are running high. I often describe this sensation to less-sensitive individuals as being along the lines of "hearing" people's emotions. You wouldn't be able to get any work done if your partner was loudly telling you about their bad day – and I feel the same way sitting in a room with someone who's clearly irritable and upset, even if they're not saying a word.

Of course, it's not always practical (or desirable) to walk away every time someone else is having a rough day. Nor can we afford to put our lives on hold at the whim of someone else's mood. Instead, this spell helps you shield yourself from the negative effects of the emotions of others, so you can continue interacting with and supporting those around you without feeling pulled into their personal woes.

Ingredients

- 1 **glass jar** with a lid
- 1 tumbled **clear quartz** or **black tourmaline crystal**
- **Sunflower, coconut,** or **castor oil**
- 1 **pen**
- 1 **piece of paper**

---

16   Other esoteric books will often refer to people in this category as "empaths". I have chosen not to do this as it implies that this is a category you either belong to or you don't, and I see empathy for others as a spectrum.

To start, take your pen and paper and make a sigil to match your intent (for a refresher on how to make a sigil, see page 81). Your sigil should be unique to you, but you can use the sentence "I am shielded from other people's negative emotions," if you don't want to write something more specific. Don't forget to charge your sigil before moving on to the next step.

Once your sigil is ready, open your glass jar and place your crystal at the bottom. Now, fill up the rest of the jar with your oil of choice. (In this spell, using coconut oil is a double-edged sword. On one hand, you may need to lightly melt your coconut oil to be able to use it, but on the other, the solidifying oil is a nice visual representation of your intent.) Close the jar and set it on top of the sigil for one day.

At the end of the day, remove the crystal. Use the oil on it to moisturize your hands and body, then use a cloth to remove any excess oil from the crystal. Carry it with you whenever you need emotional shielding. As a bonus, use the oil post-shower or bath for an extra, magical buffer.

Chapter Four: Bath & Shower Magic

Establishing the Blog

Our first year of practicing had been a whirlwind – a sort of platonic romance between me, Rhea, and witchcraft, with our other lovers orbiting around us like supporting characters.

The year started off with my breakup with Nate, and we dove immediately into magic like we were on the rebound. We blood-bonded ourselves with Kaia, then cut her out of the coven soon afterwards; we began hoarding all kinds of herbs, spices, crystals, glass bottles, natural ingredients, divination decks, apothecary tools, and anything else we thought might come in handy, and stored it all inside Rhea's house; I started dating someone new – Sarah – but was planning the perfect curse to get revenge on Nate; Rhea and I scoured the Internet for a virtual space for witches where we felt like we could belong, reading everything we could along the way; we used magic to get summer jobs; Nate was finally cursed (more on that later), and watched his socials meticulously for signs that it was working (or not); we taught ourselves how to read tarot; we became avid weed smokers; we started our sophomore year of college; Rhea started a path towards green witchcraft and soon had three huge basil bushes in her front yard; I messaged Nate at Thanksgiving, asking if he "wanted to talk" while he was in Phoenix; we met up for coffee, stayed through lunch and dinner, and made out in my car; I broke up with Sarah. Then, I split that Christmas break between seeing Nate and tinkering around with magic with Rhea.

In some ways, everything was very much the same as the year before, and in others, I had flipped the script. For one, I came back to Nate as a different person. Sure, I might have been completely stupid and naive to date him again, but I had met his move and one-upped him. I had cursed him, and now we were even.

Better than being even, I felt more confident in myself. I was not the frail teenager who had encountered Nate the year before – I was strong, powerful, and wicked if I wanted to be. I was the witch who demanded the universe give me vengeance, and the universe had answered my call. So why stop there?

Finally, I believed that I could assert my desire to be happy in this experience, too.

And I *was* happy. To the dismay of all my friends and family, I was overjoyed to be dating Nate again. I let that joy fill my entire body and spill out of me. I wasn't just happy about my relationship – I was brimming with new ideas and possibilities in all areas of my life. I was in love, and that love made me feel like I could do anything.

One day that December, Rhea and I were smoking weed as we always did: in her bathroom, with the shower running hot to fill the room with steam. (We read somewhere that the steam would dampen the smell of smoke.) I held the small pipe in my hand, striking the wheel of the lighter with my thumb and carefully lighting the bowl.

"I can't believe the most popular witch blog in the game is just some Wiccan teenager who reposts everything she sees," Rhea complained. "There's no curation. No style. I'm pretty sure my *brother* could write better spell posts."

I laughed, coughing on some smoke as I exhaled.

"I know I've said this before," she said, "but I'm positive we could run a better blog."

I passed her the pipe.

We had talked passively several times about the idea of starting our own witchcraft blog. We both loved reading and engaging with this type of content; for my part, fashion and DIY ideas, and for Rhea's, makeup and the general "alt-girl" scene. There was something special about blogs that almost tricked your brain into believing you knew the blogger personally – like you were somehow friends.

Practically speaking, no one in the witch community at the time was publishing anything that resembled curated, polished content, so the opportunity was glaring. Meanwhile, Rhea was studying photography, I liked to write, and we knew we were funny as hell together. It was like the most perfect, ripe fruit had dropped right into our laps.

"Then let's do it," I said, as Rhea took another hit. "We keep saying we could do this if we wanted to. That we *should* do it. So, let's commit to doing it."

Rhea smiled but hesitated. "It'll be a ton of work, you know."

"This girl runs the most popular blog just by reposting trash content. She's barely even trying." I took the pipe back from Rhea's outstretched hand. "How hard can it be?"

With a fine haze drifting over our surroundings, and a soft overconfidence settling into our bodies, we agreed to set up a blog before we started the upcoming spring semester.

§

By far the most challenging aspect of starting the blog was figuring out the name.

Rhea and I knew from the outset what we wanted the blog to be: It should be witty, down-to-earth, accessible but not boring, useful but not prescriptive, inclusive but not pedantic, and, above all else, it should look *good*. We wanted to take the prevalent early 2010s Internet aesthetic – pastel pinks, glitter, flowers juxtaposed with weapons, wistful sunsets and beautiful women lounging in lingerie – and blend it with our own personal tastes. It should be feminine and girly, but with a harsh edge, plenty of marijuana motifs, and a touch of earthiness (after all, we were going to be selling ourselves to people who thought the word "natural" was a unique selling point). In short, we were going to craft the type of blog we had desperately wanted to find but never had.

Plus, we already knew that we had interesting stories to tell. All we had to do was transpose our real-life friendship onto the Internet and we'd be golden.

And yet, the name was an ongoing problem.

For full transparency, it was almost exclusively Rhea who proposed name ideas for the blog. I mostly spent my time critiquing her suggestions.

"Two Broke Witches?" *Too forced.*

"Bitchcraft?" *Too obvious.*

"Craft-y?" *Too punny.*

"It's just not quite right," I would tell her. "It's not a bad option, it just doesn't really feel like *us*."

It felt like we were going around in circles for days and I was wearing Rhea's patience thin. I was tempted to cave in and pick a subpar name just to get ourselves out there, but then the moment finally arrived.

We were slowly trudging out of Rhea's steam-and-smoke-filled bathroom one bright afternoon when I saw her face light up. "I think I have it. I think I have the name for the blog," she said.

"Well, go on. Tell me."

"*Recreational Witchcraft.*"

I loved how it played on the idea of recreational marijuana, how it sounded when she said it, and how it looked on the page. It seemed like the kind of thing that would show up on the evening news as the dangerous new fad that teens were getting into. Even better, the URL was still free.

"It's perfect."

And so, almost precisely one year after jumping head-first into magic, *Recreational Witchcraft* went online.

An Introduction to Bath Magic

For me, bath magic stands alone because it's more than just a conduit to send your spell out into the world.

Like kitchen witches or green witches, the medium you use can totally transform your relationship with magic – regardless of the type of spells you're casting. I feel connected to bath magic because it's something that I can experience by myself – a bit of pure selfishness – and it's magic I can physically surround myself with.

I can literally cleanse my entire body or submerge myself from head to toe in a glamour, and then rub a protection oil all over my body afterwards to make it stick. As an Aquarius (or as an air sign generally), it's easy for me to get lost in my thoughts or have a hard time grounding myself while practicing magic. With bath magic, I can easily change my state of mind by changing the temperature of the water or by adding ingredients like Epsom salts that change the consistency of the bath. You're also casting a spell while you're naked, and I believe in the power of starting from that place of the raw self. Plus, I like that bathrooms are typically confined spaces, so you can fill them to the brim with candles, incense, and other magical trinkets.

Simply put: It's a magical *experience*.

Whatever the rationale, I used to do a bath spell before (or as part of) every major ritual I've ever conducted. It's true that the bath witch lifestyle isn't as useful as being a green witch or as enjoyable for your loved ones as being a kitchen witch, but I think that after you see how wonderful it is to be naked with yourself in warm water once per week, you might be convinced to call yourself a bath witch as well.

(Now, if you just read all of that and you're saying to yourself, "But what if I don't have a bathtub?" Trust me, I hear you and I empathize – I'm writing this now from my apartment without a bathtub. I'll get to the section on shower magic shortly.)

As a final bonus, bath magic is one of the most inconspicuous types of magic if you're not open about your practice. It's not uncommon in today's "self-care" rhetoric to hear celebrities and normal people alike espousing the benefits of taking long, luxurious baths, so your bath mixtures and candles won't raise an eyebrow. Also, "Hey, I'm going to be taking a bath for a while," sounds a lot less weird than: "Don't come into my room while I sit in the dark with my candles for several hours."

On that note, let's get into some of the details.

The Basics of Bath Magic

s with everything else in this book, I'm going to sketch out what I usually do for bath magic, but I encourage you to change the steps, details and ingredients as you see fit.

Your Tub is the Altar

One of my favorite aspects of bath magic is that *you get to be inside your altar*. Instead of being the puppet master leaning over your creation, you're right at the center of the action. If your tub has a rim, I encourage you to decorate it in a way that gets you in the mood to do magic. I always filled the rims of my tubs to the brim with candles, crystals, and other beautiful objects. If you're lucky enough to have a free-standing tub, try to prop some items around you on the sink or other objects (like a stool) so that you can see some of your trinkets from your position in the bath.

Here's what I like to add to the rim of my tub:

- 🌿 **Something to dedicate the bath to *me*.** Usually this was a talisman or crystal I wore frequently, but this could change based on the spell.
- 🌿 **Lots of candles.** I had bigger candles (in corresponding colors to the spell I was casting) present, and as many tea lights as I could fit in without it becoming a fire hazard.

- *Incense*. If you use incense for your other spells, you might as well burn some here, too.
- **Specific objects for the spell**. If I'm doing a glamour, then I add flowers and jewelry. If it's for protection, then I'd add thorns or shells. You get the idea.

What About Inside the Bath?

In the water is literally where the magic happens. What you add to the bath will have the biggest effect on the spell you're casting, so this is where you can really play around – but you also need to be careful that what you're adding is safe for your body.

First and foremost is the water itself. In general, you'll want your water to be quite warm so that you can stay in for 40-60 minutes without it getting too cool, but not so warm that you burn your skin or are standing outside your tub naked for 15 minutes waiting to begin your spell[17].

Now, on to the fun stuff. Here are some of the things that I regularly added to my bath:

- **Salt**. As in other parts of magic, salt is one of your best friends here. I'm partial to Epsom salts because 1) they help you feel "floatier" in the water (they're used in float tanks for that weightless sensation), and 2) they prevent your skin from wrinkling if you've stayed in too long. And while Epsom salt is chemically quite different from table salt, I still use it for cleansing.
- **Essential oils**. Match the intent of your spell to the relevant essential oil(s) and add a few drops. Ideally, you should still be diluting anything you use in a carrier oil, since essential oils will sit on top of the water during the bath.

---

17   A practical tip for achieving the right temperature is that you should first test the running water with your hand to see if it feels good, then let it fill up until you have a couple inches of water in the tub. At this point, test the water again with your foot. If it feels too hot, now's the time to adjust the temperature. (Trust me, if you wait too long to test the temperature, you will need an unbelievable amount of ice or cold water to make it comfortable.)

- **Homemade bath salts.** This is basically the first two items on this list combined, but you can also throw in dried flower petals or herbs, body-safe glitter, oil, and so on. The real benefit of making your own bath salts ahead of time is that you can then dedicate and charge them simultaneously and store them with a crystal for extra *oomph*. I would make a big batch of Goddess Glamour Bath (page 194) every couple of months, charge it, and then use it every other week until I ran out.

- **Tea bags.** Yes, you can add whole herbs and flowers to your bath (more on that in a minute), but the upside of using tea bags is dramatically shortened clean-up time. If you want to attract love into your life, throw a couple of bags of chamomile into your bath. If you're looking for a lazy cleansing spell, add a handful of Epsom salts along with a few peppermint tea bags to your bathwater.

- **Herbs, flowers and other plants.** If you're looking to have a beautiful bath, you can add in free-floating botanicals. I will warn you that as stunning as it looks, petals and leaves will stick to your skin and it'll be a pain in the ass to clean up afterwards. If you go down this route, I recommend purchasing a fine mesh strainer that you can keep by your bath to help sift everything out afterwards. You can also buy drawstring organza or muslin baggies to hold your herbs as they infuse the bath.

- **Milk.** You've probably heard of one powerful, historical woman or another taking a milk bath. That's because milk contains lactic acid, which can gently exfoliate away dead skin and leave you feeling beautiful and smooth. If you don't want to add liquid milk to your bath, you can always add powdered milk instead. Don't want to use animal-based products in your magic? Try adding powdered coconut milk for protection or almond milk for prosperity.

- **Colloidal oatmeal.** Colloidal oatmeal is a finely ground oat mixture that can be dissolved in water for skin-soothing and moisturizing effects. Add it to your bath for the cosmetic benefits; enjoy the association of abundance as a convenient byproduct.

- **Pre-made bath bombs, melts, soaks, etc.** Yes, bath products that you make and dedicate yourself will be more magically potent, but this book isn't titled *Spells for the Witch Who Does the Most*. Magic is for everyone, including people who just want to pick up pretty bath bombs at LUSH and charge them with a sigil. As long as you take note of the ingredients and match them to your intention, you'll do just fine.

🌿 **Charged water**. Did you charge several gallons of water under the light of the full moon and don't know what to do with it? Throw it in your bath. Do you want to give a big curse some extra *oomph*? Add in some storm water. Think your Yule bath is missing something? Take some snow, charge it, and add it to your bath. You get the picture.

Mix and match ingredients so that you get the desired practical and magical benefits you're looking for. I often mixed pre-made bath bombs with my own ingredients or purchased locally made bath salts and added them to my workhorse spells for extra power.

Once you've set up your altar and added ingredients to your bath, I recommend turning off the lights and doing the rest of the spell by candlelight.

During Your Bath

Ironically, even as a bath witch, I often find the most difficult part comes once I'm finally in the bath. If you have trouble sitting still for longer periods of time, sitting in a big batch of warm water, naked, for nearly an hour, can take some getting used to, which is why you need to take a few moments before jumping in to set yourself up for success.

I always liked to make a playlist that matched my intention ahead of time – sometimes I'd even go to the trouble of setting the exact queue of songs so that my mood would follow a particular trajectory. This is especially important for glamours, where you want to be leaving the bath with Beyoncé-level confidence in yourself, but any spell can benefit from extra atmosphere and emotional stage management.

You can also make additional magical bath products to take into the bath with you, such as salt- or sugar-based scrubs for your skin. (I've included several of these spell additions later in this chapter.) These can be extra beneficial for cleansing or curse-removal spells.

Otherwise, spend your time in the bath visualizing your intent (duh), doing normal bath stuff (washing your hair, shaving, relaxing, etc.), or engaging in trance work. For the uninitiated, trance work is considerably less daunting than it sounds. The goal of trance work is to disassociate from your current surroundings in order to do some type of esoteric task, like astral travel or communing with deities. If you add a ton of Epsom salts and draw a slightly warmer than comfortable bath (the key word is *slightly*; if you draw it too warm, you will be fixated on unpleasant bodily sensations), it becomes especially easy to forget about your body and enter a trance. Close your eyes and visualize a spiritual plane just beyond your body, where all types of energy are connected on some "higher" level than the one we're on right now. When you try entering your trance, imagine drifting from our current plane to that one, and you'll see that in a couple of tries it's fairly easy to get going.

After the Bath

When the water's started to cool, it's probably the right moment to drain and leave your bath.

If possible, it's preferable to let your skin and hair air-dry after the bath so that whatever magical infusion was in the water lingers after you get out. That said, if you live in a cold climate (or are a baby about feeling cold, like me) then you can dry off with a clean towel and it's probably fine.

At the point when I'm about 80% dry, I like to seal in the magic with some oil that matches my intent. Coconut oil is great for protection (and very dry skin), almond oil for prosperity (and more sensitive skin types), sunflower for energy or power (and acne-prone skin), grape seed oil for fertility (and dry, sensitive skin), avocado oil for sex and love, and so on. Of course, if you do have acne or another skin condition, don't feel obligated to put this oil on affected areas.

You might have noticed that I left oils out of the ingredients that you can add to your bath. This shouldn't stop you from adding them if you enjoy doing so or if you have very dry skin; I personally find that the oil doesn't disperse very well in water (which makes sense, because oil and water don't mix – the oil just sits on the surface in globs), and I always put it on afterwards, so for me, it always seemed like overkill. Also, when you add oil to your bath, it once again makes cleanup more difficult.

And so, to my last point: A bath witch keeps her bathtub clean. You don't want lingering magical energy interfering with your next spell, and you certainly don't want any kind of bacterial growth in your relaxing, magical space. Take the time after you've patted yourself down with oil and pulled yourself together to take your tea bags and botanicals out, rinse the tub down with water, and spray a cleaning product on the surface to sit for a while. It might seem like a lot of effort in the moment when you're feeling warm and sleepy, but it'll be a lot less work for your future witchy self.

Simple Cleansing Bath

As noted in the beginning of this book, it's essential that you perform a cleansing ritual semi-regularly when doing magic, or else you run the risk of contaminating your spells with whatever energy baggage you've been toting around with you. This is especially important before engaging in any rituals or casting serious spells.

This next spell is based on a bath mixture that Rhea and I would buy from a local apothecary and use before conducting our two-woman coven rituals. We'd meet at Rhea's house where her bathroom was connected to her bedroom and cleanse the entire space. Then, we'd set up the bathroom for the ritual, draw the bathwater really warm (borderline scalding for the first bather, if I'm being honest), and take turns cleansing ourselves before we began. It helped set the mood for the rest of the evening and guaranteed that we were both cleansed for casting any of our crazy spells.

That said, doing an energy cleansing outside of a ritual can feel like a chore (much like cleaning your house) and therefore it's best to make the experience as simple and enjoyable as possible. This self-cleansing spell is super easy, as you can make a big batch of the mixture in advance and then unceremoniously dump a handful in your bath when the time is right. The smell of rosemary, too, is deceptively heavenly for how simple it is.

The only extra step I recommend here is going out of your way to find fresh rosemary, wash it, pat it dry and roughly chop the needles to release their sweet smell. If you're in a pinch, dry cuttings from the store are, of course, fine.

Bath Salt Mixture

Combine the following ingredients in a bowl:

- 1 part **sea salt**
- 1 part **Epsom salt**
- A palmful of roughly **chopped rosemary**
- **Rosemary essential oil**
- Optional: a pinch of ground **fennel** or dried **peppermint**

For best results, store in a glass container with a piece of clear or smoky quartz. Charge under the energy of a new moon and then keep in a cool, dry place until needed.

Bath Ritual

When you're ready to start your cleansing, gather:

- ✏ The **bath salts** you prepared
- ✏ Lots of **white candles**
- ✏ **Frankincense, dragon's blood,** or **benzoin resin incense**
- ✏ **Something to dedicate** the bath to you (e.g. talisman you wear, tarot card that represents you, etc.)
- ✏ **Coconut** or **sunflower oil** for after your bath

Make sure your bathtub is clean (if it's not clean, take care of that first), then start lighting your candles and your incense. Begin drawing a warm bath and throw in a handful of your bath salts. Add the object that represents you to the rim of the tub, undress, and try to clear your mind in order to prepare yourself for the bath.

(Note: If you're doing this cleansing as the first part of a larger ritual, cleanse and protect your entire bathroom using the same method that you're using to cleanse your ritual space. Once both spaces are prepared and ready, draw and dedicate your bath.)

Once the bath is ready, slowly lower yourself into the water, trying to submerge as much of your body as possible. (If, for whatever reason, you usually don't like to get your hair wet when bathing, try and coordinate this ritual with your hair wash day for best results. If you can't do that, just use your hands to get the bathwater onto as much of your skin as possible.) Envision the water washing away any lingering negative energy from your body and returning you to a clean state. Spend the rest of your bath washing your body and hair as normal. If you think you need an extra magical *oomph* to banish gross energy, see the Purification Scrub on page 150.

When the water starts to cool, exit your bath and try to let yourself air-dry. Take the oil and rub it into your skin to seal the energy and protect yourself. Once that's done, either start the rest of your ritual or begin cleanup.

Power Bath Spell

In my experience, most women, queer people, and other marginalized individuals undervalue the feeling of power. It makes sense, because so many of us have had power systematically denied to us, and we're otherwise not encouraged to seek it out in our personal or political lives. But even when we do speak about it, power isn't something that we encourage people to have. We associate having power with having power over others (and probably also with the misuse of that hierarchy).

But power isn't just something you can leverage over others. There's power in knowing ourselves. Power in knowing what we really want. Power in knowing our bodies and how to use them – whether we use that knowledge to push ourselves to excellence or to make ourselves feel pleasure. There's power in standing up straight and knowing our worth. Power in knowing what we have to offer. Power in knowing that our voices matter and that we can use them to change the course of history.

Magic is about reclaiming power. But if you're just stepping into magic, it can take a while to get used to the fact that you are the woman (or man, or person) in charge. This spell is to help you center yourself, know yourself and give yourself a little magical boost if you're about to start on some complicated spellwork (like a curse). That said, it'll work just as well for your big presentation at work, or if you need to speak uncomfortable truths.

Bath Salt Mixture

In a bowl, combine:

- 1 part **black lava salt** or **sea salt**
- 1 part **Epsom salts**
- **Neroli essential oil**
- 1 teaspoon of ground **ginger**
- A palmful of dried **calendula** or **honeysuckle blossoms**
- A dash of **cinnamon**[18]

---

18   If you're performing this spell before cursework, swap in ground cloves instead.

Mix thoroughly and store in a glass jar. (If you're concerned about the free-floating flowers in your bath, you can also store bath portions in organza or muslin bags.) Charge under the light of a full moon if possible, then keep in a cool, dark place until you're ready to use this mixture. If using as a precursor to serious spellwork, I'd also recommend charging it with a sigil that is powerful for you.

Bath Ritual

When you're ready to start the ritual, gather:

- ⌀ The **bath salts** you prepared
- ⌀ Lots of **candles**
- ⌀ **Cedar incense**
- ⌀ **Storm water** [19]
- ⌀ **Sunflower oil**
- ⌀ Optional: an **empowering playlist**

Light your candles and your incense, then start drawing a warm bath. As the tub is filling up, pour in the storm water and bath salt mixture. (If you're using this spell before performing a curse or summoning any spirits, it would also be beneficial to line your tub with onyx or smoky quartz stones.) When the bath is ready, start your playlist and enter the tub.

As you sit in your bath, envision yourself pulling energy out of the warm water, the candles, and the air into your body. You're sitting here to charge yourself for any obstacles ahead. If you're performing this ritual before a specific spell or challenge, imagine yourself going through the action step by step and being successful in your endeavors.

When the water begins to cool, exit the bath and try to let yourself air-dry if possible. Use the sunflower oil that you brought to your bathroom earlier to moisturize your skin and lock in the energy from the bath. Remember: You can do this.

---

19   If you live in a climate with few storms, you can swap this out for water charged under a full moon.

Self-Love Bath

Everyone needs self-acceptance, self-love, and self-forgiveness in their life. While this comes to some individuals fairly easily, others need a bit of a helping hand. This spell is for those who need a boost. And because these bath salts are naturally relaxing and look beautiful in a jar, they also make an excellent magical gift for someone in your life who needs more "me time" (like your mom, your selfless partner, or your best friend who puts up with you whining about your ex all the time).

Bath Salt Mixture

To make the bath salts, combine the following in a bowl:

- 2 parts **Epsom salts** (as base)
- 1 part **pink salt** to promote love
- 1 part **colloidal oatmeal** (as base)
- **Lavender essential oil** for healing
- A sprinkle of **lavender buds** or **pink rose petals** for love

Pour into a glass jar and store with a piece of rose quartz or a dried bloom of your favorite flower. Charge under the light of a full moon and keep in a cool place until you're ready to use (or gift) it. At this point, the bath salts themselves should do most of the magical heavy lifting, but if you want to go all-in on being kind to yourself, add a few ritual elements to help the magic along and make your bathroom feel like a spa.

Bath Ritual

Gather:

- ⊘ The **bath salts** you prepared
- ⊘ **White**, **pink** and/or **purple candles**
- ⊘ **Vanilla incense, copal resin**, or your favorite incense
- ⊘ **Something to dedicate** the bath to you
- ⊘ A **playlist** that makes you feel good about yourself

(Note: Your playlist can be music from any genre so long as you feel better about yourself after listening to it. You shouldn't feel compelled to listen to folk or Celtic music just because you associate it with witchcraft. Your spells will work just as well – if not better – with songs from Lady Gaga, Cardi B, Gloria Gaynor, or Nina Simone.)

When you're ready, light your candles and your incense, then start drawing the bathwater at the temperature you like best. Add the item to dedicate the bath to you to the rim of the tub and toss in a handful of bath salts. Press play on your playlist and enter your bath.

As you're relaxing in the water, close your eyes and envision a soft, warm light slowly emanating from your chest. Take slow, deep breaths and make sure your muscles are relaxed. See the light slowly spread throughout your body, moving into your arms, your belly, your head, and down your legs until it has enveloped you entirely. Sit with this warmth as long as you need, then open your eyes and enjoy your bath, doing as much or as little as you'd like.

Violation Bath Salts

An unfortunate reality of life is that we occasionally cross paths with people who violate our boundaries. This could be our physical boundaries being crossed, our emotional boundaries not being respected, or even just some creepy guy on the street not understanding basic human decency.

Rhea originally made me these bath salts along with the matching salt scrub (page 154) after I had a really gross sexual encounter with an ex-boyfriend. It goes without saying that these bath salts are not a substitute for therapy or other types of deep healing, but they take the edge off if you have the feeling that you want to crawl out of your skin and feel icky all over. They're a great way to *start* the healing process, but they're not a one-and-done solution for years of trauma.

Because people often violate us without warning, I typically had a batch made ahead of time so that I could use it or give it to someone on short notice.

To prepare, combine the following ingredients in a bowl:

- 1 part **coarse sea salt**
- 1 part **Epsom salts**
- 1 part **baking soda**[20]
- A palmful of dried **basil**
- **Eucalyptus essential oil**
- 1 tablespoon of finely grated **lemon rind**

Store in a glass jar with a piece of smoky quartz, onyx, or labradorite for best results. If possible, charge under the energy of a waning moon. Dissolve in a warm bath to use.

---

20   Make sure you're using baking soda and not baking powder. This unfortunately can't be substituted because of how baking soda works chemically.

Letting Go Bath

This bath spell is for when you want to let go of something in your life, but you can't seem to release it on your own. This can be a memory, person, dream, or anything else that's weighing you down and preventing you from fully healing. Like the other bath spells, you can make this bath salt mixture and gift it to someone else who's going through a difficult time (like a breakup).

Bath Salt Mixture

To prepare the bath salts, gather the following ingredients:

- 2 parts **sea salt** for cleansing
- 2 parts **Epsom salts** (as base)
- 1 part **arrowroot powder** for purification and healing
- Dried **linden flowers** for releasing energies
- **Chamomile buds** for peace
- **Cypress essential oil** for overcoming pain
- **Lavender essential oil** for healing

First add the sea salt, Epsom salts, and arrowroot powder to a bowl and combine. Then, stir in the chamomile and dried linden flowers, and finish off by adding in a few drops of each essential oil. (If you're making this bath salt mixture in order to get over a former lover, add in a pinch of coriander seeds.) Store in a glass jar with a piece of clear or smokey quartz, and charge under the light of a new moon.

Bath Ritual

For best results, perform the ritual at night during a new or waning moon. When you're ready to start your ritual, gather:

- ⊘ The **bath salts** you prepared
- ⊘ Lots of **white candles**
- ⊘ **Dragon's blood incense**
- ⊘ **Almond oil**

Start by lighting your candles and your incense, then draw a warm bath. Add your bath salts and slowly enter your tub. Spend the first few minutes in the bath with your eyes closed, slowly breathing in through your nose and out through your mouth. Notice if there's anywhere in your body that feels rigid and release the tension accordingly. Let your body feel heavy and relaxed in the water.

Once you're comfortable, take a deep breath and envision the heaviness in your body is slowly being transferred to the water. You're releasing your burden into the water so that you can leave the bath lighter and more at peace.

Exit the bath once the temperature begins to cool and drain the water immediately. Air-dry if possible, and once you're 80% dry, smooth a few drops of almond oil over your skin to continue healing after the bath is over.

Inner Clarity Bath Spell

A s we get older, there are less and less "obvious" choices to make about our future. We don't automatically move up a grade just by doing what we're told to do. We don't have a syllabus for the next six months at work. We're no longer just ticking off classes we need to take to fulfill a degree or professional certification requirements. Whenever we finish the level of education that we are expected to complete, we're essentially thrown into the deep end of adulthood and we can only hope that we figure things out sooner rather than later.

I know in my own experience that life has played out very differently in my young adulthood to how I initially thought it would. I've come to several forks in the road where I had two clear options that would take my life in very different directions. It was times like these when I needed to sit with myself and try to figure out what I really wanted out of life.

This spell is for those moments when you need to connect with the deepest parts of yourself in order to act on that knowledge (although it also works well just for inner exploration). So, whether you're contemplating changing careers, moving across the world, or simply wondering whether to end a long-term relationship, this bath spell should help you find the answer.

Bath Salt Mixture

To prepare the bath salt mixture, gather the following ingredients:

- 1 part **sea salt** (as base)
- 1 part **Epsom salts** (as base)
- **Clary sage essential oil** for clarity
- **Cypress** or **sandalwood essential oil** for perseverance
- **Rose essential oil** for self-love
- 1 tablespoon of ground or rubbed **sage** for wisdom

Mix the ingredients together in a bowl. Add the essential oils so it's a ratio of two parts clary sage to two parts cypress (or sandalwood) to one part rose. Store in a glass jar for best results and keep with a piece of quartz or amethyst until you're ready to use. If possible, charge under the light of a waning moon.

Bath Ritual

When you're ready for your bath, gather:

- ❡ The **bath salts** you prepared
- ❡ Lots of **white candles**
- ❡ **Benzoin** or **frankincense resin**
- ❡ **Clear quartz, smokey quartz,** or **amethyst**

Light your candles and your resin as incense. Draw a warm bath and add the bath salts you've made. Take your crystals and line the rim of the tub with them. If you only have one or two, place them on the end where you'll rest your head.

Once you've entered the bath, try to submerge your head for a few seconds (try to line this spell up with a wash day for your hair if necessary). Take a few minutes just to relax, then start exploring possible routes for your life in your mind. See where different decisions take you and what kinds of obstacles you'll face.

Leave the bath when you have an idea of how you'll proceed, or once the water is cool. If you're still unsure of which direction to take, follow this spell up with some divination in a ritual space. (For more information on divination, see Chapter Ten.)

How to Use a Bath Bomb for Bath Magic

So, you have a beautiful bath bomb, and being the easy-going, indulgent witch you are, you say, "I bet I could make this into a spell." And you're absolutely right.

Of course, you're not obligated to make it an enchanting affair every time you get into the bathtub. (If someone has any good time travel magic, please go back five years and tell me that.) But if you love doing bath magic and you want to up the ante with a bath bomb, I want to walk you through a few of my tips on how to do it.

(Just as an FYI, while I'll refer to bath bombs specifically here, these tips also work for bath melts and oils, bubble bath soaps and bubblers, pre-made bath salts and so on.)

1. Match the Ingredients to Your Intent

It's true – you probably saw this one coming. Still, it's worth repeating that the easiest way to set yourself up for success is to align the ingredients with your spell intent. Let's go through a couple of examples.

If I bought a bath bomb with lavender, ylang ylang, benzoin and tonka essential oils in it, I would use it in a recuperation spell after a particularly long and demanding week. That's because lavender and ylang ylang promote peace and tranquility, while tonka (and ylang ylang) are good for love spells. Add in benzoin, which is ideal for soothing tensions and reducing anger, and you have a nice foundation for self-love and self-care.

Meanwhile, if I purchased a bath bomb with bergamot and lemongrass essential oils, avocado oil, and olive oil in it, I would probably use it to spice up a long-term monogamous relationship. Lemongrass and avocado promote lust, while olives support fidelity, and bergamot increases prosperity.

Of course, ingredients might sometimes conflict with one another's intentions because the shop probably just wanted something to smell nice. Fear not – there are ways around this.

2. Cleanse It Ahead of Time

It's in your best interests to cleanse items before using them for magical purposes, especially when buying something pre-made. Even something as seemingly simple as a bath bomb was probably manufactured thousands of miles away, packed up, shipped to you via planes, trains, and automobiles, and then delivered to a storefront where a salesperson placed it on the floor. By the time it's reached your bathtub, it's undoubtedly been handled by dozens of people – each with their own lingering energies that can rub off on your bath bomb in small amounts. You don't know what they've got going on, so you might as well wipe the slate clean with some simple purification.

To do this, either submerge the bath bomb in salt for 24 hours (which is probably kind of tricky unless you have a ton of salt lying around) or give it a simple smoke cleansing with whatever incense or cleansing herbs you have on hand.

3. Charge It With Your Intent

You might be wondering why you need to charge the bath bomb after you've already aligned the ingredients with your intent. While I won't stop you from just plopping it into your bath (I've done that more than just a few times), if you want to increase the odds of your spell actually working, you'll need to tell the ingredients what to do together.

Remember the bath bomb I mentioned previously with bergamot and lemongrass essential oils, plus avocado and olive oil? The same associations that I listed out to make a spell for spicing up a monogamous relationship could easily be spun the opposite way: they'd make a nice base for someone looking to get away with having several extramarital affairs. Your ingredients have the energy charge, but *you* need to point them in the right direction.

I'd recommend either making a sigil for your bath bomb, charging it under a related moon phase, or surrounding it with crystals that represent a similar intent (but really, a sigil is probably the safest bet).

4. Combine It With Other Elements

Aside from charging it, the next best way to ensure your spell fires in the right direction is to combine it with other items. I would often use a bath bomb and my Goddess Glamour Bath spell together to make a more intense spellcasting experience (and for an even more luxurious bath). I encourage you to pull out your candles, incense, crystals and even botanical elements if you think they'll work well together.

For example, if I use my bath bomb with bergamot, lemongrass, avocado and olive, I might set up the rim of the tub with pieces of jewelry that my partner and I have gifted to each other so it's clear the spell is referring to the two of us. I could also sprinkle rose petals onto the bathwater, and/or burn a red pillar candle carved with a sigil to heat up our relationship. Just as when you craft a spell from scratch, use your imagination to find ways to associate the magic with your desired outcome.

Other Bath Spells

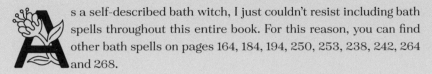

As a self-described bath witch, I just couldn't resist including bath spells throughout this entire book. For this reason, you can find other bath spells on pages 164, 184, 194, 250, 253, 238, 242, 264 and 268.

Enchanting Your Shower

f the last few pages have been borderline torturous for you because you don't have a bathtub or otherwise can't take a bath, have no fear: There are ways to do magic in the shower instead.

I will say at the outset that shower magic misses some of the ritual aspects of a bath (if for no other reason than because it's probably not safe to do by candlelight), and so I tend to think of shower magic as better for mundane magic. Still, if it's impractical to aim for creating a ritual space, the best alternative is to create a spa-like experience with some magic sprinkled in.

Here are a few ideas for how to enchant your shower.

How to Make Magical Shower Disks

 ne of our best (and most popular) innovations on the blog was this spell recipe. I credit this to several aspects of the setup: 1) It takes some of the *magic* (if you will) of bath spells and successfully transports them to the shower, 2) it's easy, and 3) it's endlessly customizable.

Shower disks were first developed as an aromatherapy treatment for when you're feeling tired and congested during a cold. We took this concept and figured that they'd be ideal for shower magic (and great at making your shower feel like a spa). Here's how to make them and use them in your own shower.

Base Recipe

Essentially what you'll be making is a tough, dry tablet that you can leave on the floor of your shower and have slowly dissolve while you bathe. This requires:

- Ø **Muffin tins with liners** or a **silicone baking mold**
- Ø **Bowl** and **spoon** for mixing
- Ø 1 cup of **baking soda**
- Ø 1 tablespoon of **cornstarch**
- Ø Approximately 1/3 cup of **water**
- Ø **Spell ingredients** (see below for ideas)

When you're ready to start preparing your disks, add your dry ingredients (which include the baking soda, cornstarch and ingredients such as ground herbs or powder) to the bowl, then slowly add the water until you have a liquid-y paste (this should be closer to the texture of cake batter than cookie dough). Scoop the mixture into your lined muffin tins or silicone molds, filling them about a third of the way, and leave out for at least 24 hours or until completely dry.

When the disks feel hard and dry, carefully take them out of the liners or molds and store them in a large glass jar for safekeeping. You can add the essential oils when the disks come out of their molds, but I recommend adding them right before use so that you have the most intense aromatherapy experience. (Also, because these essential oils won't be applied directly to your skin, you can use a few more drops than you usually would.) For extra magical *oomph*, store with a crystal matching your intent and charge under the light of a corresponding moon phase.

Spell Ingredient Ideas

Like almost all of the other spells in this book, the possibilities for customization, substitution and combination are nearly endless. I encourage you to use:

- Dried and ground herbs
- Dried flowers and buds
- Essential oils
- Powdered, body-safe ingredients (like activated charcoal or spirulina powder)
- Glitter and luster dust

And so on. The only things that I wouldn't recommend using are fresh botanicals or anything you don't want going down (or getting stuck in) your drain. Otherwise, the world is your oyster for these spells.

If you want to start out by following some of the spells we already created, here are a few ideas:

Cleansing and Purifying

Who has the time to do a full cleansing bath after that curse you conducted at 3 a.m.? Use one of these bad boys instead, and pair with a cleansing scrub for best results.

- Dried **rosemary**
- Pinch of ground **fennel** or dried **peppermint**
- **Rosemary essential oil**
- **Lemongrass essential oil**
- Optional: a pinch of **activated charcoal**

Simple Protection

"Regularly cleanse and protect yourself," is easy to say but a pain to do. This should make it a little bit easier.

- Dried **basil**
- Pinch of ground **cloves**
- Dried **lavender buds**
- **Eucalyptus essential oil**
- **Lavender essential oil**

Attracting Love

Perfect for the singleton ready to get back out there or the polyamorous couple ready to add another partner. Best suited for romantic love.

- ✎ Dried **apple seeds**
- ✎ One dried **lavender blossom** (per disk)
- ✎ Pinch of ground **cinnamon**
- ✎ **Vanilla extract**
- ✎ **Jasmine essential oil**
- ✎ **Ylang ylang essential oil**

For these disks, set aside the lavender blossoms until you've poured the mixture into the tins or molds. Gently press the blooms into the surface and let them dry as normal.

Drawing Money

Whether you need to earn more commission this month, get a higher-paying job, or simply save more money, this spell is for improving the cashflow in your life.

- ✎ Dried **thyme**
- ✎ Dried **mint leaves**
- ✎ Pinch of **allspice**
- ✎ **Patchouli essential oil**
- ✎ **Juniper essential oil**
- ✎ Optional: spoonful of **spirulina powder**

Reigniting Passion

Perfect for individuals who want to bring sexual energy back into a long-term partnership. Use it either by yourself or invite your partner into the shower to share the fun with you.

- ✎ Dried **caraway**
- ✎ Ground **ginger** or ground **saffron**
- ✎ Dried or ground **passionflower**
- ✎ **Vanilla absolute**
- ✎ **Cardamom essential oil**
- ✎ Optional: spoonful of **beetroot powder**

Charging Your Soap

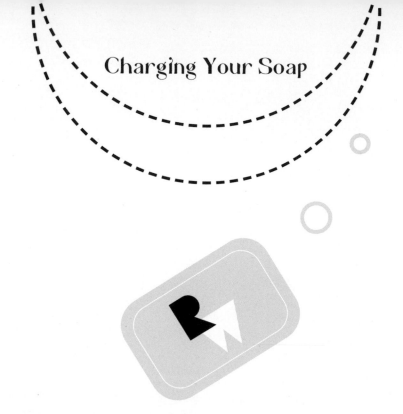

A s with all other objects, you can charge your soap to have magical significance.

Bar soap is the most obvious choice because you can simply buy an herbal soap, match the ingredients to your intent, and carve a sigil into it. For instance, if I purchased a soap that included lemon, geranium and rose essential oils (with some cute dried rose petals on it for decoration), I would charge it for a happy home spell and carve a corresponding sigil into it. You could also make your own soap (if you're not terrified of lye like I am) and add in essential oils and dried botanicals to make your own unique spells.

The same is true for liquid soap and body wash, although this is slightly more complicated. As I discussed at the beginning of this book, plastic is not considered a great conductor of magical energy, but rather a material that *contains* energy. Since most bath products you'll buy are likely in plastic bottles, it's best to decant the contents into a glass container to charge them, and then either decant them back into the original plastic container, or into a new glass bottle.

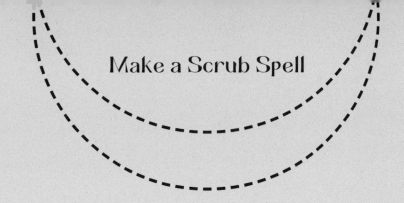

Make a Scrub Spell

nother simple way to add some magic to your shower is to make a scrub spell that is charged with your intent. What do I mean by "scrub spell"? I mean that instead of buying a jar of pre-made body scrub from the supermarket or Sephora, you make a batch for yourself and make it magical.

A scrub spell has a few clear benefits that can make up for deficiencies with the other methods listed in this section. For one, scrub spells actually touch your skin, meaning they pair well with magical shower disks, so that you *and* your environment are charged with your intent. They can also easily be made by hand and are highly customizable in terms of ingredients. Unfortunately, because scrubs often contain oil and fresh ingredients, they don't last as long as other spells we've gone through. They should be used within two weeks of preparation and kept in the fridge when not in use.

I'll be listing some of my favorite scrub spells in the following pages, but as with the bath rituals and magical shower disks we've already covered, once you understand the basic tenets of the formula, it's easy to make your own spells from scratch.

1. Pick an Exfoliating Base

In a scrub spell, obviously the most important part is the base that actually exfoliates. For magical purposes, you'll probably most often be using salt for its cleansing properties, but there is a whole range of ingredients you can use depending on the type of spell you're casting. Here are some of the most popular:

- Sea salt for cleansing
- Pink salt for love
- Black lava salt for purification
- White sugar for love and glamours
- Brown sugar for grounding
- Coffee grounds for energy and spell-boosting
- Ground oats for prosperity

The most important thing to keep in mind here is that whatever type of base you use, the grains should be fine so as to not irritate or damage your skin. If your base needs to be finer, you can always take the ingredient and either grind it down in your mortar and pestle or throw it in a food processor for a couple of seconds.

2. Pick a Binding Oil

You'll also need to pick an oil to bind the base together and provide a bit of a buffer for your skin. As with the base, the possibilities for your choice of oil are numerous, but here are a few of my favorites:

- Coconut oil for protection or purification
- Olive oil for prosperity
- Almond oil for healing and abundance
- Avocado oil for lust and glamours
- Sunflower seed oil for energy or power
- Castor oil for protection
- Grape seed oil for fertility
- Jojoba oil for healing
- Hemp seed oil for psychic ability

Additionally, you could swap all or part of the oil for honey if you're doing an attraction spell.

How much you add is up to you. I prefer to add just enough oil for the granules of the base to stick together, but others might prefer their scrub to have a more liquid-y texture.

3. Choose Your Essential Oils

I won't go through all the possibilities for essential oils and their associations here because I detailed the most popular ones in Chapter Two: The Lazy Witch's Toolkit, but I do want to make a note about essential oils generally. You should have already read my warning in that chapter, but scrub spells are really the place to exercise caution when using essential oils. You'll be putting the mixture *right on your skin* (with abrasive ingredients, no less), so it's always better to start with 1-2 drops and work your way up from there.

Also, just because it warrants repeating: Essential oils can trigger both instant *and* allergic contact dermatitis, meaning that you can have a reaction to a substance after your skin has come into contact with it on multiple occasions. Just because that essential oil didn't bother you last time doesn't mean it can't irritate you in future. Always proceed with caution and use your best judgment.

4. Add in Any Extras

Finally, you can top off your shower magic creation with other fun ingredients. These can include (but aren't limited to):

- Crushed dried flowers and herbs
- Ground spices
- Finely grated citrus peel
- Body-safe glitter
- Pureed fruit (especially if you want some gentle, exfoliating fruit acids)
- Powders (e.g. kelp powder, beetroot powder, etc.)
- Clay (e.g. Kaolin, French Green clay, etc.)

As with the other steps in this section, it's important to exercise good judgment when adding these kinds of extras. These will go directly on your skin, so it would be wise to skip the chili powder or other obvious irritants. When in doubt, do a patch test of your scrub before you use it all over your body.

One final note: While it can be tempting to put these scrubs all over your body, it's best to avoid putting salt and essential oils on your face or near your sex organs. I think it's magically sufficient to avoid these sensitive areas of the body and still have the spell work fine, but if you want an all-over experience, consider making your base something gentle like ground oats or extra-fine sugar.

Purification & Protection Scrubs

Since you're likely taking showers on a fairly regular basis, these are the perfect opportunities to perform purification and protection magic. And (just like cleaning your house) if you're habitually cleansing and protecting your body, you're less likely to need the big guns to get your slate clean again.

That said, I've listed two purification and protection scrubs here for you: one that is better formulated and is worth gathering the ingredients for, and an alternative for when you're in a pinch and you're thinking to yourself: *"I need to get this gross energy off me **now**."*

Start by gathering the ingredients for one of the variations below:

Variation 1

- 2 parts **fine sea salt**
- 1 part **arrowroot powder**
- **Coconut oil**
- A palmful of dried **hyssop**
- 1-3 drops of **lavender essential oil**
- Optional: a pinch of **black lava salt**

Variation 2

- **Fine sea salt**
- **Coconut oil**
- A palmful of dried **basil, rosemary**, or **peppermint**
- A palmful of finely grated **lemon, lime**, or **grapefruit peel**
- 1-3 drops of **lavender essential oil**

First, take whichever dried herb you'll be using and grind it in your mortar and pestle until the pieces are much finer (ideally, you would get them to a powder consistency) while visualizing your intent. Then, transfer the ground herbs to a bowl with the fine sea salt and stir together. If you're using the arrowroot powder, black lava salt or citrus peel, add it during this step. Slowly add in the coconut oil until the scrub is just combined, and finally, top it off with one to three drops of lavender essential oil.

When you're ready to use your scrub spell, start by gently massaging it over your skin in a counterclockwise direction, all the while visualizing the scrub drawing negative energies from your body and sloughing them away. Since this recipe only keeps for about two weeks, you can be generous with the amount of scrub you're using. Once you've finished the counterclockwise motion, massage the scrub in a clockwise motion and visualize the ingredients forming a protective barrier on your skin. Consider yourself cleansed and protected for the days ahead.

Warm Glow Shower Scrub

nstead of wanting to change something about your life, sometimes you just want to do magic to make yourself feel warm and content inside. This scrub is the equivalent of eating your favorite CBD gummies and then wrapping yourself in a cozy blanket on the couch.

To prepare, gather the following ingredients:

- 1 cup of raw **sugar**
- ½ a teaspoon of ground **cloves**
- 4 drops of **sandalwood essential oil**
- 3 drops of **vanilla absolute**
- 2 drops of **neroli** or **tangerine essential oil**
- 1 drop of **clove essential oil**
- **Sweet almond** or **sunflower seed oil**
- Optional: 1 tablespoon of finely grated **tangerine peel**

Stir the sugar and ground cloves together in a bowl, then slowly add either sweet almond oil or sunflower seed oil until the dry ingredients are just coated. If you're using the finely grated tangerine peel, add it now. Finally, slowly add your essential oils, and be extra careful not to add too much clove essential oil – it can easily overpower the other scents.

Store in a glass jar with a lid and place a piece of rose quartz on top for best results. Use the spell within two weeks of preparation.

Energy Shower Scrub

his spell is perfect for those dark winter mornings when you can't seem to fully wake up. Make it the night before and leave it in the shower to use the following day.

Gather the following ingredients:

- ⫽ ½ cup of **coffee grounds** for energy
- ⫽ ½ cup of **brown sugar** for grounding
- ⫽ ½ teaspoon of ground **cinnamon** for strength
- ⫽ **Sunflower seed oil** for energy and power
- ⫽ ½ teaspoon of **vanilla extract** for restoration

Combine your dry ingredients together in a bowl, then add the vanilla extract. Stir together and breathe deeply. Feel the energy of your breath move from your lungs to your chest to your arms and into your hands, then into the mixture you're preparing. Slowly add just enough sunflower seed oil for the dry ingredients to stick together.

Store in a glass jar with a lid and set a piece of citrine crystal on top to charge overnight. In the morning, remove the crystal before starting your shower and using the scrub spell.

Violation Salt Scrub

uch like the matching bath salts on page 132, this spell is to help ease unpleasant feelings that linger after someone has violated your boundaries. As with the other scrub recipes, it's best to make this when you need it and use it within two weeks.

Gather the following ingredients:

- ½ cup of **fine sea salt** for cleansing
- **Coconut oil** for purification and protection
- **Eucalyptus essential oil** for deep healing
- **Lavender essential oil** for peace
- 1 teaspoon of dried **basil** for courage and protection
- 1 teaspoon of finely grated **lemon peel** for cleansing

Add the sea salt, basil and lemon peel to a bowl, and add in one to two drops of each essential oil. Slowly add the coconut oil one teaspoon at a time until you form a scrub-like paste.

When you're ready to use it in the shower or bath, gently start massaging it into your skin. Visualize the negative emotions and memories sloughing off with your dead skin and imbuing the healthy skin underneath with a subtle armor. You have been through hard times, but you are strong, and you will persevere.

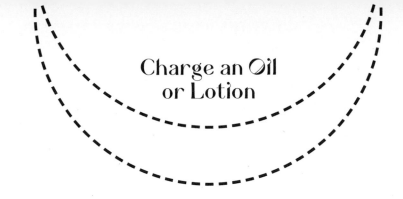

Charge an Oil or Lotion

A s with bath magic, it's ideal to use an oil after your spell to "lock in" the magic from the spell you just cast. However, with shower magic, the oil (or lotion) can take on a more active role since the magic is less complicated. In other words, you should ask more from your oil than simply locking in the magic you already sent out into the world.

As we touched on before, charging an object can be as easy or as complicated as you make it (and I'm always voting for easier). If you always take your showers in the morning, take some sunflower seed oil, decant it into a glass bottle and charge it with a sigil for more energy. If you like to always look your best, pour your avocado oil into a glass bottle you find pretty and charge it as a glamour under the light of a full moon. You can do the same with a pre-formulated body oil. Simply match the ingredients up with your intent and charge accordingly.

And like I mentioned above, you can also charge lotions with magical energy. The issues with this are the same as with body wash: these items are typically sold in plastic and will need to be decanted before charging. After that, the steps are the same as if you were charging anything else.

Make a Pourable Infusion

If push comes to shove and you don't have any time to charge your soap under the light of a full moon or wait for your shower disks to dry completely, you can always make an herbal infusion. I left this spell idea for the very end of the chapter because I think it's the least glamorous option, and because it lacks any obvious ritualized element, I also think it would be difficult for the average person to direct this energy accordingly. Still, it's up to you if you think this could work for you.

An infusion is simply a large container of warm water (probably a bucket) that has herbs stewing in it in order to charge it with an intention. (Think of it like a tea, but you're going to pour it over your head while visualizing your intent.) Theoretically, you could take any of the bath salt mixtures and dissolve it in a bucket in order to create an infusion, or you could create something from scratch.

I'm not going to list out any combinations for spells here because I think I've given you plenty of ideas in this chapter, but rather, I want to end with a reminder of how spells work. Spells are a combination of your intention with various sources of energy (e.g. crystals, herbs, incense, etc.). Your intention – and your ability to focus it – sets the direction that the energy moves in so that your desires are manifested. If you're using an infusion, make sure to make generous use of visualization at each step of the process so that you have a good chance to set your magic off in your desired direction.

Chapter Five: Love Spells for the Modern Witch

On the Ethics of Love Spells

f you bring up the topic of love spells with a group of witches, you'll usually be inundated with opinions from all sides. The traditional Wiccan brand of witchcraft is in one corner, stating that because love spells interfere with an individual's free will, they are inherently bad and should be avoided at all costs. In another corner, we have a group of modern secular witches who think the world's their oyster, and while love spells might be a little questionable, who's really to say what's right and wrong? And finally, there's another part of the modern witch community, engaged in social justice conversations, that is deeply troubled by how consent factors into love spells. Clearly, it's a complicated and fraught topic.

But seeing as I've written a chapter on love spells for this book, I'm evidently not completely against them. So, let's briefly chat about some of the potential issues at hand so that you can decide for yourself how to proceed.

In my opinion, all magic – with love magic being one of the most extreme examples – is in some way ethically dubious with regard to free will. Even if you're not directly trying to make a specific person fall in love with you (or hire you, or give you a bigger tip), you are asking the universe to change the course of events for your benefit. Maybe that cute girl at the bar notices you first and buys you a drink instead of bumping into her future spouse on the other side of the room. Maybe you get your dream job, but that might mean that a more suitable candidate who had to work harder for their position in life will miss out on that opportunity. This isn't to say that we shouldn't cast these types of spells, but rather that *we should be aware of the unintentional consequences of what we do,* and shouldn't be so ignorant as to think that there is any such thing as "good magic" or "bad magic."

Whenever you cast a spell, you are stacking the deck of life in your favor and you need to be prepared to accept responsibility for whatever the outcomes of that decision may be.

Free will is an especially thorny topic because love spells intersect with other cultural conversations about consent. What does "consent" really mean if you've changed someone's mind about what they want? What kind of harm has been done if someone who wouldn't have had sex with you or fallen in love with you under normal circumstances is now interested? Does it matter if they don't feel violated – or is that beside the point?

These are complicated ethical questions that I don't have all the answers to (although I do have a lot of thoughts). In magic, the likelihood that someone will find out that you cast a love spell on them is pretty slim unless you tell them, so these are more philosophical questions that I want you to ask yourself rather than definitively telling you what to do one way or the other. There aren't any magical police officers or juries, and I won't know what you ultimately decide to do. Just ask yourself: Will you be able to reconcile with yourself if you start a relationship based on magical coercion? Are you okay with sleeping with this person if they wouldn't normally be interested in you?

I also think it's worth considering the practical downsides to love spells – because personally, I was never convinced by the love spell shaming in traditional magic books. Setting aside the ethical issues: Love spells typically end in disaster because they're difficult to maintain.

Sure, it's easy enough to convince that person to go on a date with you, or even fall into a brief infatuation with you. Everyone has positive qualities, and the beginnings of a relationship are almost always sunshine and rainbows. But if that person wouldn't normally have fallen for you, what does that say about your overall compatibility? Perhaps they have a different communication style to you. Or different values to you. Or different life goals.

If a person wouldn't have wanted to date you in the first place, you'll have a hard time getting them to stay because you probably just weren't that compatible to begin with. You could always do further magic to aid communication, to strengthen your bond, or to put some passion back into your relationship, but you'll just be slapping bigger and bigger Band-Aids onto an underlying issue that can't be fixed. Plus, wouldn't you rather just date someone who was naturally enthusiastic about you?

Still, I know the feeling of being deep in the throes of infatuation, when you'd pay just about any price to get a taste of what you want. This chapter covers the full spectrum of love spells for the modern individual, from love attraction spells to sex spells to breakup spells. Not all of them are ones I would use myself, but I think that it's always better to have an honest conversation and offer good resources than leave people to their own devices to create more disastrous spells.

With that out of the way, let's dive into some love spells for the modern witch.

Love-Drawing Bath Soak

I f you're looking for more love in your life but are unsure about the ethics of more targeted love spells, love *drawing* spells can be a gentler alternative. These types of spells aren't focused on a particular person, but rather, encourage love to come into your life. (Although as I noted before, you are not totally off the hook regarding the potential consequences.)

I've constructed this spell in such a way that you can either use the bath salts on their own (or gift them to a lonely heart in your life), or use them as a base for an additional ritual that will strengthen the spell.

Bath Salt Mixture

Gather the following ingredients:
- 1 cup of **coarse pink salt** for love
- ½ cup of **baking soda** (as base)
- A palmful of **lavender buds** and/or **dill seeds**[11] for attraction
- 1 tablespoon of finely grated **orange zest** for beauty
- A handful of **miniature rosebuds** for long-lasting love
- **Sweet orange essential oil** for attractiveness
- **Rose absolute or essential oil** for lasting relationships

Start by adding the pink salt and baking soda to a bowl, then slowly stir in the lavender buds and/or dill seeds while thinking about the warm glow of good love. Keep thinking about the love you want to bring into your life while adding the orange peel and miniature rosebuds. Finish with a few drops of each essential oil, then store in a glass jar with a piece of rose quartz. Charge under the light of a full moon for best results.

If you're simply using the bath salts, then draw a warm bath and dissolve the salts in the water. Bathe until the heat dissipates.

---

11   Historically, lavender is associated with attracting men, and dill with attracting women. If you're bisexual or like otherwise gender non-conforming individuals, add in both.

Optional Bath Ritual

If you want to increase your odds of bringing love into your life, you can turn the bath into a full ritual. For this, you will need:

- The **bath salts** you prepared
- **Pink** and **red candles**
- **Gardenia** or **jasmine incense**
- **A piece of jewelry** you don't mind getting wet
- **Avocado oil**
- Optional: **fresh flowers** to add to the bathwater

Begin the bath spell as you would any other: Light your candles and your incense, then start drawing a warm bath. Position the piece of jewelry on the rim of the tub so that you can easily reach it while you're in the water. Add the bath salt mixture. If you're going to use fresh flowers in this spell, add them to the water right before you enter the bath.

While you're relaxing in the tub, think about the qualities you'd like to attract in a future partner and envision how a new romance would alter your life. When you're almost ready to get out of the bath, take the piece of jewelry and submerge it in the water. Feel the last bit of energy from the bath charge the jewelry, then remove it from the water when it feels energetically full.

Exit the bath when you feel ready and let yourself air-dry. When you're mostly dry, massage your skin with the avocado oil. Once you've cleaned up after your ritual, take your piece of jewelry and wear it until you find your new love.

Simple Love Attraction Jar

s mentioned before, the least "ethically problematic" type of love spell is one that simply draws love towards you. This spell is a simple but effective start for someone looking to add a little bit more romance to their life.

For this spell, you'll need:

- ⌀ A **clear glass jar** (ideally one you find nice to look at)
- ⌀ **Himalayan pink salt** for attracting love
- ⌀ Pieces of dried **orange rind** for happiness in love
- ⌀ Dried **hibiscus flowers** or dried **rosemary** for lust and love
- ⌀ 1 dried **red rose blossom** for a lasting relationship

For best results, create a sigil from scratch for drawing love into your life and place at the bottom of the jar. Then, layer the following ingredients on top, starting with the pink salt, then adding the orange rind and following with the hibiscus or rosemary. Finish by adding the red rose on top and position it so it's facing outward.

Place the jar in a part of your living area that you notice frequently. If you haven't found a romantic interest in three months, change out the ingredients but keep the same sigil at the base.

First Date Charm

 o, you have a first date coming up, and you *really* like them. They're just *so cute*, and *so funny*, and like all the same things that you do, and you'd like a bit of magical luck to help this date go as well as possible. This little charm is for exactly such a scenario.

Ingredients

- A 1-inch piece of fresh **ginger**
- 1 **whole clove**
- 1 or 2 of the following, preferably fresh:
    - **Jasmine bud**
    - **Cowslip**
    - **Blue violet**
    - **Gardenia petal**
    - **Hibiscus**
    - **Lemon balm**
    - **Marigold petals**
- A small, pretty **piece of cloth or lace**
- A piece of **string**, or other item to tie your charm together

In a perfect world, you would cast this spell by candlelight during the night of the new moon (with some incense and in a cast circle for good measure), and then go on the date within the following two weeks, before the full moon. That said, we all live in the *real world* and I'm not about to recommend moving your date with your Big Crush to the night after the new moon, because an unexpected and unexplainable schedule change might cause the intended effect to backfire. So, simply cast the spell whenever you have time.

You might also have noticed that you have a fair degree of freedom regarding one of the primary spell components. I've provided you with a list of popular flowers (and herbs) that are ideal for attracting or promoting new love. I'd recommend picking one or two that are best suited for you (mostly based on which of them feel the most *right* to you). As I mentioned in the Mechanics of a Spell (page 22), your own personal associations can make a big difference in the success or failure of a spell. Worst case scenario, you can pull a "me" and just use whichever ingredients are easiest to get your hands on.

Ritual

Take your gathered items to a flat surface that can serve as your workstation. Take the piece of ginger into your hand and think about your crush. Feel the attraction you have towards them and visualize the best-case scenario attraction between the two of you.

Now, take your flowers and/or herbs and place them on top of the ginger, imagining a bit of real romance blossoming between you both. Think for a second about what that love would feel like. Take the clove in your dominant hand, and slowly drive the pointy end through the flower and into the ginger. You've fastened them together and given yourself a bit of luck.

Hold the charm in your hands one more time, visualizing the best possible outcome of the date. Take the piece of fabric and wrap the charm inside. Fasten it with the string.

On your date, take the charm with you in your purse or in your pocket.

Dating App Spell

As I was sketching out the major aspects of modern love so that I could best provide spells for the modern witch, it seemed impossible to get around the issue of dating apps.

Nearly everyone is using them, and likewise, nearly everyone seems to hate them. At face value, this should be excellent topic to write a spell for, since the potential number of people I'd be helping would be huge. But unfortunately, it also seems that everyone hates dating apps for different reasons. Some people get too many people interested in them; others get too few. Some complain that the quality of connection is low; others complain that the girl simply wasn't as hot as she was in her pictures. There's too much casual sex. Or too *little* casual sex. Or too much effort just to get to the casual sex. The list goes on.

So, before we dive into this spell, I want to briefly play the role of the grandma in your friend group. I want you to ask yourself what you want to change about your dating experience online. At first glance, it might seem like you and all your friends are griping about the same things, but that's probably not the case if you really listen. Figure out what you're really hoping to get out of dating apps, and then we can move on to this simple sigil spell.

Ingredients

- 1 piece of **paper**
- 1 **pen**
- 1 **pencil**
- A pinch of ground **cinnamon**
- A pinch of dried **saffron** or ground **cardamom**
- 1 **candle**

Now that you have your ingredients and your crystal-clear intention, you're going to make a sigil! Write out what you want your online dating experience to be, and frame it in a positive, present-tense sentence (e.g. *"I am meeting people who I am compatible with for a long-term, loving partnership,"* or, *"I am hooking up with fun, good-looking people who respect my boundaries."*).

Next, you're going to make a sigil, first sketching it out in pencil – so you can erase it when you hate the first version – and then making a version in ink. (If you need a refresher on how to make a sigil, refer to page 82 for detailed instructions.) Once you're happy with the final version, make a copy of your sigil.

Light your candle and gently tear your sigils out from the paper. Visualize your intention clearly, then take one of the sigils and set it aflame (you might need a heatproof dish to let it burn completely). Right after the sigil is burned, drop a pinch of ground cinnamon into the flame, followed by a pinch of saffron or ground cardamom.

Finally, take your remaining sigil and put it in your phone case so that the sigil is facing upwards, towards the phone. Extinguish the flame.

Love-Strengthening Bath for Couples

Another way to partially circumvent the ethical issues of love spells is to cast them on a willing participant – your partner. It's totally normal and expected to have the intensity and passion of a relationship diminish over time as you cultivate stability and love for each other. This spell is for the couple[12] who wants to keep their love and passion strong as they build their relationship over time.

I will note at the outset that this spell calls for a few more ingredients than usual (and you can always substitute or omit as you see fit), but I think it's worth it because you're investing a bit of extra time and energy into someone you love. Gather the following ingredients:

- 2 cups of powdered **milk** or powdered **coconut milk**
- 1 cup of **pink salt**
- 2 teaspoons of ground **cardamom**
- 1 tablespoon of dried **raspberry leaves**
- A pinch of **saffron**
- A handful dried **rosebuds** or dried **rose petals**
- Optional: a handful of dried **marigold petals**
- Optional: **ylang ylang** and/or **lavender essential oil**

Combine the ingredients together in a bowl, then funnel into a glass jar or other large glass container. Charge under the light of a full moon for best results.

When you're ready to use the mixture, draw a warm bath and light some candles to set up a romantic atmosphere for you and your partner. Put on some music that the two of you find relaxing and add the bath mixture to the water. (If you don't want to have extra cleanup work after your spell, you can also put the mixture in large muslin bags before tossing it into the water.)

Once you're both in the bath, spend time gazing at each other, softly touching each other, or gently washing each other in the water.

––––––––––––

12   I say "couple" here because most bathtubs can barely fit two people. That said, if you're in a romantic relationship with more than two people, the spell will still work as long as your bathtub is big enough.

Romance Sprays

We might think of romance as being "in the air" on Valentine's Day, but what if you could take this sentiment and transport it wherever you wished, like in your living room before setting your friends up on a date, or in your bedroom for your anniversary? Enter these romance sprays.

These little room sprays not only smell lovely but fill the air with a subtle charge for love (and maybe some passion). I've provided a couple of variations on the ingredients, depending on your intended purpose.

On a practical note, because this room spray doesn't include any preservatives, I highly recommend storing it in a small bottle, using it liberally, and keeping it in the fridge for maximum longevity. Unrefrigerated, you should expect the room spray to last about a month before you'll need to toss the rest.

Base Ingredients

- *Distilled water*
- **Witch hazel** (or vodka, although it has a much stronger smell)
- Small **glass spray bottle**
- Optional: 1 small piece of **rose quartz**

To prepare, take your glass bottle and fill it with equal parts witch hazel and distilled water. Leave enough space for approximately 30-40 drops of essential oil, plus the piece of rose quartz (if using). For best results, charge under the light of the full moon and/or set it on top of a sigil matching your intent.

Shake the room spray each time before use.

Falling in Love Blend

You know that new relationship energy where everything is exciting, and your brain is drowning in feel-good chemicals? This blend is that feeling in a bottle.

- 10 drops of **ylang ylang** essential oil
- 15 drops of **lime**
- 15 drops **patchouli** essential oil

Aphrodisiac Blend

Whether you're looking to turn up the heat with your spouse or you want a little help setting the right mood for your ritual orgy, you can't go wrong with this lust-inducing blend.

- 10 drops of **tonka** (or **vanilla**)
- 10 drops of **cardamom**
- 5 drops of **clove**
- 5 drops of **patchouli**

Date Night Blend

The perfect date night with a long-term partner is fun, loving, sexy, and reminds you why you picked them in the first place. This blend helps set that tone, and you can choose to swap the jasmine for ylang ylang if you want your evening to skew more towards sexy than comforting.

- 🌿 15 drops of **sweet orange**
- 🌿 10 drops of **sandalwood**
- 🌿 5 drops of **jasmine** or **ylang ylang**
- 🌿 5 drops of **cinnamon**

Love-Strengthening Blend

Sometimes, even the best relationships go through periods of tension and disconnection. Spray this blend in your space to welcome in a peaceful, loving atmosphere.

- 🌿 15 drops of **sandalwood**
- 🌿 10 drops of **gardenia**
- 🌿 5 drops of **jasmine**
- 🌿 5 drops of **patchouli**

Witch Tip:

You can easily make your romance sprays more queer by swapping the floral notes of blends! Use violet for queer women, lavender for queer men, and mix both to include the entire gender spectrum.

Love Repression Spell

Yes, the heart wants what it wants, but we're here to put a stop to that. Sometimes, you just have to stamp out new-found (or still-lingering) feelings before they become a real problem. (In fact, most of the stories in this book could have been avoided if I had just used this spell from the outset.) Maybe you're falling for your very-married boss and don't want to torpedo the rest of your career. Perhaps, in your polyamorous relationship, your boyfriend says you can sleep with his ex, so long as you two don't start dating. Maybe your best friend is about to totally screw herself over by dating that douchebag again and you want to step in. Whatever the reason, this spell nips blossoming love right in the bud so it can't grow any further.

To perform the spell, you will need:
- 🌿 1 **flowerpot**
- 🌿 Enough **soil** for your chosen pot
- 🌿 1 teaspoon of **Himalayan pink salt**
- 🌿 1 **apple seed** or an **avocado, cherry,** or **peach pit**

Start by filling your flowerpot with the soil. Then, take your seed or pit and visualize the love starting to grow in your (or someone else's) heart. Bury the seed in the soil.

Now, take the pink salt and slowly sprinkle it over the soil: You are making the soil an infertile place for this love to grow. Slowly mix the salt further into the dirt and envision this love slowly fizzling out and going nowhere.

Keep the pot and soil nearby until you're sure that the love has died down. If you still feel your love lingering, add more salt (and block them on social media while you're at it).

Repel an Unwanted Lover Powder

aybe you've caught the eye of your company's newest bright-eyed and bushy-tailed intern, or your best friend's ex keeps leaving vague but suggestive emojis in the comments of all of your selfies. Perhaps you just don't have the heart to tell your weird neighbor down the hall that you will always be too busy to have a drink with them.

You surely *could* tell them that you're very flattered by their attention, but you're not interested in dating them – but why set clear boundaries when you could let magic do the hard work for you?

Ingredients

- 1 piece of dried **orange rind**
- 3 dried **red rose petals**
- A **heatproof bowl**
- A **lighter** or **matches**
- A strip of **paper**
- A **pen**
- ½ teaspoon of **fine sea salt**
- ½ teaspoon of ground **pink pepper** or **black pepper**
- A small **glass vial** or other container
- Optional: **mortar and pestle**
- Optional: **baby powder**

Gather your orange rind, rose petals, heatproof bowl, lighter, pen, and paper and take them outside (because this part creates a bit of smoke, and you care about your lungs and your smoke detectors not going off).

With your lighter, carefully light the piece of dried orange rind, then set it in your heatproof bowl to smolder. Do the same thing with your three dried red rose petals. Finally, write the name of the person you want to repel on the paper, and burn that, too. Imagine your target slowly losing interest in you and going on their merry way with someone else. (Note: If you want to repel romantic attention from your life completely, you can simply omit adding someone's name here.) Let the mixture smolder and burn until everything is turned to ash, then take the bowl back indoors.

At this point, there are two different ways to proceed, depending on how you want to use the powder. The easier way is to take the ashes and combine them with the salt and pepper, then store them together in the glass vial. To use, simply sprinkle over your surroundings when you're mostly likely to run into your unwanted suitor.

To up the ante, you can also take your salt and pepper and add them to your mortar and pestle, slowly grinding them into a powder consistency. Combine this mixture with the ashes, then stir in at least a cup of baby powder and mix until everything is evenly distributed. Store in a larger glass vial or a small glass jar. Apply the mixture to your skin before you're most likely to encounter your unwanted lover.

Spell to Prevent Cheating

would personally not use this spell, because if you're in a position where you think your partner is cheating or is likely to cheat, you'd probably be much better served by renegotiating the terms of your relationship, going to couple's therapy, or simply finding a new partner who shares your values. That said, sometimes it doesn't hurt to buy a bit of time before initiating a difficult conversation.

Ingredients

- ½ teaspoon of **cumin seeds**
- ½ teaspoon of **caraway seeds**
- 1 to 2 tablespoons of **olive oil**
- **Self-lighting charcoal**
- A **heatproof bowl**
- **Tongs**
- A **lighter** or **matches**
- A strip of **paper**
- A small **paint brush** or **makeup brush**
- Optional: ½ teaspoon of cut **licorice root**

At night, gather your ingredients and take them to a suitable workstation. (As a precaution, this spell creates quite a bit of smoke, so you might want to do it outside for the sake of your lungs and your smoke detectors.) Light a few candles if you'd like.

Take your tongs and pick up a single piece of self-lighting charcoal. Carefully light the piece of charcoal[13], then set it in your heatproof bowl and slowly add your cumin seeds, caraway seeds, and licorice root (if using) on top. Let the mixture smolder and burn until all of the seeds and root pieces are turned to ash, then remove the piece of charcoal and set it aside somewhere safe. Take a small amount of the ashes (about a quarter of a teaspoon) and set them aside.

Next, add your olive oil to the ashes and use your brush to mix them together in the bowl. Take your slip of paper and, while envisioning you and your partner being completely faithful to each other, write your names together with the oil. (For practical reasons, you might only want to write first names down, e.g. "Barack + Michelle," but ideally you should use full names, e.g. "Barack Obama + Michelle Obama.") Wait for the oil to dry, then roll up the paper and store it somewhere safe in your home.

Once you've cleaned up your spell remnants, take the reserved ashes and add one pinch to your partner's favorite pair of shoes, or the shoes you think they'd have the most opportunities to cheat in, such as their work shoes.

---

13   If you've never used self-lighting charcoal, it can be a bit difficult to get used to. Essentially, you need to hold it to a flame for several seconds until it starts to crackle and burn. You might want to watch a tutorial online before you do it for the first time.

Spell to Break Up a Couple

t's happened to everyone: Your wonderful, stunning, all-around-amazing friend has gone and fallen in love with the most inconsiderate (and perhaps downright evil) person you've ever met. You were patient for the first few months, quietly hoping that they'd see just how horrible their partner really is and leave them.

Unfortunately, as miserable as their partner is, this couple just won't split on their own. You could continue to be an understanding and supportive friend – or you could go ahead and end their relationship on your own terms. This spell is for the second type of friend.

Ingredients

- 1 **apple**, preferably **red**
- 1 **turnip**
- **Twine** or **black ribbon**
- 1 **knife**
- Multiple **candles**, preferably **black**
- **Pen** and **paper**
- Optional: 2 **toothpicks**
- Optional: **potting soil** and **flowerpots**

At any point during the waning moon cycle, gather your ingredients and take them to your workspace. Light your candles so that you work exclusively by candlelight.

Start by making a simple sigil (see page 81) of your target couple's names, e.g. "Jane Doe and John Smith." Carve the sigil into one side of the apple.

While envisioning your intent of ending the relationship, cut the apple in half, positioning your knife so that you slice through the sigil. Cut the turnip in half as well. Take your piece of twine or ribbon, and tie one half of the apple to one half of turnip, and then tie the remaining halves of the apple and turnip together. (You can use your toothpicks here to anchor the pieces of apple and turnip together to make the tying easier.)

At this point, you have two options: If possible, you will close your workspace, go outside and bury the two apple-turnip bundles in the ground. You should bury them in different locations with quite a bit of distance in between (which, based on your location, might be on opposite sides of a block, or miles apart at opposite ends of a city).

If this isn't feasible, take some potting soil and two flowerpots, and bury each apple-turnip bundle in a different pot. Place them in your home so that they're as far apart as possible.

Post Break-Up Healing Bath

Whether you're the one being broken up with or the one initiating the split, break-ups can be grueling affairs. It just *is* that difficult to separate from someone that you are significantly emotionally invested in – even if you know it's the right course of action, or that your friends hate them, or you always knew it wouldn't work out long-term. No amount of rationalization is going to take the pain away.

This bath spell was crafted to give you the time and space to grieve in peace, so that you can slowly begin to process and heal. It is not a heartbreak cure-all or a magical Band-Aid to put you back together in the course of a night. After the bath, you should expect to feel calmer, more centered, and like the edge has been taken off for the worst aspects of your grief.

Because you will likely be grieving for a while, I recommend making these bath salts in a big batch and using about a cup of the mixture at a time. (And while I originally wrote this spell for break-ups, it also works for healing from the death of a loved one, or other types of major loss.)

Bath Salt Mixture

- 1 cup of **sea salt**
- 1 tablespoon of dried **marjoram**[14] or **thyme**
- 1 tablespoon of dried **sage**
- **Cypress essential oil**
- **Eucalyptus essential oil**
- Optional: **lavender essential oil**
- Optional: 1 tablespoon of **chamomile buds**

Combine all of the dry ingredients in a bowl, stirring until the herbs are evenly distributed throughout the salt. Add the essential oils in equal parts to each other (e.g. five drops of cypress, five drops of eucalyptus, and five drops lavender). Mix together, then funnel into a glass jar until you're ready to use. For best results, store with a piece of amethyst.

---

14   Marjoram is possibly unsafe for those who are pregnant or nursing, so if this applies to you, please use thyme instead.

Bath Ritual

When you're ready to start your bath, gather:

- ⌀ The **bath salts** you prepared
- ⌀ **Black** and/or **white candles**
- ⌀ Optional: **incense** of your choice
- ⌀ Optional: 1 piece of **amethyst**
- ⌀ Optional: 1 sprig of **eucalyptus** or **lavender**

Start by lighting your candles, followed by your incense (if using). Draw a comfortably warm bath, and position your amethyst, eucalyptus and/or lavender around the rim of the tub. Add the bath salt mixture and enter when you're ready.

Spend your time in the bath just sitting with yourself in peace. (Feel free to put on a sad playlist if it makes you feel more understood and validated in what you're going through.) You're free to interact with your grief as much or as little as you'd like: This is *your* time, and you don't have to pretend to be strong if you don't want to. It's okay to cry in your bath.

When you're ready to exit, take your piece of amethyst (if using) and submerge it in the water. Put it back on the rim of the tub to dry. As you get out of the bath, imagine leaving just one tiny fraction of your grief in the water. The full weight hasn't been lifted, but you're one pound lighter.

If you used amethyst in this spell, take it and bind it together with the sprig of eucalyptus or lavender. Carry it around with you for extra peace and healing.

Chapter Six: Glamours

The Making of
a Goddess

Some witches use their magical talents to try and understand themselves, to create peace and harmony, or to help those around them. I, on the other hand, used magic to make myself into my own personal version of beauty incarnate.

The Goddess Glamour Bath had been one of our staple spells since the first summer of our practice. I can't even remember what the impetus for creating the glamour was – I had monogamously coupled myself with someone who was spending their summer halfway around the world from me – but I remember standing in Rhea's kitchen, haphazardly throwing ingredients into a small piece of Tupperware, trying to make a glamour bath spell.

"Do we have any ylang ylang essential oil?" I asked Rhea, rummaging through the dozen or so small glass bottles in the overhead cabinet.

"No, I think we bought neroli last time, instead. What about jasmine?"

"You really think I should use jasmine? I thought it was better for attracting love." I pulled out the rose and sweet orange essential oils from the cabinet and set them on the counter.

"I think it'll work in a pinch."

I shrugged and pulled out the jasmine as well. In my plastic Tupperware, I poured out enough sea salt to fill the container halfway, then took three dried rose petals, crushed them in my palm, and brushed the pieces into the salt. I added a dash of ground cinnamon, followed by the rose, sweet orange, and jasmine essential oils, reattached the lid, and shook the container vigorously to mix everything together.

I opened the container again and stared at the mixture. "I feel like it's missing something," I announced to Rhea. The bath salts smelled heady and too sweet, and they looked more like fake sand than something that was supposed to make me beautiful.

She walked over to the cabinet and gently sorted through several ingredient options with her slender fingers and long, jet-black nails. I remembered how Luca used to call Rhea "Talons" as a pet name, and it seemed like a particularly apt description at that moment.

There was a long pause during which it became clear that none of the herbal ingredients we had would be the right addition. "What about glitter?" she asked. Typically, I was opposed to adding artificial ingredients, but I knew that Rhea and I could make better spells together than when we created them independently.

She added a pinch of gold glitter to the mixture, and I stirred it together to see how it looked.

Now it just looked like dirty salt with glitter in it.

"Okay, I think it's still off, but I have to run. I need to take a bath with this in it, blow-dry my hair, and reapply my makeup in the next couple of hours. I'll let you know how it goes afterwards." I reattached the lid and shoved the bath mixture in my bag, then hugged Rhea before heading out into the blinding summer heat.

Calling the bath spell that I conducted afterwards a "ritual" would be a stretch, even for me.

I lit the candles that I'd left surrounding the tub from my previous bath spell, started burning some dragon's blood incense (because I still believed that stronger always equaled better), and added some nice-looking trinkets around the tub to fill the empty space. I put on Beyonce's most recent album, and then, once the tub was mostly full, unceremoniously dumped in the bath salts.

After I got out of the bath, I didn't think much about the spell. Sure, the bright red spots from my cystic acne seemed a bit less pronounced and my hair looked shinier than usual, but I just shrugged and happily went about getting ready.

Despite whichever self-identified imperfections were bothering me in the moment, I had always considered myself an attractive person. I heard regularly from my friends that people were interested in me, and I was used to my sexual advances being reciprocated.

But the attention I received after this spell was different. There was a new sensation of other people's eyes on me – not just looking at me, not just giving me a standard once-over, but lingering on me as I moved through the room. *Following* me.

The way people smiled at me was different, too. It was wider, warmer, more enthusiastic.

The moment when everything clicked was when a stranger complimented me on my skin. *My skin?* I thought. *Is she insane?*

No, I'd just stumbled across the spell version of rose-colored glasses: I had found a way to make everyone look at me like they had just fallen in love.

❧

I'd love to say that I saved this glamour for special occasions and was simply satisfied that I'd stumbled upon this gem of a spell. But that'd be a lie.

After reporting back to Rhea about the spell's success, we tinkered around with it constantly to increase its effectiveness. I added a compact mirror to better "seal in" the glamour and increase its longevity. Rhea made a solid perfume version (page 197) that could be applied on the go. I became more discerning about the trinkets I used to line the tub and the music I played in the background. I used the base bath salt mixture alongside pre-made bath bombs, liquid bubble bath, and a variety of seasonal ingredients that I thought could boost its potency.

After a dozen iterations, I settled on the version you'll see on page 194. If performed in its entirety, the spell lasts for 10-14 days; so, for nearly two years, I re-cast the spell every two weeks to ensure that I was at my most attractive at all times. Sometimes, I cast it even more frequently if I had someone I particularly wanted to impress.

The only time I thought one of my iterations was too strong was when I mixed it with a pre-made bath salt mixture that I'd bought from a local herb shop.

It was a simple mixture for "promoting self-love," and it contained red rose petals, red rosebuds, chamomile, lavender and calendula petals, as well as lavender and ylang ylang essential oils – nearly all excellent ingredients for glamours. I added it to my bath the next time I conducted the full Goddess Glamour Bath ritual and otherwise didn't think about it for the next several hours.

My first clue that something was different was when I was at a mixer, and a man who was significantly older than me came up to me and asked for my number.

And then someone else did the same thing a day later.

And then someone sent me a drink from across the bar.

I went over to Rhea's place two days after I cast the spell, and before I could even start recounting these stories to her, she stopped me with her own observation.

"You seem different," she said.

"How so? I did a new spell of sorts a couple of days ago."

"You seem really... charged. I don't know how to describe it. Like I can see the energy coming off you."

I told Rhea about my most recent changes to the glamour, impressed with myself as I always was whenever my magic performed better than I anticipated. I was still feeling fairly smug as we went out shopping for new crystals, but my self-satisfaction turned to annoyance as a man followed us around while we were browsing, refusing to leave us alone.

"I'm a little concerned about these new additions to the Goddess Glamour Bath," Rhea told me as we left the store. "The effects are kind of predatory."

"Agreed. I think I finally found a way to make myself *too* beautiful."

In the end, the intense level of attention I received lasted for four days before returning to normal. And while I never cast that version of the spell ever again, I've always kept it in my spellbook in case I ever need to be truly irresistible.

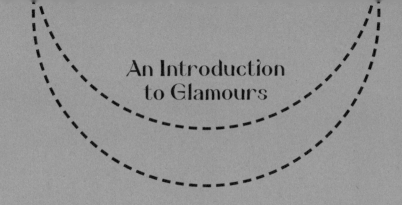

An Introduction to Glamours

or the uninitiated, a glamour spell is any spell that alters your appearance. Of course, we're limited to the confines of the practical and psychological, so you can't pull a Harry Potter and transform into your nemesis' ugly friends. Real-life glamours are much more about subtly shifting the way in which people perceive you, like the magical version of getting a good facial or putting on mascara.

And while I should note that glamours can alter your appearance in a number of ways, I chose to only tweak my appearance in one direction: to improve it.

Call me vain or superficial if you like, but once you try a beauty glamour, you never go back. Here are some of my favorite variations for you to try out for yourself.

Goddess Glamour Bath

If I could go back in time before I was running the blog with Rhea, I would have renamed this spell the "Helen of Troy Glamour," because once you've cast it, you will feel so beautiful that nations could go to war over you. When I was actively practicing, I conducted this spell at *least* once per month – but if I'm being honest, it ended up being more like once every 10 days. If you have a similar (read: *vain*) type of personality to me, I'm warning you now that there is something quite addictive about this spell. It can be hard to go from being the most beautiful person in the room to wherever you fell on the totem pole before (even though I'm sure you were always close to the top). So, with this Surgeon General's warning out of the way, let's get into the spell itself.

Like most of the other bath magic spells in this book, there are two key parts to the spell: the bath mixture itself, and the corresponding ritual. I personally think the mixture works better if you make it for yourself, but you're also free to give a batch to someone else to use. And as I noted in the introduction to bath magic, I typically liked to make a batch big enough to last for several baths so that I didn't have to re-prepare the mixture every other week.

Bath Salt Mixture

For the mixture, combine the following ingredients in a mortar and pestle:

- 🌿 2 parts **sea salt**
- 🌿 2 parts **Epsom salts**
- 🌿 1 part **baking soda**
- 🌿 3-5 dried **red rose petals**
- 🌿 **Sweet orange essential oil**
- 🌿 **Rose essential oil**
- 🌿 **Jasmine essential oil**
- 🌿 A dash of **cinnamon**
- 🌿 Optional: a pinch of **body-safe**[15] **glitter**

---

15   What's the difference between body-safe glitter and craft glitter? Body-safe glitter and craft glitter are produced differently, and craft glitter has sharp edges that can damage your eyes, skin, or other sensitive areas of your body (especially important to keep in mind for bath spells!). If you want to also minimize plastics ending up in our oceans, make sure to buy biodegradable glitter.

Grind all of these together while envisioning your intent (which is to become the most beautiful, divine version of yourself). You can either use it immediately or store it in a glass jar with a pretty crystal or a whole dried rose bloom.

The Bath Ritual

Ideally, you should do this at night or in a bathroom where you can block out natural light, so that you can bathe exclusively by candlelight (candlelight is flattering for basically everybody).

When you're ready to begin your ritual, gather together:

- The **bath salts** you prepared
- **Gold, pink** and/or **white candles**
- **Items you find beautiful**
- **Dragon's blood incense**
- A **small mirror** (ideally, one you find pretty or associate with beauty)
- A **scented lotion** you like, or **evening primrose** or **avocado oil**
- A **playlist** you find empowering

Start lighting your candles and placing them around the tub and on your countertops, then kill any artificial lights. Now's the time to start arranging the mirror and the items you find beautiful. The goal here is to embody the beauty of the objects, so it's really up to you which kinds of trinkets you'd like to select. I typically displayed crystals, ornate antiques, jewelry, flowers and an elegant robe to wear afterwards, but you should choose items that feel authentically beautiful to you. (The only type of object I'd stay away from is pictures of other people, because 1) that's not very kind to yourself, and 2) you'll always be more beautiful as a polished version of yourself than as a poor imitation of someone else.) At this point, light your dragon's blood incense to increase the potency of the spell.

Start drawing a warm bath and add the bath salts. While the tub fills, you should start playing your music to get into the right mindset.

Once the tub is full, enter the bath. Ideally, you should submerge as much of your body in the water as possible, but if you don't want to get your hair wet (I've been there) or otherwise can't submerge part of your body, just use your hands to get the bathwater on as much of your skin as possible. While doing this, envision the water transforming you into a flawless, breathtakingly beautiful version of yourself.

When you're nearly ready to get out of the bath, take your mirror and look at your dimly lit reflection. Imagine any "imperfections" you see becoming slowly less and less visible until they disappear completely. Say something empowering (I recommend "I am beautiful, and everyone knows it," if you don't have an incantation you like better), then kiss the surface of the mirror. Now, turn the mirror over and stow it away.

Slowly get out of your bath and let yourself air-dry if possible. When you're about 80% dry, apply your scented lotion or oil to lock in the energy of the glamour (and to lock the moisture into your skin). From here, you can drain your bath and clean up.

At this point, you should be an absolutely stunning version of your-self, and you shouldn't have to wait long for the compliments to start rolling in. The effects are strongest right after the spell has completed, and slowly taper off in the following days.

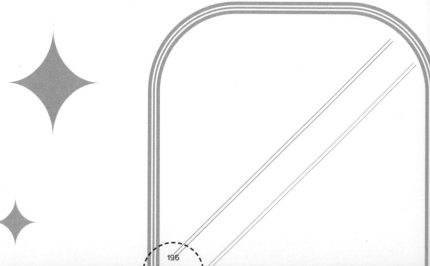

Glamour Solid Perfume

After we published the Goddess Glamour Bath on the blog, we soon received a ton of positive – and public – feedback that our spell was a miracle-worker. It made you look like you had gone to therapy, taken a tropical vacation, got a facial, and had Gwyneth Paltrow's personal chef cook for you for a year – and it could be accomplished in less than an hour, in a bathtub.

But of course, once you make something useful, people are often keen to get the benefits in an even faster, less energy-intensive way. After tinkering around with this recipe a few times for our own personal use, we followed up the GGB with this solid perfume, so you can touch up your glamour on the go.

The most critical part of this spell is finding a small container to hold the solid perfume. Ideally, it should be something you find visually pleasing (it is a glamour, after all), but aside from that, it can be any small receptacle with a lid. We used a large antique locket, but you could also use a pretty tin, or a vintage pill box, or anything else along those lines. Because the size of your item will likely vary significantly from what we produced, I wrote this spell in parts rather than fixed measurements.

Ingredients

- A small container
- 1 part **grapeseed** or **sweet almond oil**
- ⅛ part **beeswax**
- **Sweet orange essential oil**
- **Ylang ylang essential oil**
- **Rose absolute**
- Optional: a pinch of **gold glitter**

In the microwave, heat the beeswax in a short burst on a low temperature until melted down. (You can also do this in a double-broiler on the stove if you don't have a microwave.) Mix in the grapeseed or sweet almond oil. Add your essential oils until the mixture is fragrant (depending on the size of your container and the amount of wax you're using, this will likely be between 30-50 drops in total). If you're using glitter, stir it in now.

Decant the melted mixture into your container and let it solidify over several hours. Charge over a sigil matching your intent. To use, run your finger over the mixture until soft and fragrant, and dab on the pulse points of your body.

Quick & Dirty Glamour Scrub

There come times in one's life when you'd like to feel significantly more beautiful, but because of limited time, money or resources, you don't have the ability to drop a few hundred dollars at the salon or spare the time to do a full glamour bath. This spell is for those occasions when you find out two hours beforehand that your crush will be showing up to your best friend's birthday party, or your spouse surprises you with a last-minute date night.

Gather the following ingredients:

- ⌀ ¾ cup of **white sugar**
- ⌀ **Honey**
- ⌀ **Avocado oil** or **evening primrose oil**
- ⌀ 2 teaspoons of finely grated **orange rind**
- ⌀ Optional: **lemon verbena** or **ylang ylang essential oil**

In a small bowl, add the white sugar and the grated orange rind. Then, slowly stir in the honey and base oil one teaspoon at a time until you've formed a thick scrub. (If you're in a pinch for ingredients, you can substitute the avocado or evening primrose oil for sesame oil or omit altogether.) Finally, add one to two drops of lemon verbena or ylang ylang essential oil (if using).

When in the shower, gently massage the scrub spell all over your body, imagining that the mixture is slowly making any "imperfections" less noticeable and letting your true beauty shine even brighter. Finish your shower as normal, then admire what a knock-out you are when you're getting ready.

(Note: Since this is a sugar-based scrub, this spell can be used on the face if you're very gentle. That said, I'd advise omitting the essential oils and only adding in a pinch of orange rind so you don't irritate your skin. Follow up with a gentle cleanser if you're sensitive to oils on your face.)

Lingerie Glamour Spray

ne of my many non-witchcraft hobbies is buying and wearing luxury lingerie. People have pointed out to me that this is kind of a pointless hobby for how expensive it is, but so is collecting rocks or comic book figurines. At least I know I'm sexy as hell when I'm wearing it (and you can't say that about your husband's *Magic: The Gathering* collection).

But as you might be able to tell, I'm also kind of a magical maximalist. Sure, the *lingerie* is sexy, *I'm* sexy, and I've done a full Goddess Glamour Bath to amp things up, but couldn't we do *more*? Enter the Lingerie Glamour Spray, here to take you from a 9.5 to a perfect 10.

And though this spray is intended for lingerie, this glamour spell can be applied to any article of clothing to boost your sex appeal.

Ingredients

- **Witch hazel** (or vodka, although it has a much stronger smell)
- **Storm water** or **moon water**
- A small **glass spray bottle**
- 15 drops of **sweet orange essential oil**
- 10 drops of **rose absolute**
- 5 drops of **patchouli essential oil**
- Optional: 1 small piece of **red jasper**

To prepare, take your glass bottle and fill it with equal parts witch hazel and storm water. Leave enough space for your 30 drops of essential oil, plus the piece of red jasper (if using). For best results, charge it under the light of the full moon and/or set it on top of a sigil matching your intent.

To use, simply mist over your lingerie before and after putting it on. Store in the fridge for maximum shelf life.

Last-Minute Glamour

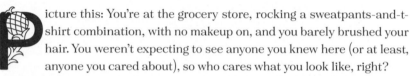

Picture this: You're at the grocery store, rocking a sweatpants-and-t-shirt combination, with no makeup on, and you barely brushed your hair. You weren't expecting to see anyone you knew here (or at least, anyone you cared about), so who cares what you look like, right?

That's the moment when you catch a glimpse of your ex, hand-in-hand with someone else, passing by the aisle. It seems like they haven't seen you yet, but it also seems pretty likely that they'll run into you eventually. Then, you'll need to talk to them, and smile, and pretend you don't look like you just rolled out of bed.

So, what do you do? This last-minute glamour, of course.

This simple spell is meant to be used in a pinch, even if that means darting to the produce section and picking up the ingredients there. (In that case, my professional recommendation is to pay for them afterwards, unless you want an extremely awkward conversation with the security guard on staff.)

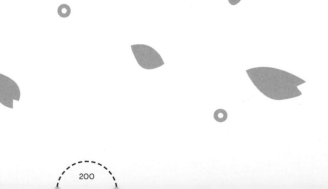

Ingredients

- 🌿 1 small piece of **ginger**
- 🌿 1 **orange**
- 🌿 Optional: 1 **petal** from a flower you like

To prepare, take your orange and dig your nail into the rind so that you can pull off a pea-sized piece of the peel. Put the peel in your dominant hand along with the piece of ginger and wrap with the flower petal (if using). Press and rub them together with your fingers as you imagine a soft filter settling over your body. You see your best features become slightly more prominent, while your flaws fade into the background. You are vibrant and confident.

Take the items and shove them into your pocket. (For practical advice, I also recommend biting your lip and adding a bit of lip balm for color and shine.) Then, when you run into your ex and their new boo, flash them a big smile – you look excellent.

Chapter
Seven:
Cursing
101

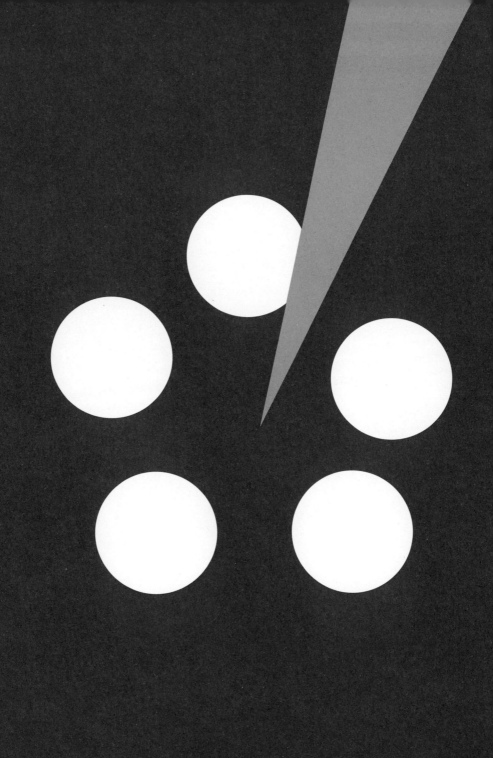

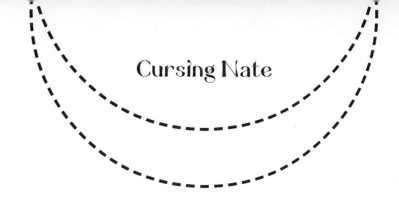

Cursing Nate

The truth is that I had considered cursing Nate right from the beginning. I had the good sense not to do it immediately, but I was not – *am not* – the "forgive and forget" type of woman. There was something about how calculated Nate's actions were that left me feeling raw, exposed, and robbed of my agency. I felt stage-managed, and a curse was the type of revenge that would allow me to regain a feeling of control.

As I was getting into witchcraft, my eyes glazed over while reading the dispassionate pleas in books warning witches not to curse. Instead, I tried to read between the lines on how I could cast one safely. I quietly researched how to curse, which ingredients I'd need to pull it off successfully, and which precautions I'd need to take.

As Nate would send back things that I had lent him over the course of our relationship, I stowed them away in sealable plastic bags so that his energy on the items would remain fresh. I knew I would use them as taglocks (items that tie a person to a spell) in the future.

One thing that was clear from the beginning is that I'd need help pulling off a big curse. I told Rhea about my intention, but I don't even think I officially asked her to help me. There was an implicit understanding that she'd help once I formulated a plan.

I started by reading lots of curses on the internet to investigate different types of symbolism, herbs, and desired effects. I wrote down ideas that I liked so that I could "Frankenstein" a curse together when the time was right.

All I needed to do was wait patiently for the perfect moment.

※

It was July and I was back in Phoenix for the summer. Although I had spent nearly a year in Tucson for my first year of college, I didn't feel anchored there, so I was back in my hometown to spend time with Rhea, my family, and friends that I was still close with from high school. My new girlfriend Sarah and I had been dating for about three months, but she was in Spain, studying abroad.

It was also Cancer season, and therefore Nate's birthday would be right around the corner.

Nate's birthday was at the beginning of July, and I had a hunch he'd be back in Phoenix to celebrate with his family in traditional Cancer fashion. I checked his social media to confirm and saw that he'd be in town with Tommy for the next week. My chest tightened slightly from the mixture of anticipation and anxiety.

I had been loosely planning on cursing Nate during this period because: 1) I figured I'd have better luck directing the curse at the right Nate if we were in closer vicinity, and 2) I was hoping his birthday would add some magical significance. July also marks the beginning of monsoon season in Southern Arizona, and I was crossing my fingers that I could charge my curse materials under the power of a massive thunderstorm.

That said, things felt very different once I knew he was actually back in the city.

It felt claustrophobic. I hadn't realized how much solace I took in him being over a thousand miles away until he was just a short drive across town. I wasn't going to run into him at the grocery store or on the street when he was in Portland and I was Tucson – but now, we were both here.

Nate was seeping back into my thoughts again, and I felt paranoid knowing that he could theoretically be around any corner. I had worked hard to build my sense of autonomy and control back up over the last half-year: I made new friends in Tucson, I started dating someone new, I dove head-first into magic and witchcraft. But somehow, practically overnight, all of that work was melting away and slipping between my fingers.

Still, I wasn't about to throw away months of planning and let him go back to Portland happier than ever. I told Rhea that Nate was officially back in the city, and she helped me finalize our plan to curse him.

The curse had several moving parts, but the idea was simple enough.

I knew that I wanted something effective, and a mechanism that would limit the risks to me, so I created a spell that would allow Nate's own vices to drag him into ruin. First, I made a poppet out of fabric to represent him, filled it with sand, and dedicated it to him through several of my saved taglocks. Then, I identified five of his major character flaws and used five stones to stand in for each of them (and used a bit of extra magic to tie each stone specifically to each vice).

From there, the plan was to go over to Rhea's house, do a cleansing and protection bath around midnight, then drive out to a park with a man-made pond (we don't have many natural standing water sources in Southern Arizona). I would cast a circle with the elements while Rhea protected the space around the circle to guard me. Then, I'd open the poppet at one of its seams with a blade, pour out some of the sand, fill the cavity with the five stones and sew it back up again. I'd say a small incantation about how Nate's vices would metaphorically drown him, then I'd toss the poppet in the water and we'd dissolve the circle. Finally, we'd take the written incantation and any scraps from the spell, drive all the way to Nate's parents' home on the other side of Phoenix, and bury the spell elements in their front yard. If we timed it correctly, we would leave Nate's parents' house right around 3 a.m. – the Witching Hour.

To be honest, by the time I was driving over to Rhea's house with the poppet and stones in tow, I was pretty impressed with the spell we had cobbled together. Unfortunately, the curse didn't exactly go according to plan.

The cleansing bath was straightforward and went off without a hitch, but we quickly realized by the time we reached the park that we hadn't quite thought everything through. For one, it was only a couple of days after a full moon, which was great for the magic itself, but we could see everything like it was nearly daylight – and that also meant that anyone in the surrounding neighborhood could see us.

Feeling extremely self-conscious, Rhea and I got to work as quickly as possible. We cast a circle near the water, and as Rhea started burning protective herbs around me, I started work on the poppet.

That's where the second misstep of the evening occurred: I had brought a small pocketknife to the pond with which to cut open the poppet, but it was immediately clear that the blade wasn't sharp enough. I struggled with it for several moments, pressing harder and harder into the thread at the seam, until at last, it sliced into the doll.

It took me less than a second to register that the knife hadn't *just* cut into the poppet – it had passed through the body of the doll and sliced into my palm.

"Oh *shit*," I said. "I just cut my hand."

"Jesus," Rhea replied. "Are you okay?"

My blood was seeping into the poppet and dripping onto our ceremonial blanket. "I think so. I don't think we have any other option at this point except to continue." Looking down at the poppet covered in my blood, it suddenly occurred to me that, magically speaking, I was about to foray into another round of blood magic. *Goddamnit.*

I hurriedly dumped out as much of the sand as I could, added the stones, and sloppily sewed the poppet back up as best I could. I read the incantation I wrote and took a deep breath. *Here goes nothing*, I thought as I tossed the doll into the water. "Okay, let's get out of here as quickly as possible."

We quickly closed the circle and carried our items out of the park. I had wrapped my bleeding hand in part of the ceremonial blanket, but somewhat miraculously, the bleeding had already started to subside. Rhea drove us north to Nate's house.

"I get the distinct feeling that this was the price I paid for the spell," I said, motioning to my hand. Big, complicated spells come with big, complicated price tags, and it seemed that the price I paid to curse Nate was putting my own blood and skin in the game.

"Yeah, I'm getting the same feeling."

It was some 30 minutes later by the time that we pulled up to Nate's childhood home – except there was one more problem: The light in his basement bedroom was clearly on, even at nearly three in the morning.

"Christ, what are we supposed to do?"

We decided to scratch the plan to bury the remnants in their yard in favor of leaving them under some brush closer to the sidewalk, instead. It wasn't ideal, but we were much more afraid of Nate and Tommy looking out the window and seeing us there than of the spell not working. I quickly darted out of the car, tossed the items, and scurried back. As soon as I closed the car door behind me, Rhea drove off.

We both exhaled a heavy sigh of relief that we managed to pull off the spell – even with the hurdles – and as I checked the time, I was pleased that we were indeed leaving right at Witching Hour. At that moment, I felt a sudden urge to check Nate's social media to see if he and Tommy were doing anything notable while we were sneaking around outside his house. What I saw was almost too good to be true.

Paranoid I have lost my tarot cards

02:36 AM

It is near the witching hour and there are lights on in this house that I did not think could come on #nomoretarot

02:50 AM

Just kidding, the mystery lights are flashing above the table my tarot cards are on #ididnotneedthis #nakedandafraid

02:54 AM

It seemed too wild to be a coincidence, and at the time, we took it as proof that the curse was working.

Over the following months, I watched from afar as Nate and his girlfriend broke up, several of his close friendships became strained, his grades slipped, and his overall satisfaction with life seemed to decrease. There was a large part of me that was satisfied with how the curse appeared to be going – a success by all accounts – but I still felt a nagging sense that I hadn't received everything that I wanted. There was something missing, even if I had a hard time putting my finger on it.

Around Thanksgiving, I reached out to him again and asked if he wanted to talk. As you know if you read the earlier chapters, Nate and I did get back together that winter. I'm not sure if it was the accidental blood magic or my plain, messy human feelings, but I felt a pull towards him that, at the time, seemed impossible to ignore.

And regardless of what you might think of my choice, I did eventually get to hear what he experienced that night of the curse, which he divulged to me after I confessed to cursing him:

He and Tommy had been drinking and reading tarot in the basement. At some point, they had stopped reading tarot and started communing with Nate's guardian angel and spiritual guide, the Archangel Michael, when the lights suddenly started flashing. The room they were in suddenly felt cold, like all of the energy had escaped. In its place, they felt that something malignant had entered.

At that moment, Nate told me that he felt the Archangel Michael dart out of the room, taking the dark presence with him. He said the space felt empty, that they were scared out of their minds, and that he wasn't able to commune with Michael for many months after that – he had the feeling that he was busy dealing with something else.

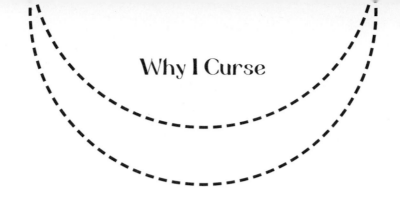

Why I Curse

hether or not you have any experience with magic, you probably hold some negative beliefs about cursing.

Curses in popular culture fall along the lines of Maleficent putting a spell on Sleeping Beauty so that she'd prick her finger and fall into a deep sleep, or the killing curses cast by Voldemort in the Harry Potter series. Characters in pop culture who curse are all undoubtedly evil, unredeemable, and never to be emulated.

So why do some witches curse, and what does this say about them as practitioners?

The truth is that cursing is complicated and not as black-and-white as we'd like it to be. It's undeniable that cursing has ill intent behind it: If you cast a curse, you're attempting to harm someone in some way. But I don't believe that all harm is inherently bad. Whatever you think of my decision to curse Nate for the ways that he hurt me, you might still take a pause and think about whether it's wrong to curse a rapist, or an abuser, or someone who exploits other people for personal gain.

Maybe this still doesn't convince you. "But why don't you let the criminal justice system handle these cases?" many people would retort. Even without opening up the entire Pandora's box of whether certain people – based on their identity, their income level, the country they live in, or the level of corruption in their local government – can even rely on police officers, many types of crimes are notoriously difficult to prosecute. The Rape, Abuse & Incest National Network estimates that for every 1,000 sexual assaults, 230 are actually reported to the police, of which 46 will lead to an arrest, 9 will be referred to prosecutors, 5 will be charged with a felony, and 4.6 will actually go to prison. The other 995 will walk free. I don't know where you fall on that issue, but these numbers make me deeply uncomfortable. And while I'll continue to vote for better District Attorneys, support police reform, and speak openly about changing the culture of sexual violence, I'm also 100% okay with cursing rapists.

If you're a Wiccan (or follow a similar Neo-Pagan faith), you might have a fundamental issue with cursing because it interferes with the Rede. (For the uninitiated, the Rede is the religious principle *"An it harm none, do what ye will."*) As I briefly touched on in other parts of this book, there isn't any type of magic that is truly benign or doesn't influence someone's free will.

If you cast a spell "attracting more money" to your business, that extra money doesn't come out of nowhere. Perhaps it was intended for someone else's college savings fund, or to pay back someone's debt. Your lucky break is a missed opportunity for someone else. Even outside of magic, most of our interactions with other people impact the people around us, and something as simple as selecting the wrong shipping address on your order could set off a chain of events that radically changes someone's life. Yes, cursing is a bit more obvious because we get to see the harm unfold directly in plain view, but almost all spells have unforeseen consequences. At least when I cast a curse, I'm being honest about what I want these consequences to be.

Finally, you might tell me that cursing is wrong because you're concerned about *me*. "What about the Threefold Law? Aren't you concerned that this negative energy will come back to you three times stronger?" I don't want to insult anyone's religious beliefs, but no. For one, nothing else in nature works like this, let alone by a factor of three. I believe that curses are risky because you're calling out into the world for some spirit, energy or deity to do something malicious on your behalf and that's not typically the type of attention most people want to attract – but I don't believe that bad just begets more bad. Secondly, I wasn't asking for your permission. You can pipe down and mind your own business.

For me, cursing is just another tool in my wheelhouse. It's a tool that I prefer not to use because it's risky and labor-intensive, but it's a tool nonetheless. So, if you've read this far and are at least a little bit curious about how to cast a curse, keep reading.

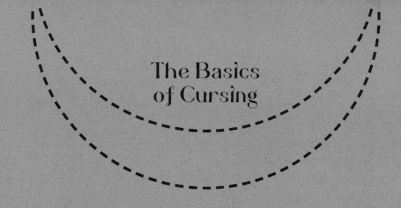

The Basics
of Cursing

So, at this point, you at least have a working understanding of how a curse can unfold, as well as some of the ethical dilemmas that accompany cursing (and my corresponding rationalizations). But how does one go about actually casting a curse? Let's go through the main steps and precautions you should take.

1. Committing to Cursing

Seems obvious, no? But seriously, just because I condone cursing doesn't mean I take it lightly. You're about to go down a path where you intentionally harm someone, and you'll probably need to invoke some magical, malevolent help to get that done. You're doing the magical equivalent of going to a shady part of town and loudly asking, "Hey, who'd like to beat someone up for me?" Sure, someone will probably take you up on your offer, but you don't get a lot of choice in who that is – and do you really want to be on their radar in the future?

Even putting those first two points aside, it's a very laborious type of spell to cast and I'm going to insist that you double- and triple-check everything you're doing. It's not for the faint of heart, so if you're at all doubting whether or not you should be doing this, the time to bail is now. (Plus, there are always alternatives to cursing, which you can find later in this chapter on pages 221 and 223.)

2. Write a Curse That Fits the Crime

For better or worse, being a witch who curses is essentially playing judge, jury, and executioner all at once. No one appointed you, and you're not accountable to anybody but yourself. But that doesn't mean that you shouldn't try to be fair and find punishments that are proportional to the misdeeds someone's committed.

For example, if someone is bullying you or putting you down, perhaps you'd cast a spell that makes them feel socially isolated and ridiculed. If your shitty boss is stealing your work and taking credit for it, perhaps you cast a spell for people to find out that they're a fraud, or for them to royally mess up in a way that puts their job in jeopardy. Meanwhile, a common punishment for a rapist is to cast a curse so that their genitals burn whenever they try to use them.

I won't actually be giving out curses in this chapter because I don't think the paint-by-numbers approach to spellcasting works well here. You should read other witchcraft books and blogs for their curse ideas, then write an original spell that you think fits the crime you're trying to punish. When in doubt, use symbolism that references the reason why you're cursing them. And if you're on the fence about whether a spell is too harsh, it's probably better to pull back and go too soft instead of too hard.

3. Find a Taglock for Your Target

All spells need a direction and a taglock in order to hit the right target – and this is especially true with curses. But what is a taglock? A taglock is something that ties a spell to the intended target. In a perfect world, you'd have fingernail clippings or hair (i.e. something with DNA) that you could add to the spell, but most of us are going to have a difficult time procuring that. In this case, I try to make a sigil to represent them, and I include as many details as possible. For example, I don't just make a sigil with someone's first and last name, but also include their middle name or other names if possible, their birthday, the city they live in, and so on.

Additionally, if they've recently given me something – or I've taken something – I'll store it in a plastic container so that their energy stays on it. Then, if I make a poppet or something else to represent them, I can put it in the container and it'll pick up some of their "magical scent" (if you'll humor the comparison).

Why go through all this effort? Well, presumably you want to actually punish your target, so that should be good enough motivation right there. But what if your curse hits the wrong person, like someone in their life or a stranger with the same name? That would be devastating and it's your responsibility to go through every precaution to make sure that doesn't happen. Worst case scenario, the curse can also *backfire*, so that you end up cursing yourself instead of your target. Needless to say: Don't cut corners on the taglock step.

4. Make a Plan for Conducting Your Curse

So, you have a rough idea of what your curse is going to entail and what you want to accomplish. That's great – but also not nearly enough of a plan.

I want you to walk through what you intend to do, starting with your prep work and then going step by step, from circle casting to closing, and ending with aftercare. Because of the risks we've already touched on, a curse is the wrong type of spell for you to realize, while casting, that a key ingredient is on the kitchen table, outside of your circle. This is also not the time to wing it and make it up as you go along. You need to have total focus during your casting, and you need to be prepared to think on your feet if necessary. Run through your curse plan and imagine a couple of likely hurdles and how you'd address them. You should also use this time to write down any ingredients or tools you'll need so that you don't accidentally forget anything in your prep stage.

Take it from someone whose 80% curse planning effort caused them to blood-bond themselves to their target: Be serious about the planning stage.

5. Add in a Duration

No spell should last forever, a curse least of all. For one, part of your energy will likely be siphoned off for as long as the spell is working, and it would be exhausting to maintain a curse for a lifetime. Additionally, if you find out later that this person wasn't as bad as you imagined, or it misfires and affects the wrong person, you can at least limit their suffering. That's why it's key to write in a time limit (e.g. six months) or to specify that the curse is over once the desired effect has come to fruition.

6. Do Your Prep Work

Prep work can be divided into two categories: prepping your materials and prepping yourself.

Prepping your materials is more or less self-explanatory, as you'll simply be gathering all the ingredients and tools that you'll need to cast your curse, and cleansing and/or charging them if necessary. That said, this is always easier said than done, especially if you're trying to time everything to a particular date or phase of the moon. Curses often call for specialty ingredients, and if you're adapting the spell from another source, you might want to double-check that none of the herbs could cause you harm. If you're tied to a particular date, it's ideal to have a couple of substitution ideas in your back pocket in case you can't track down that specialty root (or whatever you're still looking for). As for tools, run through exactly how you'll be using each object to make sure you're not missing anything. For example, I should have anticipated that the pocketknife I had brought along for Nate's curse would be dull and needed to be swapped out for something with a sharper blade.

Now, prepping *yourself* is a little more involved. Hopefully, you heeded the first step and only got this far because you're already emotionally ready to curse someone, but you still need to cleanse yourself, protect yourself, and get yourself into the right headspace to cast.

As I've already touched on several times, cleansing and protecting is something that you should ideally be doing regularly, but it's all the more important during cursing. Cleansing is key because you don't want to accidentally be dragging any strange or conflicting energy into your spellwork (the fewer variables you're working with, the better). Meanwhile, I cannot stress enough the importance of doing some protection magic before casting a curse. What you're doing has a high likelihood of backfiring, or otherwise just attracting the wrong type of energy (e.g. the spirit doing your bidding for you decides you'd be fun to hang around afterwards). You could use whatever standard protection spell you typically use, but I prefer to bathe in angelica before cursework as it's an extra powerful cleansing and protection herb.

And finally, if you're not doing your cleansing and protecting right before casting your curse, you'll want to do some other warm-up spell to get you in the right space. Your intention will need to be crystal clear in order to pull this off.

7. Cast Your Curse

Okay, you have all your items assembled, you're in the right headspace, you know what you're going to do, and you're wearing the magical equivalent of a bulletproof vest. Now all that's left to do is cast your curse.

Cleanse and protect your space, then cast a circle. When you're ready, start your cursework. Go slow, be deliberate, and send out your intentions clearly. You can do this – you've certainly prepped accordingly.

After the Curse

s much as we'd like to close our circles, dust ourselves off, and call it a day after the curse has been cast, that's unfortunately not the best idea. You still have a bit of work to do – and it's worth doing for your own health and wellbeing.

Cleanse Your Space and Your Tools

Yes, you already cleansed your space before casting your curse, but you need to cleanse afterwards as well. Pull out your incense, your cleansing stick, your herbal infusion, or whatever you used to purify your space the first time around and do it again.

Depending on their size and material, burying your tools in salt is a great way to perform a deeper cleansing. Otherwise, an infusion of hyssop will work quite well, and if all else fails, you can smoke cleanse them, too.

Cleanse Yourself

I hope you saw this one coming. Pull out the strongest self-cleansing magic you have (if you need ideas, check out the Purification & Protection Scrub on page 150) and get purifying. This is also the time to double- or triple-up on your magic if you have the time. For example, I'd probably do a cleansing bath ritual, bring a purifying scrub with me into the bath, and also make a peppermint and basil tea to purify my energy from the inside out.

Protect Your Space

In a perfect world, you have standing protection spells around your home that you can simply "top up" after a big spell like this. If you don't, you'll need to do some protection magic so that your home base doesn't become a cesspool of negative energy.

If it's right after the curse and you already feel emotionally wrecked (or it's 3 a.m. and you're just exhausted), just ward[16] the walls of your room or home and push the bigger protection magic to the following day. Additionally, you could plan ahead before your spell and charge a batch of stones or crystals with protective qualities and then place them around your home before you cast your curse.

If you need further suggestions, don't forget to check the section on protection, which you can find on page 45.

Protect Yourself

My pro tip for all true recreational witches out there is to bundle your personal cleansing work with protection work so that you don't have to do them in separate steps. Still, if you left it out before, here's your not-so-gentle reminder to get on top of protecting yourself.

---

16   Here, I simply mean using energy from your body to create a short-term barrier. You can do this by standing in front of a wall and centering yourself. Feel the energy gather in your chest, then touch the wall to funnel that energy from you, through your arm, into the wall itself. When the wall feels "full" of energy, move onto the next one. When you have a full perimeter, you're done.

Relax and Regain Your Strength

If you actually followed all of the steps I've laid out here, you should feel properly exhausted – both physically and in terms of spiritual energy. This curse is going to be sapping your energy for quite a while, so take a break from any major spellwork for at least a few days (and ideally, a few weeks).

In the immediate hours after your curse, I'd recommend taking it extremely easy. If you cast your curse at night, you should try to sleep late the follow morning so you can regain your strength, then spend the next day relaxing and doing something mindless. If you really get the urge to do more magic, try something like the Self-Love Bath Spell (page 130) or Letting Go Bath Spell (page 134).

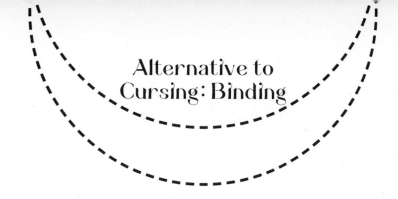

Alternative to Cursing: Binding

inding is hands down one of my favorite types of spells to cast because it contains almost all of the benefits of cursing without the risks.

Binding is essentially when you have a target who's a horrible person, but instead of sending an external magical force to fuck this person up, you simply turn that person's own toxicity in on themselves. You are "binding" their toxic traits to them, instead of letting them negatively affect other people.

This type of spell is a great alternative to cursing because almost anyone who you'd want to curse could probably benefit from a taste of their own medicine. (And if binding wouldn't work on them because they aren't toxic enough, are you sure you'd really want to cast that curse after all?) It is also significantly less risky than cursing because you don't have to make any Faustian deals to make it happen. And if you *do* believe in laws of returning energy? You *technically* didn't send out any negative energy: You just made this person's actions that much more impactful on *them*. From my perspective, the only real benefit of cursing over binding is that, if you have a vindictive streak (like me), cursing feels more satisfying than binding.

How to Bind Someone

While there are undoubtedly numerous, effective methods you can use to bind someone, I primarily use three ways to perform simple bindings.

1. The Vinegar Method

The first option is the easiest. As if I were making a taglock for a curse, I create a very detailed sigil with someone's name, birthday, city, and other information so that I'm tying the magic to the right person. Then, I'll write the sigil again on a small piece of paper with ink that can smudge (in other words, this isn't the place for a sharpie). After that, I simply fill a small bowl with white vinegar and place the sigil in the liquid. I leave it in the vinegar until the sigil has disappeared, then toss the mixture. Easy-peasy.

2. The Mirror Method

The second and third options are slightly more complicated – but more fun to do, in my humble opinion.

If you consider yourself crafty or otherwise good with your hands, you can bind someone by taking a box with a lid and covering the inside of the container with mirrors on all sides. For extra insurance, you can make a sigil with a binding intention and either draw or carve it on the underside of the box. When you're ready to bind someone, simply make a poppet for your target and dedicate it as usual. Then, leave the poppet in the mirrored box for as long as you want the binding spell to last.

3. The Physical Binding Method

Finally, the last option is quite similar to the second, in that you make a poppet to represent your intended target and dedicate it accordingly. Next, find some long, skinny material that you can use to physically bind the poppet, such as twine, a ribbon, or something metallic (like tinsel or aluminum tape), and charge it for the purposes of binding. Wrap it around the poppet, taking care to secure the "arms" down so that they can't hurt other people, and secure the ends. Leave the poppet bound for as long as you want the binding to last.

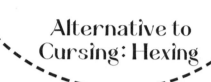

Alternative to Cursing: Hexing

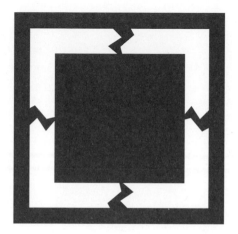

S o, you've read the suggestions for bindings and they're not tough enough for your cold heart, but you still want to torment someone – gently. Enter hexing, the more low-key, younger sibling of cursing.

Technically, many witchcraft books use the terms "cursing" and "hexing" interchangeably to refer to malevolent spells, but for me, a "hex" is more akin to a "jinx" than a full-blown curse. Plus, etymologically speaking, the German word "hexe" refers to witches themselves, so it has a soft spot in my heart.

As we'll be referring to them here, hexes are more like ready-made bad luck spells that you can pull out in a pinch and don't require as much investment on your part; they also don't pack as much of a punch as a curse. I've chosen to make all of these powders for ease of use, but there are other low-investment ways to hex someone if these aren't your thing.

1. Simple Bad Luck Powder

That lady who treats service industry workers horribly? This spell is for her, along with people who steal your parking spot, old men who talk down to young people, and anyone else who needs a taste of their own medicine. This bad boy is best suited for doling out standard "bad days" to your unsuspecting recipient.

To make the Simple Bad Luck Powder, gather:

- 1 teaspoon of **mustard seed**
- 1 teaspoon of **black pepper**
- 1 large, dried **basil leaf**

Burn the basil leaf in a small heatproof container and sprinkle the mustard seeds into the flame. Once the leaf is burned to ash, transfer the remnants of the leaf and mustard seeds to a mortar and pestle, and grind into a powder. Add the black pepper, then store in a vial. To use, covertly sprinkle a small amount of the powder in someone's path or onto something they own.

2. Simple Banishing Powder

Sometimes, you really just want someone to go away (and preferably never come back). Of all the hex powders, this is the most gentle. To make, combine:

- 1 teaspoon of **black pepper**
- **Tobacco** from 1 cigarette
- 1 pinch of ground **cloves**

For easier use, grind the tobacco with your mortar and pestle until it has a finer consistency. Otherwise, store the powder in a vial until you're ready to use. To banish someone, take a pinch of the powder and flick it in their direction, ideally getting some of it on them or in their path. They won't stick around for long.

3. Fighting Powder

This powder is to encourage bickering and arguments for those you use it on. You'll need:

- 1 large **basil leaf**, burned to ash
- 1 teaspoon of **sand** or **infertile soil**
- A sprinkle of **cayenne pepper**

Combine the ingredients while thinking about your intention, then store the mixture in a glass vial for future use. Sprinkle on someone's property or in their path to use, and watch their close relationships devolve into a series of petty arguments.

4. "F*** You" Powder

If you don't want to commit to fully cursing someone, but you want a hex to hit someone where it hurts, this is your powder. Just one word of warning: Don't use this lightly, as it packs the kind of punch that can turn into job losses and divorces. Gather:

- Roasted **chicory root granules**
- **Blueberry powder** (can be purchased, or you can dry blueberries in your oven and then grind them into a powder)
- Dried **wormwood**

Lightly burn the chicory root granules on a piece of charcoal so that they start to smoke, then remove them from the heat and let them cool completely. While the chicory is cooling, grind together the blueberry powder and wormwood with a mortar and pestle until broken down and powdery. Once they're cool, add the chicory granules, then store the mixture in a glass vial until you're ready. Sprinkle in a person's path to use.

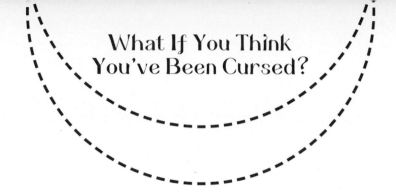

What If You Think You've Been Cursed?

inally, no chapter about cursing would be complete without the ever-present question: "But what if *I've* been cursed?"

This question arises for even the best witches among us and seems to pop up after a few too many instances of bad luck unfold in quick succession.

Let me start by saying that you probably haven't been cursed. Being cursed requires quite a few ingredients, most notably someone to curse you in the first place. (And if you think about it, there aren't that many witches in the world, few that curse, fewer even that know you, and least of all, *care* about cursing you.) Still, people do occasionally cast curses (guilty as charged), so we need to discuss a plan of action for when these types of things occur.

Verify That You've been Cursed

First of all, start by checking if you're actually cursed. The best way to do this is with divination via whichever method you're most comfortable with. Afterwards, if you come to the conclusion that you've been cursed, ask for a second opinion from someone you trust (again, with divination). You could always ask for a third opinion, too, but I'm of the mindset that two pairs of eyes are probably enough to start the purification and cleansing process. Worst case scenario, you went a bit over the top for some standard lingering negative energy, but that's still preferable to letting a curse stick around.

From here on out, many of the steps are quite standard (and will look very similar to the After the Curse instructions), but I'm going to recommend pulling out the big guns. That means more powerful herbs and, ideally, enlisting another witch to help you out, if possible.

Cleanse Yourself

If you've been cursed, now is the time to pull out the big guns. The magical version of bleach, if you will.

I can recommend bathing in an infusion of angelica – which has the added bonus of also being a protection herb – along with a generous amount of sea salt. You can do the same with Yerba Santa, although it's typically a milder cleansing. Finally, chamomile can also work in a pinch, but I'd follow up with something stronger if possible. And of course, any of the other cleansing bath spells and scrubs I listed earlier in the book will also work, but you might need to layer several methods together to completely cleanse yourself of the curse's energy.

Protect Yourself

This is a kind of "put your own oxygen mask on before helping others" type of deal. Curses do have a nasty habit of seeping over to others around you, but you're going to want to be in tip-top shape before moving on to helping anyone else who's affected.

So, while cleansing was a great start, now you will want to seal yourself off from any future reverberations or additional cursework sent your way. Some of the cleansing herbs listed above do double-duty for cleansing and protecting, which is handy, but it's best to combine several layers of protection. Charge an oil like coconut or sea buckthorn with a powerful protective sigil, then massage it into your skin after every shower you take for at least several days.

You should also carry some physical object with you, like a piece of obsidian or black tourmaline crystal. Or make a charm out of herbs (like eucalyptus, marjoram, or nettle) and keep that on you, instead.

Cleanse Your Space and Others

Now that you're cleansed and protected, you're in a good position to start ridding your environment of this malignant energy (and gods forbid, your loved ones, as well).

For cleansing your space, I'd recommend an infusion of rue sprinkled around the home or used as a floor wash (but do **not** burn it or bathe in it, as rue can be toxic to humans). An infusion of fennel seeds can also work well but is less potent. Another very effective – but extremely annoying – cleansing option is to buy a lot of salt, mix it with ground chili or cayenne pepper, sprinkle it throughout your home, and then vacuum it all up. (Of course, you'll need to dispose of the used salt mixture immediately afterwards.) You can also combine several simpler methods.

Cleansing others, meanwhile, is a bit more difficult. If grandma's down for taking a full-on purification bath, that's the best way to go. Unfortunately, that's typically not the case. In this situation, you'll want to go for some more covert methods, like a cleansing tea made out of angelica (although this should not be given to those who are pregnant). You can also serve someone the cleansing cocktail from page 292, or give someone a cleansing scrub under the guise of it being a beauty treatment.

Protect Your Space

Lastly, it's time to protect your space. At this step, the goal is to turn your home into the magical, modern equivalent of a medieval castle. You'll want to dig a moat, have a big set of castle walls, have those walls monitored by archers, and finally have another, inner set of walls. In other words, you'll want to layer your protection methods very thoroughly.

As a suggestion, I would start by smoke-cleansing with cedar, or another strong botanical that you associate with protection. Follow this by sprinkling an infusion of angelica around your home or using it in a floor wash. If you have a green thumb, grow a couple of the suggestions I made on page 46 in or around your space. If not, I'd recommend placing charged obsidian or black tourmaline in the four corners of your home. And finally, make a protection sigil for your place and charge it.

As a general rule of thumb for protection after a curse, more really is more. This is not the place to scrimp or cut corners.

Chapter Eight: Sabbats and Celebration

Why Celebrate Festivals as a Witch?

n modern paganism (and most notably in Wicca), it's common to celebrate the "Wheel of the Year." Supposedly, these dates correspond with celebrations that ancient pagans once observed; mostly, they're tied to the changing seasons, e.g. the summer and winter solstices, the spring and fall equinoxes, and the midway points between each of these markers, so that there are eight celebrations in total throughout the year.

Now, you might be asking yourself why I'm bringing this up when I've mentioned many times my discontent with Wicca and how it crowds out other forms of magic within the community. While I stand by everything I've said so far, I have also found that it's worth carving time out to celebrate and be grateful for what we have.

Even as a recreational witch, I often found myself constantly keeping an eye on the current moon cycle so that I could optimize my spells to match the stage of the moon or trying to "fix" issues I saw in my life (or watching those spells misfire, and then trying to fix them with more magic). Witchcraft can easily become an overwhelming way of life that adds more items to your to-do list.

That's why I believe that it's important to set time aside from all the mundane magic and just have fun. For Rhea and me, that meant celebrating the Wheel of the Year, but depending on your background and the type of witchcraft you practice, that could mean observing any number of holidays. If you're a Christian witch, perhaps you observe Christmas and Easter with special rituals. If you were raised Hindu, maybe you weave in magic while you observe Diwali and Holi. Meanwhile, if you were raised in a religion that's tied to your Indigenous community or ancestors, you can celebrate with whichever local practices you grew up with. Or, if you don't have any religious beliefs, you can pick other days that have personal or cultural significance to you. The point isn't to celebrate *particular* festivals throughout the year to feel more authentically magical, but to take time for yourself and your loved ones to enjoy the present moment.

When I was practicing with Rhea, I loved that we would build a day around enjoying the season and each other's company. For one Ostara (the spring equinox), we just packed a picnic basket and spent time picking flowers in the park. For a Midsummer (the summer solstice), we woke up while it was still pitch black outside so that we could hike up a small mountain at dawn and watch the sun come up from above the valley. Whatever holidays you observe, they're just about spending time with the people you love.

And so, while it'd be embarrassing to have me tell you how to celebrate Diwali or a local festival you observe, I want to take you through the major holidays in the Wheel of the Year. I personally don't believe in almost any of the pagan lore behind these dates, but I do think that observing the passing seasons helps me feel grounded and connected to the world around me.

Imbolc

"Hell yeah, it's almost spring."

February 1st

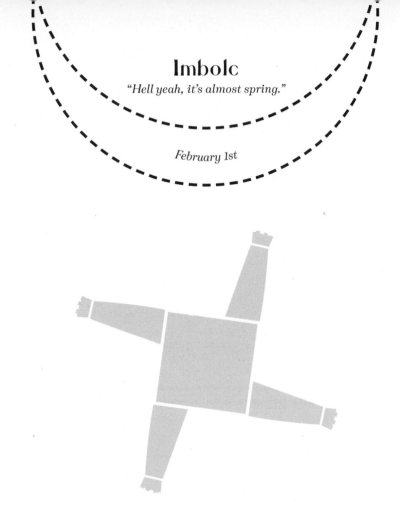

Like many of the other holidays in the Wheel of the Year, Imbolc was originally a Gaelic holiday celebrated in Ireland, Scotland, and the Isle of Man. And while the historical details are muddled, it seems likely that this celebration was originally associated with the Celtic goddess Brigid and then later Christianized into Saint Bridgit's Day.

Since I'm not Wiccan, Gaelic Pagan, or Catholic, the historical specifics are less important to how I observe it. Instead, I view Imbolc simply as a preparation for the arrival of spring. If you live in a northern latitude, the end of January and beginning of February can be a bleak and depressing time. Imbolc fits in nicely for this part of the year as a time to sit in peace and be grateful for what you have.

Ways to Celebrate in the Home

In my humble opinion, Imbolc is a better inside holiday than an outside one (unless you're a farmer or otherwise rely on your land). My perfect Imbolc is one where I'd wake up early, make a humble breakfast, pick one deep-cleaning project in my home and tackle it, then light a bunch of white candles and some incense, and finish the day relaxing with a joint, a cup of herbal tea, and a bath ritual.

Here are some other ideas for observing it in your home:

- Sweep your home with a besom[17]
- Go through clutter in your home and find items to give away
- Start your spring cleaning
- Cleanse your home with rosemary or myrrh incense
- Use your fireplace for for what might be the last time this season
- Enjoy a hot drink to prepare for the warming weather

Ways to Celebrate Outside the Home

As someone born and raised in the desert, I'm not particularly keen on going out in the cold for this holiday, but here are a few ideas if you're differently inclined:

- Take a walk or a hike and take notice of the changing season
- Gather melting snow or icicles for future spellwork
- Leave an offering for the soil so that it's fertile come springtime
- Prepare flowerbeds or your garden soil for the coming season
- Light a fire in a fire pit during the evening

---

17   A besom is simply a broom that you keep for more ceremonial purposes. Practically speaking, I still clean with my vacuum cleaner and then metaphorically cleanse my space with the besom.

Celebrating With Bath Magic

Since Imbolc is more of a solitary holiday (and it's cold outside), this is one of the best celebrations to observe with some relaxing bath magic. Here's what I've done:

- Prepare an Imbolc Ritual Bath (on following page)
- Add a few drops of rosemary or myrrh essential oil to your bathwater
- Add ice to your warm bath to symbolize winter melting away
- Take a colloidal oatmeal bath to honor the goddess Brigid
- Bathe surrounded by white candles

Decorations and Altar Adornments

Whether you want to add these items to your altar or just around your home, here are a few ways to make your space feel more festive:

- Make ice bowls or ice luminaries to decorate the outside of your home
- Decorate your space with white candles and white crystals
- Sprinkle seeds on your altar
- Lay out bundles of dried lavender stalks, rosemary branches, or other dried green herbs

Imbolc Ritual Bath

n my mind, Imbolc is a time of gentle cleansing and relaxation. It's a moment of peace and quiet before the joyous spring arrives, so this bath serves as a warm hug on a cold winter's day.

Bath Mixture

Gather the following ingredients:
- 🌿 1 cup of powdered **whole milk** (or powdered **coconut milk**)
- 🌿 1 cup of **colloidal oatmeal powder**
- 🌿 1 handful of **Epsom salts**
- 🌿 **Lavender essential oil**
- 🌿 **Clary sage essential oil**

Mix together the dry ingredients in a bowl, then add several drops of the essential oils in equal amounts. Keep in a glass jar with a piece of amethyst until you're ready to use the mixture.

Bath Ritual

When you're ready to bathe, gather:
- 🌿 The **bath mixture** you prepared
- 🌿 Several sprigs of **rosemary**
- 🌿 Several large pieces of **lemon peel**
- 🌿 Lots of **white candles**
- 🌿 **Myrrh** and/or **frankincense incense**
- 🌿 **Almond** or **coconut oil**

Start by lighting your white candles and your incense, then draw a warm bath. Add the bath mixture, then toss in the pieces of lemon peel and sprigs of rosemary. Once you've entered the bath, take a few minutes to center yourself in the water. Think about which issues from the previous calendar year are lingering around in your life, and how you would like to address them in the coming months. Visualize the purifying energy of the white, restorative water flowing through your body and preparing you for the year ahead.

When the water starts to cool, exit the bath and gently pat your skin dry with a towel. Finish by massaging a few drops of almond or coconut oil into your skin.

Ostara

"Hell yeah, it's spring."

Spring equinox: March 19th–23rd

Much like Imbolc, Ostara has a complicated historical legacy. Wiccan tradition would tell you that the day is a celebration of the Germanic goddess Ostara (or Eostre), and that Christianity has simply reappropriated many of the traditions of this pagan holiday to fit another religious festival: Easter. Meanwhile, academics are split about whether the goddess Ostara was ever celebrated by pagans in the first place; there isn't much evidence to point to her existence in pagan sources and she's only mentioned in one 8th century writing by a Christian monk.

Regardless of where the historical truth actually lies, Ostara is a celebration of the spring equinox and is a time to revel in the new energy of the season. If you were raised Christian, then you'll probably recognize many of these themes and traditions.

For Rhea and me, Ostara was already quite a warm time of the year and so we'd make a picnic and take it to a park with a stream to enjoy the weather. Then, we'd fill up the empty picnic basket with freshly plucked flowers and spend the rest of the day at home.

Ways to Celebrate in the Home

Unlike Imbolc, Ostara is a good indoor/outdoor holiday. Personally, I like to spend the morning and evening indoors (when it's cool outside), and try to enjoy as much of the afternoon outside as I can if it's warm and sunny.

Here are some other ideas for observing it in your home:

- Open your windows to let in the fresh spring air
- Dye and decorate eggs to celebrate fertility
- Start your spring cleaning, if you didn't during Imbolc
- Bake something delicious in your kitchen
- Burn floral incense, like rose, jasmine, or violet

Ways to Celebrate Outside the Home

If the weather permits in your area, Ostara should be celebrated at least partially outside.

- Go for a walk or lounge in a field to enjoy the spring weather
- Collect spring flowers (in accordance with local laws) to decorate your home or dry for later use
- Leave offerings in your garden
- Scatter eggshells in soil you till to fertilize it
- Leave out offerings of sweet food for the Fae (a.k.a. fairy people)
- Witch Tip:
- Flowers and herbs gathered on holidays are traditionally thought to be more magically potent than other herbs.

Celebrating With Bath Magic

Ostara often involves spending quite a bit of time outside, but that doesn't mean that you can't carve out some "you" time inside. Plus, you can switch up your usual bathing rituals and bathe during the day. Here's what I suggest:

- Hold an Ostara bath ritual (on following page)
- Add fresh flowers to your bathwater
- Surround yourself with pastel-colored candles
- Buy a brightly colored bath bomb or bubble bath mixture and enchant it with your intent

Decorations and Altar Adornments

Whether you want to add these items to your altar or just around your home, here are a few ways to make your space feel more alive with the spirit of spring:

-  Fill vases with freshly cut flowers
- Put out dyed eggshells as decoration
- Sprinkle fresh flower petals on your altar
- Decorate with yellows, blues, greens, and soft pinks
- Add rose quartz, citrine, or aquamarine to your altar

Ostara Ritual Bath

This Ostara bath is mostly to help you connect with and observe the passage into spring, but it's also good for some light healing and attracting happiness into your life. And unlike most bath rituals, it also works equally as well when done during the day as it does at night.

Bath Mixture

Similar to the Imbolc bath, the ingredients for the bathwater are split up into a shelf-staple bath mixture and fresh ingredients that you'll add just before entering the water.

To prepare the mixture, gather:

- 1 part **Epsom salts**
- 1 part powdered **milk** or **coconut milk**
- **Orange blossom** or **neroli essential oil**
- **Jasmine** or **ylang ylang essential oil**
- **Rose absolute**
- **Sandalwood essential oil**

Mix together the Epsom salts and powdered milk in a bowl. Then, add one drop of each of the floral essential oils, and three drops of the sandalwood essential oil. If it's not fragrant enough for you, add one more drop of each floral essential oil, and three more drops of sandalwood. Store in a jar with a piece of rose quartz before using.

Bath Ritual

When you're ready to start the ritual, gather:

- The **bath mixture** you prepared
- Several large pieces of **orange peel**
- Fresh **flowers** that you've rinsed ahead of time
- **White** and **pastel-colored candles**
- **Frankincense** and/or **myrrh incense**

As always, start by lighting your candles and incense. Draw a warm bath and stir in the bath mixture, then add the pieces of orange peel and fresh flowers. As you sit in the water, think about what enabled you to survive another winter, and feel gratitude for the warmer weather.

Beltane

"Hell yeah, it's almost summer."

May 1st

 ompletely unsurprisingly, Beltane has a complicated history when examining the convergence of its Gaelic roots, similar European celebrations, Neo-Pagan and Wiccan reconstructions, and modern May 1st celebrations. (Are you noticing a pattern?)

Beltane, like Imbolc, is one of the four Gaelic seasonal festivals that has been incorporated into the Wheel of the Year. It seems to have primarily been concerned with protecting crops and livestock, marking the beginning of summer, and perhaps also fertility. The best-known tradition for Beltane is holding a large ceremonial bonfire, but it's also celebrated by decorating "May Bushes" (summer's answer to Christmas trees) and hanging flowers around the home.

Meanwhile, celebrations on or around May 1st have taken place throughout much of Europe going back to at least Roman times, and include a wide range of rituals, from dancing around Maypoles, to making flower crowns, to crafting items that protect people *from* witches, to prohibiting people from working fields. Each locality has a slightly different custom and intention, although many of these celebrations share a theme of fertility. Fast-forward to the modern era, and many of these same countries now also observe May Day as International Workers' Day.

It shouldn't be surprising, then, that I'm in favor of a more relaxed observation of this holiday. Since I don't live on a farm or cultivate any food for a living, the traditional Beltane celebrations are a little hollow for me. But having lived in Berlin for several years as I write this, I can't deny that May 1st has a certain energy about it: the weather is beautiful, everyone is anticipating the arrival of summer, and there's something in the air that is a chaotic type of fun. Based on that, here are my recommendations for this holiday...

Ways to Celebrate in the Home

Yes, you'll probably want to spend most of Beltane outside if the weather's nice, but that doesn't mean you can't enjoy some festivities indoors, too:

- Make flower crowns
- Arrange a floral bouquet (or several) for decoration
- Burn sweet, fruity, and/or floral incense
- Donate to organizations that support workers' rights (including but not limited to: minimum wage increases, mandated paid holidays, mandated paid vacations, mandated parental leave, affordable healthcare, and so on)
- Spend a little *quality time* with your special someone to connect with the fertility associations of the day (even if babies aren't on the agenda)

Ways to Celebrate Outside the Home

As noted above, Beltane really should be celebrated outside unless the weather is truly horrible. Here are just a few ideas:

- Wake up early and go for a walk while there's still dew on the morning's flora
- Pick colorful flowers for flower crowns, flower baskets, and bouquets
- Have a picnic with lots of fresh food, fruit, and sweets
- Have a small fire at night in your fire pit
- Attend a local protest or march for workers' rights or other related causes

Celebrating With Bath Magic

While the bath magic spell I wrote is actually a shower spell, here are a few ideas if you're really married to the idea of taking a bath:

- Start the day with an early morning bath
- Cast your favorite glamour or self-love bath spell
- Bathe with fresh flowers you've picked that day
- Have a bath with a colorful, enchanted bath bomb

Decorations and Altar Adornments

In my mind, Beltane marks the day when the Northern Hemisphere officially comes back to life after a cold and dark winter. It's time to have fun and bring some of this uplifting, free energy indoors. Here's how:

- Decorate with bright colors and colorful crystals
- Bring the outside in with fresh flowers
- Any items that make you feel more connected to your sexuality (go ahead – add your cute vibrator)
- Put out bowls filled with vibrantly colored fruits (both to eat and to look at)

Beltane Shower Scrub

or me, Beltane just has this anxious, borderline frantic energy about it that is poorly suited to a bath. It's also a modern democratic holiday, and your modern working person is much more likely to take a shower than a bath. A shower scrub spell was simply a much better fit thematically.

Use this scrub on the morning of Beltane before celebrating the rest of the holiday to get a boost of uplifting energy that lasts all day long.

To prepare, gather:

- ½ cup of **fine sea salt**
- ½ cup of **white sugar**
- 3 tablespoons of **sweet almond oil**
- 4 drops of **frankincense essential oil**
- 2 drops of **patchouli essential oil**
- 2 drops of **lemongrass essential oil**
- 2 drops of **rose absolute**
- Optional: a pinch of **body-safe glitter**

Start by adding the fine sea salt and sugar to a bowl, then stir in the sweet almond oil until combined. (If you think your scrub texture is a bit dry, you can add more almond oil a few drops at a time.) Finally, add your essential oils and body-safe glitter (if using). Give it one last good stir, then bring it into the shower for an extra burst of spiritedness.

Midsummer

"Hell yeah, it's summer."

Summer solstice: June 20th–22nd

 alfway through the Wheel of the Year, we reach Midsummer, the longest day of the year. Luckily for us, Midsummer has been celebrated by numerous cultures all around the world for a very, very long time, so I'll spare you the history lesson for each and every variation.

Most celebrations for this festival focus on the sun, energy, and liveliness, and you're probably familiar with the Nordic traditions that include celebrating with large bonfires. It has the energy of one giant party, but it also has a bittersweet edge: Because it's the longest day of the year, every day thereafter will become shorter and colder until we arrive at Yule, the winter solstice.

Still, it's only Midsummer once every 365 days, so you should try and make the most of the extra sunlight and festive energy.

Ways to Celebrate in the Home

Like Beltane, Midsummer is essentially an outdoor holiday (since you'll be spending most of the year inside anyway), but spending a little time indoors preparing food and snacks can be a great way to kick off the day's lively celebration in the open air. This includes:

- Starting off your morning with a cup of chamomile tea
- Cooking recipes that call for honey
- Making (and enjoying) fruit and herb-infused water
- Burning sandalwood, frankincense, myrrh, or rose incense
- Making homemade lemonade or sun tea

Ways to Celebrate Outside the Home

The possibilities for enjoying Midsummer outdoors are practically endless. Here are some of my favorite suggestions:

- Go for a hike at dawn and watch the sunrise
- Collect as many herbs and flowers as you can carry
- Sunbathe (but with sunscreen, because there's nothing magical about getting skin cancer)
- Cleanse and charge magical items under the energy of the sun
- Swim in a natural body of water
- Watch the sun set in the evening
- Build a small bonfire to enjoy with your friends

Celebrating With Bath Magic

Whether you carve out time in this long day for a bath is up to you, but if you do decide to bathe, here are a couple suggestions:

- Charge a bowl of water in the light of the sun and add it to your bath at the end of the day
- Take a Midsummer Ritual Bath (on following page)
- For the lazy witch, enjoy a chamomile-infused bath
- Finish off your bath with sunflower seed oil

Decorations and Altar Adornments

Maybe you decide all of Mother Nature is your altar today, and that's a choice I respect. If you go the traditional route, however, here are some ideas for decorating your indoor altar:

- Decorate with gold, yellow, orange, and white
- Incorporate solar imagery where possible
- Use fresh flowers, especially daisies, sunflowers, or other flowers that resemble the sun
- Put out a basket of fresh fruit and vegetables to snack on throughout the day

Midsummer Milk & Honey Bath

I f there's any day to be a little luxurious with yourself, it's surely the summer solstice. Take this bath in the morning as a bit of self-care so that you feel relaxed, centered, and pampered throughout the rest of the day's festivities.

This bath spell is also a bit different from the other spells we've encountered so far, since you aren't going to be making any bath mixture ahead of time. Instead, this spell calls for liquid milk and honey, and it's worth the time and effort to dissolve the honey in hot water beforehand. (You could also add the honey directly to your bathwater *without* dissolving it ahead of time, but it might have a hard time dispersing evenly.) Additionally, dairy milk is preferable here because it contains lactic acid, which acts as a gentle exfoliating agent, but if you don't want to use animal products, you can substitute with oat milk.

For the bath, you'll need:

- 1 cup of **honey** (hard, crystalized honey that is hard to cook with is perfect here)
- 1 liter of **whole milk**
- A **small pot**
- **Bergamot essential oil**
- **Tangerine essential oil**
- **Sunflower seed oil**
- **Frankincense** and **myrrh incense**
- A few **white, yellow or gold candles**
- Optional: dried **calendula** or **marigold petals**

When you're nearly ready to begin your bath, take your pot and heat a few cups of water on the stove. Once the water is just shy of boiling, slowly add the honey and stir until it's all dissolved.

Take your dissolved honey to your bathroom and start drawing a warm bath. While the bath fills, light your candles and your incense. Once you have some water in the tub, pour the honey mixture in along with the milk and gently mix them with the bathwater. Slowly add a few drops of your essential oils in a ratio of two drops bergamot to one drop tangerine. If using, sprinkle in a handful of dried calendula or marigold petals.

Enter the bath when you're ready. Relax in the water until it starts to cool, then exit the tub. Let your body air-dry, then massage a few drops of the sunflower seed oil into your skin to seal in the energy from the bath.

Lammas

"Hell yeah, it's the first harvest."

August 1st

ammas, also called Lughnasadh in the Wheel of the Year, marks the halfway point between the summer solstice and the fall equinox. Technically, in some Christian denominations, the name "Lammas" refers to the older holiday "Loaf Mass" (like Halloween was originally "All Hallow's Eve"), but many Neo-Pagans and witches use this and "Lughnasadh" interchangeably. (I choose to use "Lammas" because it's easier to write and say.)

It's also colloquially referred to as the "First Harvest," since it's the first of three sabbats – Lammas, Mabon, and Samhain – which are all essentially harvest festivals. Compared to Mabon and Samhain, Lammas still has one foot in summer, and the celebration is comparatively lighter and more laid-back.

Besides all the more traditional ideas I've listed below, I personally believe that Lammas is a great time to reevaluate your romantic relationships. Historically, some villages in Ireland celebrated Lughnasadh by having people wed in "trial marriages," in which young people would be handfasted and then married for a year and a day. If the trial went well, the marriage would become official, and if it didn't, both parties could walk away without consequence. I think almost all of us could do better at more consciously thinking about our relationships, and so I've used this as inspiration for my celebration suggestions.

Ways to Celebrate in the Home

Depending on where you live, the weather may already be cooling down by August 1st. If that's the case, you can celebrate inside with these ideas:

- Bake bread from scratch with a loved one
- Leave bowls of nuts and seeds around the house to snack on
- Drink beer or other grain-based alcohols
- Burn frankincense or sandalwood incense
- Hold a relationship check-in with your partner(s) to discuss what you'd like to keep doing, and what you'd like to leave behind

Ways to Celebrate Outside the Home

If the weather is still nice where you live by the time Lammas arrives, you can make your celebrations more outdoor-oriented with these suggestions:

- Gather fruits and vegetables from your garden or a local farm
- If you tend land, collect seeds that you can use for next year's harvest
- Pick herbs and flowers to dry and use for the cold months ahead
- Visit friends or neighbors and gift them freshly baked goods as a gesture of good will

Celebrating With Bath Magic

If you're looking to take a ritual bath on Lammas, here are a few ideas:

- Pour a liter of beer in your bath and bathe in it (bathing in beer is a thing – Google it)
- Take a re-dedication bath with a partner (instructions on the following page)
- Bathe surrounded by warm-colored candles

Decorations and Altar Adornments

To bring the festive spirit of the First Harvest to your altar, try some of these recommendations:

- Use colors like yellow, orange, red and green
- Incorporate woven baskets or wooden bowls into your setup
- Display apples, grapes, grains, and other seasonal foods
- Decorate with seasonal flowers like sunflowers, heather, poppies

Lammas Re-Dedication Bath

The thing about Lammas is that, historically, it's all about bread – but bread and baths do not go well together. I'm sure I could have shoe-horned something in there to reflect the traditional associations for the holiday, but instead of making Lammas a completely lackluster, minor holiday with a forgettable bath spell, why not focus on one of the more interesting aspects of its history and make a new ritual, instead?

Hence, I've chosen to create a Lammas Re-Dedication Bath for you and your partner[18]. Inspired by the concept of Trial Marriages, held by some Irish towns on Lammas in times past, this bath is for those who want to reaffirm their bond, perhaps on a yearly basis each August 1st. I'd recommend holding a relationship review earlier in the day so that you can talk about how things are going for each of you. Then, assuming both partners want to continue the relationship, you share the ritual bath in the evening.

For the bath mixture, you'll need:
- 1 cup of **colloidal oatmeal**
- 1 fresh **orange**, cut into slices
- 2 tablespoons of dried **skullcap**
- 2 tablespoons of dried **yarrow**
- A handful of dried **chamomile flowers**
- Optional: **honey**
- Optional: **avocado oil**

---

18   As with the Love-Strengthening Bath for Couples, this ritual also works well for multiple individuals. You're only constrained by the size of your bathtub.

When you and your partner are ready to begin your ritual, start by lighting some incense and candles together, then begin drawing the bath. Add the colloidal oatmeal, mixing either with your hand or a wooden spatula to disperse it in the bathwater. If you're using honey, stir that in now, too. Next, add the dried skullcap and yarrow (I recommend using a fine mesh baggie to make clean-up easier). Finish by gently placing the slices of orange and the chamomile flowers on the surface of the bathwater.

When you're ready, climb in with your partner. You can choose to either sit quietly in the bath and just enjoy each other's company, or you can use the time to explore how your relationship might look different in the future. You've created a ritual space outside of the everyday – you can speak about your sexual fantasies, your needs, how you divide labor, how you might open or close your relationship in the future, or any other topics you have a difficult time discussing day-to-day.

After your bath draws to a close, I encourage you to spend a bit of time massaging each other with avocado oil. This last step encourages physical intimacy, as well as bringing some of the magical energy from the bath back into your daily life.

Mabon

"Hell yeah, it's the
second harvest."

Autumn equinox: September 21st–24th

By the time this festival rolls around, we're officially into autumn. Unfortunately for poor Mabon, it's not as well loved as the other solstices and equinoxes, and that's in large part because Samhain (the following holiday) steals all the fun six weeks later. In the Wiccan tradition, the history behind Mabon is also weaker and comes with less mythology: Basically, Wicca went looking for a Western European holiday for the autumn equinox and could only find a minor Welsh celebration that fit. However, because of a lack of historical sources, no-one is sure if "Mabon" is a God, a Demigod, or just Some Cool Dude. This isn't actually unusual for ancient pagan festivals and deities, as these cultures relied on oral storytelling, rather than writing things down for the reference of future witches.

Still, many cultures celebrate this time as a harvest festival or a general time of giving thanks. There's the Moon Festival in China, Taiwan, and Vietnam; Navaratri in Hindu-observing India; Oktoberfest in Germany; and the United States' original Thanksgiving date was October 3rd before it was changed by President Lincoln. For all these reasons, I'll be treating Mabon as a standard harvest festival in my suggestions below.

Ways to Celebrate in the Home

Unless you live in a desert (as I did), the end of September is the perfect time to start cherishing calm and cozy moments indoors. To celebrate Mabon indoors:

- Make a wreath out of foraged autumn leaves and pinecones
- Burn spicy incense varieties like cinnamon, frankincense, or myrrh
- Fill your home with warm-scented candles
- Bake an apple pie or other apple-based pastry
- Enjoy a glass of wine or cider in the evening

Ways to Celebrate Outside the Home

If you enjoy spending time outside on a crisp autumn day, here's how you can observe this holiday outdoors:

- Go to a local apple orchard and go apple picking
- Take a walk and notice the changing colors of the season
- Collect leaves, pinecones and acorns you find on the ground
- Harvest other seasonal fruits, vegetables, and herbs

Celebrating With Bath Magic

A cool, perhaps dreary day outside is the perfect excuse for a warm bath inside. Here are some of my ideas for bath magic on Mabon:

- Add oil to your bathwater to protect your skin from the changing seasons
- Conduct a Mabon Ritual Bath (following page) for increasing protection and prosperity
- Bathe surrounded by warm, fall-colored candles

Decorations and Altar Adornments

The good news about the three harvest festivals is that you can simply build on the decorations you took out for the previous ones for each successive holiday. To update your altar for Mabon:

- 🍃 Make a dried floral arrangement with flowers you gathered from the summer celebrations
- 🍃 Set out pumpkins and gourds in your home
- 🍃 Decorate your space with warm fall colors, like orange, red, purple, and yellow
- 🍃 If you want to run wild, get a cornucopia and fill it with seasonal produce
- 🍃 Incorporate quartz, amber and/or citrine crystals

Mabon Ritual Bath

abon marks the time after the school year has started, when there's a chill in the air, and you can finally buy a pumpkin spice latte. If you're still in school or you have children in school, this time of year can be like a mini New Year: You're resetting your goals and intentions, and you need to put your best foot forward. It's also historically when farmers would start harvesting a large round of crops and hoping that they had produced enough food to last through the winter.

For these reasons, I've designed this ritual bath to focus primarily on protection and prosperity. May you set yourself up for success in academics, may your family be protected, and may you have enough food and resources to last until next summer.

Bath Mixture

For the bath mixture, gather the following ingredients:

- ½ cup of **colloidal oatmeal**
- ½ cup of **sea salt**
- ½ teaspoon of ground **cinnamon**
- ⅛ teaspoon of ground **ginger**
- ⅛ teaspoon of ground **nutmeg**
- ⅛ teaspoon of ground **cardamom**
- 1 pinch of ground **cloves**
- 2 drops of **frankincense essential oil**

To prepare, combine all dry ingredients in a bowl and stir to combine. (If you have especially sensitive skin, halve all spice ingredients.) Add the two drops of frankincense essential oil and store in a glass jar until needed. For best results, charge under the light of the full moon preceding Mabon.

Bath Ritual

When you're ready to start the ritual, gather:

- ⌀ The **bath mixture** you prepared
- ⌀ **Red**, **orange**, **yellow**, and/or **brown-colored candles**
- ⌀ **Cinnamon** or **frankincense incense**
- ⌀ **Sweet almond oil**
- ⌀ **Trinkets** that you value, like jewelry, crystals, small gifts you've received, souvenirs, etc.

Start by lighting your candles and your incense, then draw a warm bath. Add the bath mixture and stir it into the water until it's evenly dissolved. Once you've entered the bath, take a few minutes to relax in the water. Reflect on the year ahead, looking around at the tiny pieces of abundance you've already surrounded yourself with. Visualize the prosperous and protective energy of the water flowing through your body and preparing you for the months ahead. Even if times are tough, you will pull through and succeed.

When the bath starts to cool, exit the tub and gently pat your skin dry with a towel. Finish by massaging a few drops of the almond oil into your skin.

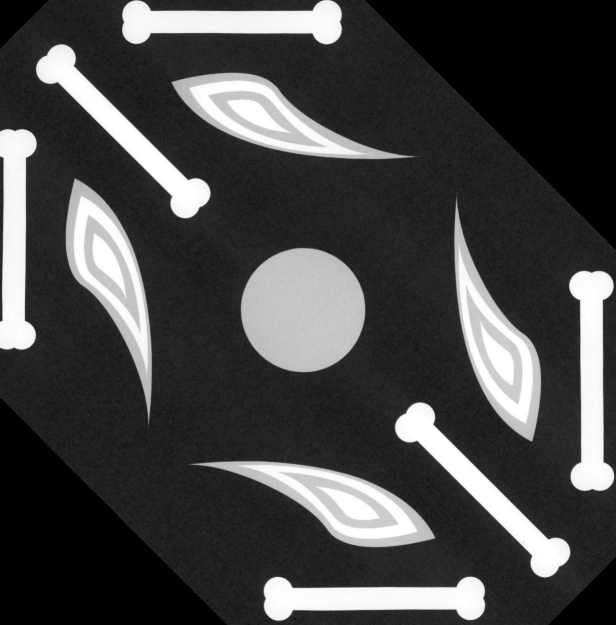

Samhain

"Hell yeah, it's the third harvest."

October 31st–November 1st

Along with Midsummer and Yule, there's a good chance you've heard of this Wheel of the Year holiday. That's because it heavily influenced another major (and more mainstream) holiday that we celebrate today: Halloween.

Samhain is the last of the four Gaelic festivals incorporated into the Wheel of the Year (after Imbolc, Beltane, and Lammas), and it was celebrated in varying ways across much of the British Isles. You probably know some of the mythology behind this festival already: This was when people believed the "veil" separating our world from the spiritual world was at its thinnest, that spirits could more easily "cross over" into our world, and that this was a good time to give offerings to spirits. People of Gaelic descent also used to carve turnips (before the much-more-carvable pumpkins were discovered by Irish immigrants to the Americas), and it was considered polite in several Samhain traditions to cook for and entertain your dead relatives on this day.

Truth be told, Halloween always freaked me out as a kid and I'm probably one of a dozen witches alive who doesn't love Samhain. In the same way that hardline introverts prefer not to interact with people, I'm a witch who prefers not to interact with spirits. (They're draining!) With that in mind, here's how I celebrate Samhain – without a single ouija board in sight.

Ways to Celebrate in the Home

Samhain is all about getting cozy indoors. Here are my favorite ways to observe this holiday while inside:

- Light a fire in your fireplace
- Set up some spice-filled stovetop incense and let it simmer all day
- Knit or crochet hats, scarves, or mittens to keep warm in the coming winter
- Tell stories with loved ones about those who have passed away
- Bake a classic pumpkin pie and inscribe sigils into the crust before adding the filling
- Do a spell to honor your deceased ancestors

Ways to Celebrate Outside the Home

If you're looking for a breath of fresh air during this holiday, here are my suggestions:

- Carve a pumpkin and leave it outside your front door
- Have a bonfire in the evening with your friends
- Visit a local cemetery and leave an offering for the dead
- Harvest the last of your herbs before winter

Celebrating With Bath Magic

Samhain is the perfect holiday to sit and reflect by yourself for a few hours. Here's how to do that with bath magic:

- Have a Samhain Ritual Bath (on following page)
- Buy yourself a very cool black bath bomb
- Use cypress and clary sage essential oils if you've recently experienced a loss

Decorations and Altar Adornments

Is there anything better than decorating for Halloween? Yes, it's called decorating for Samhain. Here are my recommendations:

- Incorporate harvest foods like dried ears of corn, gourds, and apples
- Decorate with symbols of death, such as bones or the Death tarot card
- Pull out pictures or personal items from loved ones who have passed away
- Burn spicy, woody incense, like pine, cedar wood, myrrh, or cinnamon
- Use colors like black, brown, red, orange, and dark purple

Samhain Ritual Bath

Whether you prefer the imagery of the "veil" between the physical and spiritual world being thinnest at Samhain, or something more akin to the "gate" of the underworld opening, it's clear that the threshold between our world and the next is most blurred the night of this holiday. This bath spell is designed to make reaching across that threshold as easy as possible, whether you want to connect with a deceased loved one, explore the astral plane, or simply do some amazing divination later in the evening. There are several different ways to prepare this bath: First, you can steep the herbs in one to two liters of boiling water and strain the mixture before your bath (which will give you a stronger infusion and make cleanup easier); second, you can throw the herbs into a muslin bag and let them steep directly in the bathwater itself. Third, you can choose to let the herbs float freely in the bathwater if you don't mind the leaves sticking to you and having extra work afterwards. Choose the method that is most appealing to you.

This bath should also be performed the night of October 31st and be completed entirely by candlelight. It also works well as a base for astral travel or scrying.

Bath Infusion

- 1 cup of dried **mugwort**[19]
- 1 tablespoon of **anise**[20] **seeds** or **star anise**
- ½ cup of dried **sage leaves**
- Optional: tablespoon dried **chervil** (if you'd like to commune with a deceased loved one)
- Optional: **cypress essential oil** (if you're still grieving someone's passing)
- Optional: a sprinkle of dried **calendula** or **marigold petals**

---

19   Those who are pregnant or are trying to become pregnant should avoid mugwort. Also, try to patch test first if you're allergic to ragweed, chrysanthemums, marigolds, daisies, tobacco, or similar plants, as you have a higher chance of also being allergic to mugwort.

20   Anise can have estrogen-like effects on your body when taken in large quantities. If you're taking certain birth control pills or have an estrogen-caused medical condition like breast cancer, uterine cancer, ovarian cancer, endometriosis, or uterine fibroids, you should check with a doctor before using large quantities of anise.

If steeping the herbs before your bath, combine your mugwort, anise seeds/star anise, sage and any of the optional herbs in a teapot or other heat-safe container that can contain one to two liters of water. Cover with boiling water and let them steep for 15 minutes to an hour. (If you're not using a teapot, strain the herbs out once they're done steeping.)

Bath Ritual

When you're ready to bathe, gather the following materials:

- The **infusion** you prepared or its ingredients
- Two handfuls of **Epsom salts**
- Lots of **candles** (preferably **black**)
- **Cinnamon, myrrh,** or **gum arabic incense**
- **Coconut** or **hemp seed oil**

Start by lighting your candles and incense, then draw a warm bath. Add the infusion (or the muslin bag with the herbs) to the bathwater, then toss in the Epsom salts. If you're using essential oil, add a few drops. Enter the bath when ready and use this either for traveling to the astral plane, or as a precursor to practicing divination afterwards.

Stay until the water starts to cool, then leave the bath. Once you're out, finish with either coconut oil or hemp seed oil – coconut oil for those who need protection when talking with spirits and hemp seed oil for those who want to do divination.

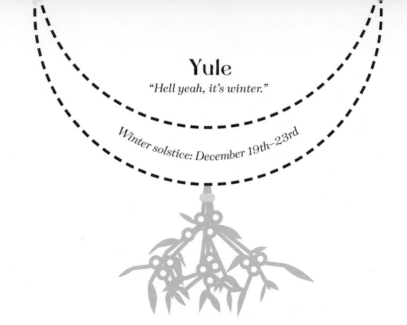

Yule

"Hell yeah, it's winter."

Winter solstice: December 19th–23rd

ast but not least, we arrive at Yule. In the literal sense, Yule is a modern reconstruction of several Norse and Germanic traditions that involved burning Yule logs, gathering mistletoe, singing, and decorating trees to name but a few activities you might find familiar. In a broader sense, however, Yule is a celebration of the winter solstice, which was popular – and remains popular – across a variety of cultures, from Ancient Rome to the Incas to the Zuni people of the American Southwest to modern Iran. There is something about the shortest day of the year that draws people indoors to celebrate.

With that in mind, here are some more and less traditional ideas for how to observe Yule in your practice.

Ways to Celebrate in the Home

With only a few hours of sunlight available on this day, you'll probably want to spend most of the day celebrating indoors. Here's how:

- Make gifts (or spells) to give to loved ones
- Simmer some stovetop incense as an alternative to smoke incense
- Hang mistletoe around your home for protection (and some kisses)
- Prepare some mulled wine for the adults in your life
- Do some holiday baking and carve sigils into the items before sending them into the oven

Ways to Celebrate Outside the Home

Just because it's freezing outside doesn't mean you can't celebrate Yule outdoors as well. Here are my suggestions:

- Go for an early morning walk and observe the darkness on the shortest day of the year
- If it's snowing or there's snow on the ground, collect some for snow water
- After the sun has gone down, burn a Yule log in a bonfire
- Leave out an offering of seeds for the wildlife in your area

Celebrating With Bath Magic

The Yuletide season can be a hectic time of year, but it can be great to set aside an hour just for yourself. Here's how to do that with bath magic:

- Have a Yule Abundance Bath (on following page)
- Take a lazy witch's Yule bath with fresh orange slices and frankincense essential oil
- Enchant a holiday-themed bath bomb

Decorations and Altar Adornments

One of the best things about the holiday season is the decorating and the warmth it brings into the home. Here's how to do that, but with a touch of magic:

- Use colors like reds, greens, white, and metallic hues
- Stash some magic in your Christmas tree by enchanting the different glass ornaments
- Set out oranges, pears, nuts, and berries to snack on
- Lay out snowflake obsidian, clear or smokey quartz, and bloodstone

Yule Abundance Bath

Seeing as the time around the winter solstice is both traditionally a time for gift-giving in many religions *and* it's close to the end of the calendar year (in the Northern Hemisphere), Yule is the perfect time to set intentions for prosperity. This bath is for welcoming abundance into your life in the coming year and works just as well whether done in the morning before the festivities, or in the evening to close out the shortest day of the year. These bath salts also make a great gift to give to any fellow witches in your life.

Bath Salt Mixture

For best results, prepare the mixture a few days before Yule so that it has time to sit and charge before use.

For the mixture, you'll need to gather:

- 1 ½ cups of **sea salt**
- ½ cup of **baking soda**
- ¼ cup of small pieces of dried **orange peel**
- 1 teaspoon of ground **cinnamon**
- ½ teaspoon of ground **ginger**
- A dash of ground **nutmeg**
- **Sweet orange essential oil**
- **Frankincense essential oil**
- Optional: **almond fragrance oil**

Combine all the dry ingredients in a bowl and gently stir while envisioning what abundance would look like in your life next year. Be sure to focus not only on abundance of money, but also on abundance of opportunity, love, and happiness.

If using the almond fragrance oil, start with one drop of it before adding either of the essential oils (since synthetic fragrances have a tendency to be overpowering). Then, add the frankincense and sweet orange in equal amounts until the fragrance smells balanced. For best results, store the bath salts in a glass jar with a piece of citrine or jade, and charge under the light of the full moon.

Bath Ritual

When you're ready to start the bath, gather:

- ✐ The **bath salts** you prepared
- ✐ Lots of **candles** (preferably **red**, **green**, **white** and **metallic colors**)
- ✐ **Frankincense** and **myrrh incense**
- ✐ **Sweet almond oil**

As with other bath rituals, start by lighting your candles and your incense, then draw a warm bath. Add your bath salts and enter the tub when you're ready. Enjoy the comforting, warm water and envision your life in the following year being similarly warm and enjoyable with abundance. Exit the bath when the water starts to cool, and massage a few drops of almond oil into your skin to lock in the energy from the ritual.

Chapter Nine: Psychoactive Spells

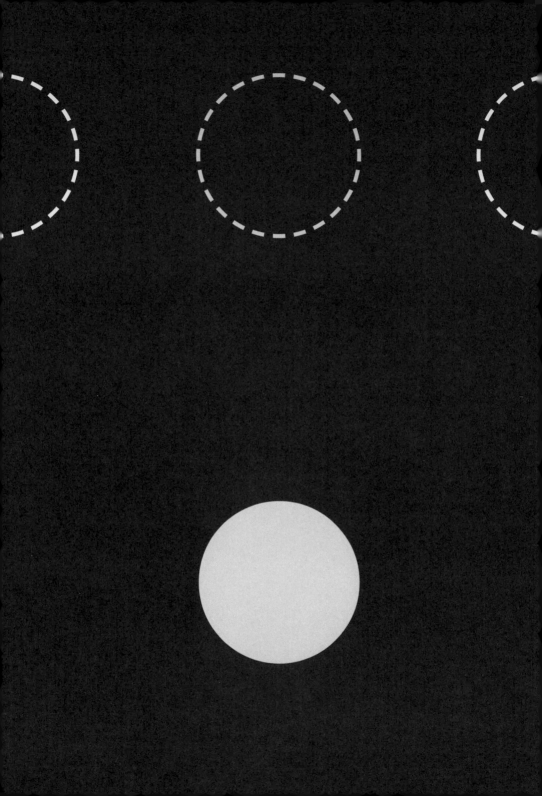

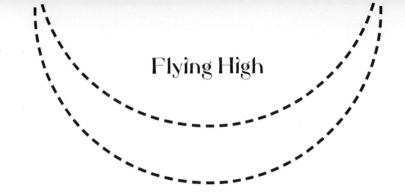

Flying High

hea and I had been toying with the idea of journeying into the astral plane together for quite some time.

She had purchased a "flying ointment" (a balm applied to the skin said to have hallucinogenic properties) from Etsy a few months back, and we kept saying we'd try it *next time*. The particular flying ointment Rhea had picked up had great reviews online for actually causing some hallucinations; unfortunately, that was because it contained belladonna, the highly toxic but mind-altering plant in the tomato family. After finding a reason to miss half a dozen opportunities, it was obvious that we were both going to chicken out.

"We could try to astral project after smoking some weed, and then just see if we meet each other in the astral plane," I suggested to Rhea.

"Yeah, alright. Let's try that."

We had both semi-successfully visited the astral plane on separate occasions – both during bath magic – but neither of us felt particularly good at it.

The first time I visited was during my prep work for the curse on Nate: I journeyed to the astral plane and tried to find some kind of a connection to him. I wanted to flex my magical muscles and see if I could siphon off any additional energy from him that I could funnel into my poppet. Mostly, it was a disorienting experience, as I felt other entities passing me by, and I tried to stay as unremarkable as possible. I prayed that none of them would try to interact with me.

At the end of that journey, I had halfway succeeded in finding him, but it was more like finding an echo of someone you once knew. It was as if he had been to this place in the astral plane sometime before, and I was just seeing a shadow slowly fade out of view. Or maybe a ghost.

Whatever it was, it mostly just made me sad (and a little horny – but as it turns out, fantasizing about the ghost of the ex you encountered on the astral plane is not a sexy setup). More than anything, I was just happy to have somewhat achieved my goal and finally be able to leave.

Rhea, meanwhile, hadn't told me what she had done while she was there. Neither of us told the other. I figured she had explored like I had, but what for was entirely unknown to me. It seemed that what each person was looking for on the astral plane was an extremely personal thing.

By now, however, it was a year since our first attempts, and things were different. Rhea and I were deep into magic, and we were both constantly pushing each other to try new things so that we could write about it for the blog. Nate and I had also gotten back together, which also meant that we had another magical source of knowledge that we could tap into.

If there was ever a moment for projecting into the astral plane together, this was it.

We set up Rhea's room so that it was filled with glowing candles and incense. She always kept her space clean and well-decorated, but we tucked away any loose items of clothing and straightened the objects on her desk.

Then, we both went into the bathroom, pulled out her pipe and grinder, and started running the shower hot. While we hadn't projected using marijuana before, we figured we should smoke enough that we were noticeably intoxicated, but not so high that we couldn't think straight. The goal was to lose the definite edges of reality but keep our cognition mostly intact.

Once we thought we'd reached the appropriate level, we slowly made our way out of the bathroom and onto Rhea's bed, where a mound of fluffy pillows awaited us.

As I closed my eyes, I drew my sensory awareness inwards. I imagined that the lines of my body were fuzzy and amorphous, slowly bleeding into my environment like pigment spreading in a watercolor painting.

At the same time, I conjured a duplicate image of my surroundings, set off from reality by just a few inches. There was Rhea's bed, and then the softer, floatier version of Rhea's bed. There was me, and then there was the gossamer version of me. Everything had a diffused version of itself.

Once I felt detached enough from my body, the window of opportunity slowly came into view. I gradually nudged myself from the definite, material world and flowed into the second, nebulous one. There was a slight tingle at the back of my skull, moving into my neck, like I was entering a warm bath.

After that, the transition to the astral plane was quick. I imagined myself moving *up* and *up* until I reached a dark, vast place filled with points of light and segmented into a large, three-dimensional grid. It felt like being inside a dazzling star navigation chart from a science-fiction movie – except the light and lines of the chart were behaving strangely, as if I were underwater.

I could feel the presence of other entities moving past me in different directions: some quickly, others slowly. Some were represented by points of light; some were invisible to my eyes. Some, I didn't dare to look at for fear that they might notice me. I glanced around to see if Rhea was nearby, but nothing that looked or felt like her was in my vicinity. Perhaps she was still in the room, or perhaps she had entered another part of the vast plane.

I contemplated going off to find her, but I figured that she was fine, wherever she was. Rhea was just as smart and powerful a witch as I was. She could handle herself.

There was, however, another person I was curious to see if I could find: Nate.

I had felt slightly embarrassed by my first foray into trying to find him on the astral plane; I couldn't even tell Rhea about how it had really unfolded. Now, however, I was a more experienced witch with a better intuition about these things. It was time to try again.

Intellectually, finding any one entity on the astral plane should be as difficult as locating a needle in a haystack – it should be filled with spirits, demons, deity-like beings, and at least some number of people who died long ago. Any one person should get lost in the noise of everything else.

In my experience, however, it's much easier. I started by intuitively heading to where I thought he'd be, as if there were a variety of centers of gravity on the plane, and some would likely appeal to him more than others.

I drifted to a place where I could feel a semblance of his energy, and from there, it was more like looking out on a crowd from a high perch. Sure, there might be hundreds of other people in that crowd, but from on high, you can see how each person moves. If you know someone, then their gate and body movements are distinct.

Sure enough, there was a little pinprick of light that seemed like Nate.

As I moved towards "him," I felt the astral plane fading similarly to how I had entered it. The large, dark grid slowly faded out of my field of vision, and in its place, I could see Nate in a room. The details were fuzzy, and the colors didn't seem quite right (everything was covered in a light wash of red). But there was Nate: moving and smiling, sitting on a couch. I could feel that there were other people nearby that he was interacting with, but they were outside the plane, and I didn't know who they were. Someone passed him a pipe filled with weed, and as he exhaled, he laughed.

Instinctively, I smiled and squeezed my hand. I had done it – I had found him.

Unfortunately, the squeeze to my own hand had a grounded, bodily feeling that reminded me I was in two places at once. Before I could get my bearings, I was zooming back into the darkness, through the expanse of the astral plane, and falling back onto Rhea's bed. I half expected to feel a thud as I came back to my resting place, but instead, I just felt mildly startled. I opened my eyes.

"Jesus," I muttered.

Rhea was also stirring. She opened her eyes as if she were awakening from an intense dream. "What? Did you see something during your projection?" she asked.

Slowly, I tried to sit up. "Well, I found Nate. It looked like he was at a party."

"Is he at a party right now?"

"I have no idea. I haven't texted him for a few hours." I rubbed my eyes. "I'll ask him."

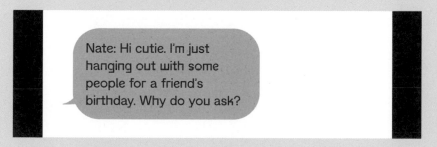

Lyra: Hey, what are you doing right now?

"What about you?" I asked Rhea as I waited for Nate's response. "Did you do anything interesting?"

"Not really. I tried talking to a couple spirits. They were fine, but mostly just talking about nonsense. I felt like I had to repeatedly politely excuse myself." We both laughed. Rhea was a typical Libra – getting herself into the exact same situations on the astral plane as she did in real life.

My phone buzzed.

Nate: Hi cutie. I'm just hanging out with some people for a friend's birthday. Why do you ask?

I showed the message to Rhea as I smiled widely, smug with myself. She smiled back.

"We really are good at this."

Why We Mixed
Witchcraft and Drugs

You might have picked up by now that Rhea and I dabbled in a bit of recreational marijuana use, drinking sporadically, and being generally curious about other mind-altering substances.

In the grand scheme of things, what we did was not particularly notable in terms of young people experimenting with marijuana and alcohol. Nor was it strange that we were two individuals in a left-of-center, spiritual space who dabbled in these substances.

What was special about it was that we dared to mix the magic itself with drugs and alcohol.

Of course, with the recent boom in various jurisdictions legalizing marijuana for recreational purposes, this all probably seems like old news. If you search for something along the lines of "weed and magick" in Google, you'll get a variety of recently published books and articles suggesting different ways to incorporate marijuana into your craft.

To go back much further, if you know anything about ancient history or anthropology, then you also know that people have been using mind-altering substances in their spiritual practices for centuries. Just to nerd out for a second, mind-altering drugs used for spiritual purposes – as opposed to the purely recreational – get their own specific term: *entheogens*.

There's fairly decent proof that humans in prehistory (and perhaps even other members of the Homo family, like Homo Erectus) used psilocybin ("magic") mushrooms. The strongest evidence for this is that there are psilocybin-containing mushrooms in almost every major region on the planet, and where there are remaining Indigenous communities in those areas, they typically make use of them for divinatory purposes with similar ritual aspects.

Another well-known entheogen of choice is ground peyote, traces of which have been found in a cave on the present-day Texas-Mexico border that date back to 3,780–3,660 BCE. Researchers think this points to a long-standing psychoactive use by communities living in that area.

A more mundane entheogen was the wine consumed for a range of religious rituals in classical antiquity – most famously in celebrations honoring Dionysus – although this concoction was also seemingly spiked with opium, hemlock, wormwood, cannabis, and various other animal venoms and toxins from plants. Because of these additives, it was standard practice to dilute the wine with water in a ratio of three or four parts water to one part wine. Drinking it straight could cause permanent mental damage or even death after a few cups.

To circle back to our particular topic at hand – witchcraft – it was documented that several women arrested for witchcraft in the 16th century had "flying ointments" in their possession when they were apprehended. When physicians of the time tested the contents of said flying ointments, they were found to produce hallucinogenic effects.

Things changed, however, around the same time as the modern witchcraft revival, with the publishing of *Witchcraft Today* in 1954 by Gerald Gardner. While he made passing comments about "certain incenses" that could assist in improving one's psychic abilities, he otherwise was extremely mum – at least publicly – on the subject of mind-altering substances.

After his death in 1964, parts of his book of shadows (now typically referred to as the *Gardnerian Book of Shadows*) began to be published posthumously. Like most books of shadows, this was originally intended only to be used by his coven rather than to be a public-facing work. In there, he wrote that "Hemp" was particularly dangerous, specifically because of how easily and quickly it opened the inner eye: Gardner urges his readers that this spiritual effect is so enticing that the drug should be used sparingly, with the supply limited and controlled by someone sober and responsible.

While this isn't an absolute ban, I think it's quite clear that Gardner was a bit of a stickler about drug use. In his paradigm, if you're using mind-altering substances at all, it should be strictly for spiritual purposes – not for recreational use.

Of course, the long-term suspension of drug use in witchcraft is not all Gardner's fault. It was also undoubtedly impacted by larger cultural shifts, including national drug bans implemented in Europe and the United States in the first half of the 20th century, the signing of the Convention for Limiting the Manufacture and Regulating the Distribution of Narcotic Drugs in 1931 by the League of Nations, the follow-up UN treaty Single Convention on Narcotic Drugs in 1961, and the American War on Drugs starting in 1971.

Broadly speaking, drug use fell out of favor in many wealthy nations at that time. Drug use for spiritual purposes is just one casualty of the larger shift.

By the time that Rhea and I fell into the witchcraft scene in the 2010s, things were just starting to change. In our small corner of the online witch community, most posts were *against* using any type of drugs during magic. Only occasionally did we see someone else post something pro-marijuana (or even pro-alcohol during rituals, for that matter).

Before I tell you why I am a fervent believer in mind-altering substances for witchcraft, I want to acknowledge some valid arguments from critics. In the slice of the online community Rhea and I inhabited for those years, the mood was very anti-risk and pro-safety – which is not a bad position to take. Drugs and alcohol do impair your judgment, and there are many occasions in witchcraft when it's good to have your wits about you (for instance, I would not have wanted to be high anytime I was using a sharp object).

Just practically speaking, even "less dangerous" substances like alcohol and marijuana can cause dependency, alter your brain chemistry for the worse, be used inappropriately by those with mental illness and trauma (which can prevent better coping mechanisms from developing), and cause negative health effects beyond your brain, as alcohol and marijuana are both essentially poisons. Almost anything that is used as an entheogen can harm you in some way.

Now, on to the good stuff.

So much of witchcraft and other modern esotericism is about trying to transcend your body, tap into a higher level of consciousness, and connect with your intuition that it's pretty shocking drug use ever fell out of favor in the first place.

Of course, many individuals can train themselves to transcend reality through meditation or trance work, but it is a long and arduous process for most. Some people believe that waiting years to experience this is the price you pay for achieving your goal – but I'm not of that school of thought.

I believe that magic is for everyone, including the person working two jobs or the stay-at-home parent of multiple children. Not everyone has the time or opportunity to go off every day to meditate for an hour, but most people can carve out a couple hours a month to smoke a joint and read tarot.

Meanwhile, it's not like Rhea and I single-handedly rediscovered drugs for spiritual purposes in the 21st century: There are still a variety of Indigenous communities and other groups that have kept up long-standing traditions of entheogenic drug use with assorted botanical ingredients. These practices have been with us the entire time, just at the margins. And even if the situation has dramatically improved for those of us who incorporate marijuana into our craft, that doesn't mean that's also the case for communities that use other psychoactive drugs for their spiritual purposes.

Like everything else in this book, my purpose in writing this isn't to say that incorporating drugs into your craft is 100% the right course of action, nor is it to say that we can't enjoy entheogenic drug use because there are communities that don't experience the same level of freedom that we do. The point is that this topic is mired in ethical shades of gray, and the more information you have access to, the better informed your position can be about using entheogens in your own practice.

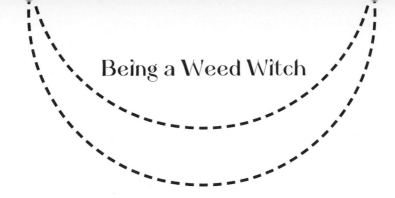

Being a Weed Witch

You might be reading this now and thinking to yourself that this is all well and good, but I haven't given you any practical information on incorporating weed into your craft.

On some level, that's on purpose. I don't feel completely ethically at ease giving a step-by-step guide on how to use drugs (apparently the D.A.R.E. program had more of an impact on me than I'd like to admit).

You might also have picked up on the fact that our use of alcohol and drugs did not fall under the strict "entheogenic" category. We smoked regularly: for fun, for ideas, for relaxation, for astral travel, for intense dreams, for rituals, for enjoying munchies, or even just for dispelling boredom. Not all of it was healthy, and large parts of what we did are not what I'd recommend to others. I smoke considerably less than I did back then, and that influences what ideas I would suggest to readers.

So, as with the chapter on cursing, instead of detailing something more prescriptive, I've outlined some broader ideas and themes for using marijuana in your magical practice. From there, you can experiment with what does and doesn't work for you.

Astral Travel

As noted by my story earlier in the chapter, I think one of the best reasons to use marijuana in your craft is to help you with astral travel. THC can give you a very floaty, ungrounded, and fuzzy feeling that perfectly sets the stage for astral projection. And even putting aside lofty statements that marijuana "opens your third eye" or something like that, it is a very mild hallucinogen which will do funny things to your synapses and help you see things in a new light.

On a related note, marijuana is also ideal for cultivating other out-of-body experiences, like working with deities. This is especially true if you'd like to be inhabited/possessed by the energy of a deity – but as noted in the beginning of this book, I don't work with deities and I won't be of any help with recommendations on this front. Use at your own risk.

Reaching Trance-like States

When I say, "reaching trance-like states," I don't actually mean going into a literal trance (although you can certainly do that). What I mean is using weed to enhance the rhythmic, flow-like mental state that happens when you set up a really elaborate ritual.

If you've never been in a full-blown ritual before, it can be hard to describe the intense feeling of energy in the air and the mystical, autopilot-like feeling that can take over your brain. It's what lots of people (including me) love about rituals, and weed can intensify this feeling further. Plus, when you're in this type of state, your magic will typically work more effectively, as you have better concentration and cultivated intent.

Even for something less elaborate than a full ritual, weed can help you get in a similar frame of mind before reading tarot or doing other divination work. But be warned: Unlike with astral travel, be careful how much THC you consume before rituals or divination work. If you smoke too much, you might get sleepy and not have the energy to execute your intended purpose.

Adding Creativity to Your Craft

While this might sound like a lackluster suggestion, one of the best outcomes of smoking weed that Rhea and I had during our time practicing together was in the creation of new ideas.

Sometimes, after reading a dozen spells that all seem kind of similar or staying too long in one part of the witchcraft community, magic can seem formulaic and rote. In reality, it's not like that at all. There are all kinds of new combinations to discover and new experiences to uncover – you just need to switch up your perspective. What I liked best about smoking weed is that it helped us spawn new ideas – several of them detailed in this book.

To tap into this benefit of weed, simply ingest a small (again, dosage is important here) amount of THC before going about some of your routine magic work, like grinding herbs or preparing bath salts. You might be surprised by what new connections your brain makes.

Making Mundane Smoking More Magical

Of course, you can also look at this the other way: Instead of adding weed to your magic, add some magic to your weed.

By this, I mean draw sigils with non-toxic ink on your rolling papers and let them be activated as you smoke. If you often mix your marijuana with tobacco, try mixing things up and smoking with ground lavender for relaxation, damiana for lust, or mugwort for better divination (just to name a few suggestions). Add moon water to your bong or enchant your CBD body balm for extra soothing effects.

To bring this back to my main point, I can't legally encourage you to incorporate alcohol and drugs into your practice (especially if you're underage) but mixing these substances with your craft might give you some new experiences and ideas that you never would have had before. They can be an especially powerful component for divination, psychic work, and traveling to the astral plane.

If you do decide to dabble in mixing entheogens into your craft, **be smart about it**, and use your brain. Always start with low doses and gradually increase from there. Do not operate any vehicles or conduct any bath magic while intoxicated. And of course, follow all your local laws.

Drunk Tarot

fter Rhea and I launched the blog, we were surprised by how fast
we were gaining followers – especially once we started publishing
our own spell content. We quickly passed 5,000 followers, then
10,000, and 20,000 came pretty quickly, too.

For both of us, however, just hoarding followers was never the point. We
wanted to build our own little brand and have a distinct personality in the
community. For that, we knew we'd need to up our engagement beyond just
recirculating other popular posts and adding controversial commentary.

Of course, there were standard giveaways, but that was too basic, too
obvious a grab for more followers, and our site platform was very good at
hunting down and deactivating accounts that held giveaways. We couldn't
post more pictures or videos of our lives, as we both wanted to be anonymous.
The same issue came along with meetups (plus, then we'd have to make small
talk with strangers).

We jockeyed ideas back and forth, trying to find something unique that
could be just ours, but we kept coming up empty-handed.

One day, I lay on Rhea's bed while browsing our dashboard. We had both
just smoked weed, and I was mindlessly scrolling through posts to add to our
reblog queue when I stumbled upon a public tarot reading someone had given.

"What if we gave away free tarot readings? That seems a little less obvious than giving away free items," I suggested to Rhea.

I saw her ponder it as she packed away the rest of her weed and her pipe into the box she stored it all in. Then her eyes suddenly widened, and a smile broke across her face. "What if we gave away free tarot readings *while high?*" she countered.

It was a devilishly good idea. "What if," I posited back, "we gave readings while high *and drunk?*"

"It's perfect."

We giggled, smug about how good we were at coming up with new blog ideas together. Doing public tarot readings in general would be great for attracting lots of community engagement, but adding alcohol and drugs into the mix was even better. For one, many people claimed that you should never read tarot while under the influence, so it'd be perfect for pissing off those people and building our reputation as rule breakers. On top of that, doing readings while we were cross-faded meant that even if our interpretations were completely wrong or off the mark, it would be fun and low stakes.

We quickly made a plan to do a trial-run that evening under the title "Drunk Tarot." Our strategy was to start early-ish so that followers on the East Coast and some night owls in Europe could participate. We wrote a post outlining the rules while we were still sober, and otherwise planned on being slightly cross-faded right as we started.

The rules we outlined were as follows:

- Followers would come into our inbox and ask a vague question about a topic they wanted our input on.
- We would do a three-card draw and then write back one quippy sentence as a response.
- We didn't want to spam our followers' feeds, so we'd only pick five or so anonymous questions that would be answered publicly. The others would
  be answered privately.
- We'd let it run for about three hours, or until we were too lazy and/or lethargic to keep going, and we'd try to get to as many people as we could in that time.

In typical "content creator" fashion, we then spent the following hours painstakingly creating photos to serve as the header image for the post: pulling out our most expensive and photogenic bottles of alcohol, making a convincing-looking faux cocktail, and arranging them with Rhea's beautiful tarot cards in various ways until we got several decent options. It was exhausting, but it would pay off.

Our rules written and the photo edited, we queued everything up so that we could publish with a single click, then turned our attention to getting intoxicated.

Rhea pre-ground enough weed for several bowls while I made cocktails. We took our two drinks to the bathroom while we smoked, and although we felt solidly tipsy afterwards, we both agreed we were not nearly intoxicated enough for the title of our event. To speed things along, we also pulled out a bottle of tequila and two shot glasses.

"Here's to Drunk Tarot," I said.

"To Drunk Tarot."

Our tiny shot glasses clinked together, and our night began.

In the minutes after we clicked "Publish" on our post, our inbox was inundated with dozens of requests. Rhea and I worked independently with our own decks to try and answer as many of them as possible, but even after we'd only answered one each, our inbox had already climbed to over 90 requests.

After we had both responded to a few more message, it became obvious that three-card draws were way too laborious to do while intoxicated, so we quickly went back and edited the post to say we'd be doing one-card draws, instead.

We also took another shot, to keep the light-hearted energy up. When we came back, our inbox had already topped 200.

At that point, we made the decision to close our inbox to stop new requests from coming in. We worked over the next hour to clear as many questions as possible, periodically taking shots and publicly posting answers to show that we really were intoxicated. Rhea also had the good sense to make an intra-community joke:

---

recreationalwitchcraft

when ur readings all in reverse caus you're drunk

12:10 AM

We closed the night after answering 80-some requests and made a public apology to everyone else we didn't get to.

In the morning, we woke up with no hangover (as early twenty-somethings) and saw that the community response looked even more positive when we were sober. People were asking when we'd do it next, we got great feedback from those we did read for, and we finally had something to offer that couldn't be found anywhere else: our intoxicated divinations.

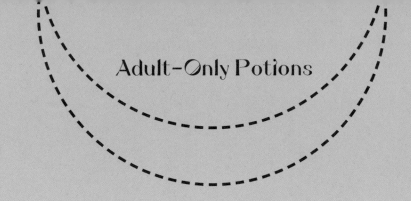

Adult-Only Potions

Real-life magic doesn't use as many potions as you might have expected from reading fantasy novels, and that's because most potions you could make are just a fast-track to producing mold.

That said, I don't think weed should get all the spiritual fun in magic. Alcohol used to be quite difficult to distill correctly in high concentrations in ancient times, and offerings of alcohol (also known as *libations*) to deities or ancestors were very popular across time and many cultures. It can be easy to forget when alcoholic drinks are now so widely available, but this stuff used to be cool for magic, too.

Needless to say, enjoy responsibly, and follow your local laws.

Lucky Night Pre-Game Cocktail

I f you live in a location where bars and clubs close around 2 a.m., you've really got to make the most of your night out. To do this, start at home with this cocktail, which maximizes luck generally (and has a little something-something in there if you're planning on gambling or looking for a hook-up). This recipe yields one drink.

Ingredients:

- 3 ounces of **bourbon**
- 1 ounce of **maple syrup**
- Juice from 1 **orange**
- 1 slice of **orange**
- A dash of **nutmeg**
- **Ginger beer**

Add your bourbon, maple syrup, and orange juice to a shaker with ice and shake vigorously for a few moments while visualizing your intent. Then, pour into a glass filled with ice. Top with ginger beer and garnish with the slice of orange.

An Incognito Cleansing Spell

n occasion, it will occur to you that you've done something that may put people in your inner circle at risk of picking up negative energy. Perhaps you played a little too fast and loose with those hexes. Maybe your spell misfired. Or maybe, you just attracted the wrong spirit to your home during a ouija misadventure.

Whatever the reason, you might need to slip a cleansing charm to someone without alerting them. This spell is intended for just that, as it's based off a tried-and-true cocktail formulation that your loved ones have likely encountered before. This recipe yields one cocktail but produces enough simple syrup for several drinks.

Ingredients:

- 1 cup of **water**
- 1 cup of **sugar**
- 3 sprigs of fresh **thyme**, plus more for garnish
- A pinch of **cayenne pepper**
- 1 whole **grapefruit**
- 2 ounces of **vodka, gin,** or **tequila**
- **Soda water**

Start by cutting and juicing the grapefruit, but be sure to keep the leftover peels. Take your water, sugar, grapefruit peels, and thyme and add them to a small pot. Heat until the sugar dissolves, stirring while thinking of your cleansing intent. Remove the thyme and grapefruit peels, then add the pinch of cayenne pepper. Remove from the heat and allow to cool to room temperature. (You can let this syrup cool on a sigil matching your intent for extra magical benefits.)

Add your alcohol of choice, plus 2 ounces of the grapefruit juice, and 1.5 ounces of the syrup you made, to a glass filled with ice. Top with soda water and stir to combine. Serve with a sprig of thyme for garnish.

A Not-Boring Protection Spell

A nyone who's spent significant time in the witchcraft community knows that most modern protection spells are a bit of a snooze-fest. This potion, meanwhile, is actually a joy to drink, and can easily be given to a friend without having to convince them to carry a bunch of loose herbs in their purse. This recipe yields one cocktail.

Ingredients:

- ⌀ 2 ounces of **gin**
- ⌀ ½ ounce of **elderflower liqueur/violet liqueur**
- ⌀ 3 **basil leaves**, plus more for garnish
- ⌀ ¼ cup of **blackberries**, plus more for garnish
- ⌀ 1 ounce of **lime juice**
- ⌀ **Soda water**

Place your basil leaves, blackberries, and lime juice in a shallow glass and muddle (a.k.a. smush) them all together as you visualize your intent. Top with ice, gin, your liqueur of choice, and soda water. Stir before serving, and garnish with extra basil and blackberries.

Lovers' Lust Potion

This cocktail is really only intended for partners or as a pre-ritual orgy drink. You could also theoretically serve it at a party if you want to create some chaos among your guests. This recipe yields four drinks.

Ingredients:

- 1 cup of **water**
- 1 cup of **sugar**
- 1 **hibiscus tea bag** (or loose flowers)
- 1 **cardamom pod**
- ½ teaspoon of **vanilla extract**
- ¾ cup of **whisky**
- ¼ cup of **lemon juice**
- Some thin slices of **pear**, for garnish

First, take your water, sugar, hibiscus tea, and cardamom pod and add them to a small saucepan. Steep over a medium-high heat. Stir while visualizing your intent until the sugar has dissolved, then remove the tea bag and cardamom pod. Keep on the heat until the mixture begins to thicken slightly into a syrup. Allow to cool to room temperature.

Next, add the ¼ cup of hibiscus syrup, the vanilla extract, whisky, and lemon juice to a shaker with ice. Shake vigorously for a few moments, then strain into a glass filled with ice. Garnish with a thin slice of pear.

Yuletide Prosperity Mulled Wine

his is a great drink to enjoy during Yule, or anytime in the colder months. This recipe also makes a rather large batch, so be sure to invite your coven over, or some fellow witchy friends.

Ingredients:

- 1 (750 ml) bottle of **dry red wine**
- ½ cup of **honey**
- 1 cup of **water**
- 4 **cinnamon sticks**
- 5 **allspice berries**
- ⅓ teaspoon of **whole black peppercorns**
- 2 whole **star anise**
- 1 **apple**, cored and thinly sliced

Add all ingredients together in a medium-sized saucepan and stir while envisioning prosperity coming to you in the new year. Keep it on the heat until steaming, and just very slightly simmering. (Be careful not to cook the alcohol off!) Then, strain out the solid ingredients, and serve in mugs.

As a bonus, this cocktail also makes for a great offering to Dionysus, if that's your thing.

Chapter Ten: Divination and Astrology

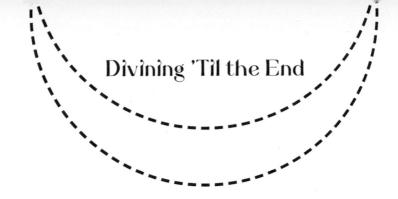

Divining 'Til the End

t was March, over a year after the blog was started, and after Nate and I had gotten back together. I sat on the bed in my second college apartment, my tarot cards in a messy heap in front of me.

"What should I do about this situation?" I asked my deck. "I want to be with both of them for very different reasons."

Three and a half months earlier (at Thanksgiving, of all holidays) I'd stumbled upon evidence that Nate had been cheating on me during the summertime. I was heartbroken, anguished, distraught, and – of course – furious. What had been the point of having a lengthy conversation about what was and wasn't out-of-bounds in our relationship if Nate was going to act unilaterally anyway?

I first considered using magic to get back at him again, but I had a more practical option this time around: I'd told him I'd be striking up a sexual liaison with a woman who I knew was interested in me – Halle – and that he could sit and loyally pine for me. Unfortunately, my revenge hadn't gone according to plan, and I caught feelings for Halle.

I looked down at my cards on the floral quilt, searching for answers. Slowly, I hovered my palms just above each card, searching for some warmth or other energy to draw me to one over the other 78. Finally, one caught my attention, so I plucked it from the pile and turned it around to see its face. The Hanged Man. *Yes, I know I'm at a moment of indecision.* Useless.

The truth was that my deck had always had an attitude. It was something I respected about her, but also made it difficult to want to ask her the tough questions.

"Okay, what about Halle specifically? What would our relationship be like?"

I quickly found another card in the pile that was burning my hand and pulled it out. Eight of Swords. *Trapped, restricted, imprisoned.* Yikes.

I had just seen Halle earlier that evening, and she had more or less begged me to be with her. She pulled out all the stops for me – gazing lovingly into my eyes, stroking my hair, reminding me about how Nate had betrayed my trust by cheating on me, not just once, but on multiple occasions. *He'll never change,* she said. *He's practically an abuser. I'm different.* She rounded out the evening by stating that if I didn't choose her, I'd lose her forever. *It's now or never, Lyra.*

I left her house feeling fairly certain that I wanted to be with her, but that sense of certainty was all too familiar: Two days prior, I stood at the airport in Portland and told Nate I wanted to be with him. *This isn't the last time we're going to see each other. I'm sure of it,* I said.

And so, there I was, sitting on my bed with my 78 tarot cards, trying to see what my deck had to say about my situation.

"Are you absolutely sure about the Eight of Swords? Like, 100% sure about Halle?"

This time, I shook out my palms a couple of times and rubbed them on my clothes to rid them of excess energy before searching for a new card. I hovered my palms above nearly every single one before going back to one card that seemed to stick out from the rest. In the same way that I wanted my deck to be 100% sure that her message was correct, I wanted to be equally sure that I was pulling the right card.

Three of Swords. *Heartbreak, sorrow, trauma.* This was going horribly.

"Alright, fine. Fine. What about Nate?"

This time I had two cards that seemed to be jumping out at me. I pulled the one with slightly more energy transfer first. Three of Cups.

"Yeah, I know he's a cheater. That doesn't help me." I went back and pulled the other card – maybe this one would help clarify. Knight of Cups.

I couldn't help but roll my eyes. I already knew he was the Knight of Cups. He was sensitive and romantic, but also self-obsessed and too involved with his own feelings to ever let me be truly close to him.

I pushed the pile of tarot cards away from me and fell back onto the bed. So, my relationship with Nate would essentially stay the same. By the looks of it, it seemed like it would mostly revolve around his charming personality and penchant to want multiple partners at once (while somehow demanding monogamy from me at the same time). I'd done that for nearly two years in total, and even though it was difficult, I thought I could come to terms with letting him go.

But Halle was different. Sure, there were a few red flags – she was eight years my senior, she had been to jail for two DUIs, she had a long history of substance abuse, she was still on probation for failing her last drug test – but I couldn't understand why my deck would harbor such a grudge against her. She had showered me with affection and romance, and she seemed to always know the right thing to say to reel me back in. I wanted to at least see what life would be like with this person.

Sitting up, I looked at my cards again. "Okay – one last try. Show me what my relationship with Halle would be like." I pulled one final card, silently praying that it wouldn't be as bad as the first two. Third time's the charm, right?

Wheel of Fortune. Good enough for me.

I grabbed my phone and opened up my texts with Nate. I tapped the empty field, then started composing my message to him. *I'm so sorry, I just can't...*

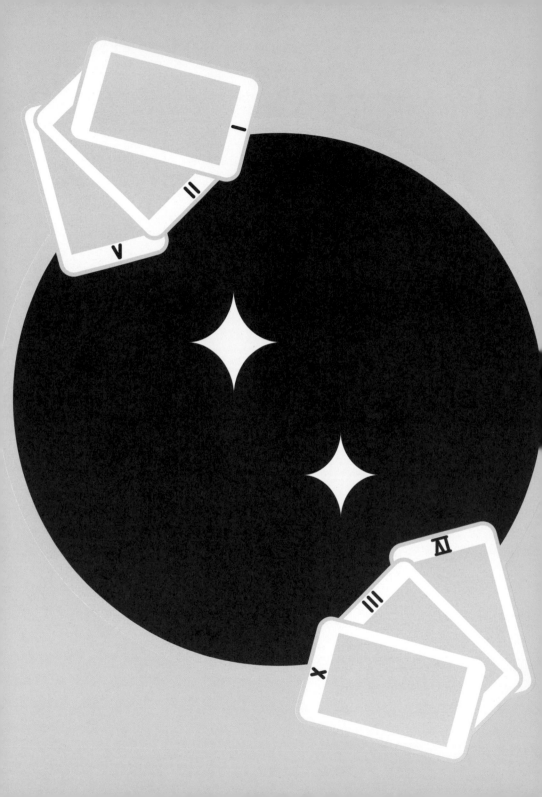

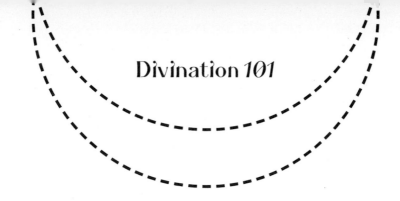

Divination 101

For the uninitiated, divination is any process by which we can gain insight into future events, or the meaning of something, by supernatural means. Tarot is probably the most popular type of divination, and you might also be familiar with palmistry, tea leaf reading, and Norse rune reading. The ever-popular astrology also fits neatly under this definition. Of course, there are literally hundreds of types of divination that have existed throughout human history (if you're ever bored, take a look at the Wikipedia article titled "Methods of divination"), so this chapter is only going to scratch the surface of what divination is and the methods I prefer.

Divination and magic have an interesting relationship. For one, you don't have to be a witch or other magical practitioner to read tarot or use other types of divination, and you don't technically have to use divination if you're practicing witchcraft.

That said, divination is an incredibly useful tool to have in your back pocket when you're a witch, because then you have some way to measure whether or not your spells have been successful. While not all methods are ideal for this, you can essentially use divination as a way to analyze magic and the supernatural world around you. In the same way that today's businesses use data to inform their decisions and help them improve, you can find weak spots in your magic, analyze your performance, and make predictions about how things will change in the near future. Sure, you could go without divination in your practice – but would you really want to?

On top of that, you're also building up your psychic skills when you divine. At least as far as I've experienced, all supernatural events and energies are connected on another plane, and when you tap into that place to practice divination, you develop a better understanding of how to get there and how this other world operates. That way, if you want to engage in astral travel or connect with other beings, you'll have an easier time making it happen than if your experiences with the "other side" were more limited.

Finally, for the recreational witch, giving tarot or astrology readings can be a way for you to feel connected to this part of your life without staging a huge, elaborate ritual. For me, even in years when I barely cast a single spell, I still read natal charts for my friends and colleagues and kept up with tarot reading.

It was my novelty party trick, but it also reminded me that underneath my professional, "adult" veneer, I was still powerful. I could see things that other people couldn't see, and I could do things that other people couldn't do. I was still a witch.

So, while I can't force you to take up divination, I highly recommend trying out different methods and ultimately settling on one or two that work well for you. I'm going to speak about my favorite methods, tarot and astrology, which I use for two different purposes, but if these don't work for you, there are literally thousands of others listed on that monstrous Wikipedia page.

A Brief Introduction
to Tarot

uckily for me, there are numerous excellent books out there on tarot that explain how it works, what all the cards mean, what all the different superstitions are about them, and so on. So, instead of going over all the basics (because that would fill a whole book on its own), I'm just going to give a brief introduction to this method of divination and how I like to use my cards.

If you're already a tarot reader, perhaps my description of sitting on my bed by myself with a large pile of cards in front of me, doing random one-card draws makes you uncomfortable. What if I told you that I bought my own deck? Or that I very rarely use spreads?

There are a lot of superstitions surrounding tarot cards, but as you may have noticed, I ignore almost all of them. (The only thing I'm specific about is that I don't want other people touching my cards.) For me, tarot is an excellent divination method for two reasons: 1) The wide variety of cards gives a lot of nuance to a reading, which I think is harder to achieve with simpler methods but is less open to subconscious feelings than, let's say, scrying (see page 319), and 2) tarot decks, in my experience, have personalities and a sense of intentionality that I don't sense as much with other methods. It's more like having a conversation with a cryptic person than piecing together the universe's puzzle.

With that in mind, let's take a look at the basic tenets of tarot.

The Basics of Tarot

Even if you've never heard of it before, it's probably contextually clear that tarot is a method of divination involving cards. That said, what separates tarot from standard cartomancy (i.e. the use of cards for divination) is that tarot involves a special deck that differs from the standard deck of 52 playing cards. Tarot decks have four suits – Wands, Cups, Swords, and Pentacles in the popular *Rider-Waite* version – that each include 10 numbered cards and four court cards, collectively referred to as the Minor Arcana, and a separate grouping of 22 standalone cards that form the Major Arcana.

Perhaps unsurprising for any history buffs out there, tarot originally started out as a normal card game that can be traced back to at least the 15th century. Meanwhile, the earliest recorded use of tarot cards for esoteric purposes wasn't until 1750. The three most popular versions of tarot decks are the *Rider-Waite* deck (published 1909), *The Thoth Tarot* deck (1969) and the *Tarot de Marseilles* deck (~1650). Of these, the *Rider-Waite* is by far the most popular, and the vast majority of modern decks use this version as the basis for their imagery, card naming, and motifs.

In tarot, the diviner pulls cards out of the deck and typically arranges them into a particular visual pattern, or "spread," wherein certain placements represent different aspects of a narrative. For instance, a simple three-card spread might represent "Past, Present, and Future," or "Thinking, Feeling, and Doing."

Most tarot readers have a shared understanding of the meanings of the cards that is supported by imagery, numerology, and tradition, but many readers also have personal associations with them that deviate from this standard. Generally speaking, the meanings of each card are always somewhat flexible, as most of the understanding you'll draw from a reading comes from the interaction *between* the cards. The card Death looks scary on its own, but if it's situated next to The Lovers in reverse and the Three of Swords, it's fairly obvious that a romantic relationship in your life is probably coming to a close. The theme and context also play a large role: Depending on which subject you're doing a reading for, a card's meaning can shift dramatically. Furthermore, the "people" cards (i.e. the court cards for each of the four suits, and, in some interpretations, the cards in the Major Arcana that show individuals such as The Hermit, The Empress, The Emperor, and so on) quite often take on the role of someone in the reader's life who possesses the same qualities as the card's character.

I'm not going to cover the meanings of each of the cards, because there are *a lot* of cards (78!), and there are already many excellent resources – from books to websites and even apps – out there dedicated solely to teaching this aspect of reading. Instead, I want to briefly cover some of the general themes of the cards.

The bulk of the cards belong to the Minor Arcana: As previously mentioned, these cards are organized into the four suits of Cups, Wands, Swords and Pentacles. Each of these pairs with an element – Cups with water, Wands with fire, Swords with air, and Pentacles with earth – so they're handy to compare with someone's astrological signs (page 314), as well as with the parts of a spell. Each suit also contains 14 cards: 10 numbered cards that start at Ace and go up to 10, plus four court cards, which are Page, Knight, Queen, and King. As I've already noted, the court cards are particularly useful for identifying people in your spread.

The remaining 22 cards make up the Major Arcana. These cards convey standalone ideas, and they're typically a bit more "weighty" when you're reading them compared to the Minor Arcana. These are also likely the cards that come to mind when you think of tarot: Death, The Sun, The Moon, The Devil, Justice, The Lovers, and so on. These cards pull your focus to a major theme in the spread and demand more attention. (They're also typically easier to learn, so I recommend starting with those if you're getting into tarot for the first time.)

Tarot Superstitions

For reasons that are completely beyond me, there's a not-insignificant subset of the tarot community that seemingly has nothing better to do than spout off arbitrary rules. Normally, this isn't that big a deal (I have been giving you license to break rules left and right for the duration of this book), but with tarot, they're especially gate-keeping in their overall impact.

The biggest superstition about tarot is that you can't buy your own tarot deck. Luckily, this myth is slowly starting to die out, but in case you haven't heard the good news yet: You absolutely can buy a tarot deck for yourself. Probably the vast majority of people who are into tarot at this moment bought their first deck for themselves, because unless you were lucky enough to have other esoteric people in your life, there wasn't another option.

Another myth, which is rarely spelled out but almost always implied, is that you should always read in spreads. It's true that spreads can be incredibly useful, as they define roles for the different cards, but you don't *need* to use them. As noted earlier, I regularly dump my cards into a pile and just pull cards out while asking pointed questions. It certainly doesn't look as mysterious as a large, complicated spread done by candlelight, but it works just fine.

There's one last big myth, although I'm more sympathetic to this one. This final superstition says that no-one but you should be touching your tarot cards, or it'll negatively impact the energy of the deck. It is true that if other individuals are touching your cards, they'll leave bits of their energy on them, but this is kind of a moot point because you should be cleansing your tarot deck regularly anyway. In fact, a friend of mine usually has me handle and shuffle their cards before they read for me because they think this is an efficient way to get their cards familiar with my life and circumstances. For me, the only reason I don't like people touching my deck is because I'm a bit of a control freak and I don't want smudgy fingerprints all over my cards.

Using Tarot in
Witchcraft

You might be thinking, "This is nice and all, but what's the upshot of all of this for magic?" Truthfully, you don't need to read tarot to be a witch – but it does make things easier and more fun.

Instead of casting a huge spell in the metaphorical dark, you can ask your deck what kinds of obstacles you might face or how likely your efforts are to succeed. If you've cast a spell on another person but they live far away, you can ask your cards how the spell is developing and how they're feeling. Really, the possibilities in terms of analysis are endless, as long as you're willing to read between the lines and occasionally put up with some cryptic answers.

Practically speaking, tarot also trains your intuition and your ability to recognize patterns – both of which come in handy during spellcasting. If you see a theme from a spread show up during a spell, that's something that should grab your attention and tell you to look closer. The more practice you get at this, the better a witch you'll be.

Finally, I use tarot (and astrology) as a kind of honeypot for magic-skeptical friends. The same person who's willing to critique your esoteric beliefs is also typically quite willing to have their future divined. Everyone loves finding things out about themselves! And if you give a good reading, you'll find that this person might just change their mind.

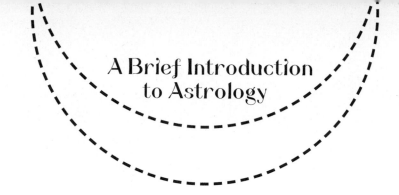

A Brief Introduction to Astrology

ot to put this too harshly, but you'd have to have been living under a rock for the last 30 years to have not heard of astrology. That said, if you're just dipping your toes into magic, you might not know that astrology can be more than unconvincing horoscopes listed at the back of women's fashion magazines, or vague memes that seeming only target Geminis and Scorpios.

As a divination tool, astrology has very different strengths to tarot. It's borderline useless for checking in on how your spells have performed because it can't change or respond to new stimuli.

What it can do, however, is tell you about your strengths and weaknesses, help you identify patterns in your craft, and illuminate trajectories in your life. But before we get to that, let's do a very brief introduction to what astrology really is.

What is Astrology?

Astrology in a general sense is using the movement of celestial bodies to anticipate and analyze events in our tiny human lives. Typically, when we say "astrology," we mean "Western astrology," because there's also Hindu astrology, Chinese astrology, Tibetan astrology, and a variety of other astrological practices that are no longer in use, but were very popular in past societies (e.g. Mayan Astrology).

In practice, astrology is just looking up at the sky from the perspective of Earth (fun fact, astrology is *not* heliocentric) and interpreting how our lives and current events will be influenced based on planets in our solar system and how they move through different zodiac signs (which roughly correspond to various constellations). You can drill down quite far into astrology to also consider houses, cool asteroids, aspects and degrees, and a surprising amount of math – but your average witch will get along fine with just a bit of casual astrological knowledge.

I'm not going to do a deep dive into the subject because, just as with tarot, people can and have filled books much bigger than this one to the brim with information on just this topic. Instead, I'm going to provide a taster in case you're totally new to the subject, a few pointers on good things to know, and some tips about using astrology in your craft.

The Signs of Western Astrology

As an overview, here are the signs and some of their main qualities:

- **Aries.** March 21st–April 19th. A fire sign, Aries is full of energy, will, power, passion, and sometimes aggression. Also, very good at getting their way.
- **Taurus.** April 20th–May 20th. An earth sign, Taurus is laid-back, hedonistic, stubborn, and somehow both lazy and hard-working at the same time. Loves creature comforts.
- **Gemini.** May 21st–June 21st. An air sign, Gemini is quick-witted, funny, flirtatious, eloquent, and notoriously two-faced. (Sorry, Geminis, it's just the truth.)
- **Cancer.** June 22nd–July 22nd. A water sign, Cancer is sensitive, family-oriented, caring, moody, and can cry in self-pity like no other sign in the whole chart.
- **Leo.** July 23rd–August 22nd. Another fire sign, Leo is bold, exuberant, loyal, lavish, selfish, and typically the life of the party. They're also the natural leaders of the bunch.

- **Virgo.** August 23rd–September 22nd. Another earth sign, Virgo is precise, loyal, hard-working, practical, anxiety-ridden and the best sidekick anyone could ask for.
- **Libra.** September 23rd–October 22nd. Another air sign, Libra is funny, eloquent, charming, intelligent, superficial, and even-handed to a fault. Also loves dating other Libras.
- **Scorpio.** October 23rd–November 22nd. A water sign, Scorpio is everything you've heard ascribed to them, which includes sexy, mysterious, vindictive, and somewhat unhinged.
- **Sagittarius.** November 23rd–December 21st. The last fire sign, Sagittarius is fun-loving, flighty, quick, energetic, and likable, but typically lacks any kind of follow-through.
- **Capricorn.** December 22nd–January 19th. The last earth sign, Capricorn is serious, family-oriented, materialistic, success-driven, and the workaholic of the signs.
- **Aquarius.** January 21st–February 18th. A surprise air sign, Aquarius is sharp, forward-thinking, stubborn, dogmatic, and contrarian. Basically, the elitist professor of the group.
- **Pisces.** February 19th–March 20th. The last water sign, Pisces is idealistic, creative, empathetic, moody, and sensitive. They can also have a surprisingly two-faced quality to them.

There is a bit of squabbling about these precise dates, as some people will tell you that Taurus actually runs until May 21, or Sagittarius really starts on November 22, and so on. I have precisely zero interest in wading into this fight, because for me (and a large portion of other astrology fans) it's a moot point anyway. That's because I believe in the concept of *cusps* – planetary placements that are between two signs and therefore which pick up characteristics from both. In this paradigm, it doesn't matter if you're "officially" a Taurus or a Gemini if your birthday is May 21, because you're going to end up being a mix of both signs either way.

Now, that might not seem all that controversial at first glance, but the concept of cusps and *cusping* (the verb form) is actually extremely contentious within the astrology community. I've gotten in my fair share of heated disagreements with people about whether or not cusping is real, but now I have my own esoteric book and I can fill it with whatever astrological propaganda I see fit.

Elements of the Signs

One clear point of overlap between the magic I've talked about and astrology is the fact that they both use elements. (The same is true of tarot, if you recall from a few pages back). If you think back to the section on building an altar (page 77), it's common for witches to dedicate our altars to the four elements: fire, air, water, and earth. These same four elements pop up here, too.

In astrology, these elements are used to group different signs together by their shared characteristics. For instance:

- The three **fire signs** are Aries, Leo, and Sagittarius. They are all marked by their action-oriented personalities, overabundance of energy, passion, and warmth.
- The three **air signs** are Gemini, Libra, and Aquarius. These signs are known for their intelligence, communication skills, eloquence, and interest in ideas.
- The three **water signs** are Cancer, Scorpio, and Pisces. These three are delineated by their sensitivity, empathy, intuition, and general connection to their emotions.
- And finally, the three **earth signs** are Taurus, Virgo, and Capricorn. They are marked by their pragmatism, work ethic, material focus, and being the most grounded.

This can be very helpful for developing pattern recognition in your craft. If you have a sign that is overly dominant in your chart (let's say Virgo), you might notice that certain tarot cards come up more frequently (like the suit of Pentacles), and that you make for a better-than-average Green Witch. This is likely because you have a significant amount of earth element in your chart. So, when these earth aspects pop up during spell casting (or divination, or dreams), you can take note of them and better contextualize them.

The Natal Chart

When someone is into astrology, they typically don't just know their Sun sign (which is what most people are asking for when they say, "What's your sign?"), but rather, their whole natal chart. Also known as a "birth chart," this is the complete list of planets in the solar system, each with their corresponding sign. To make one, you need to know your birthday, the city you were born in, and the time you were born. (And luckily for us, we live in the age of computers, so we can easily have our natal charts generated for us, and don't need to spend days doing complex math to chart it all by hand.)

To take my chart as an example, this will end up sounding something like: My Sun is in Aquarius, while my Moon is in Leo, and my Ascendant is cusping between Libra and Scorpio. (Your ascendant sign is the sign on the horizon at the time you were born.) Meanwhile, my Mercury is in Aquarius, my Mars is in Leo, and my Venus is in Capricorn etc. – all the way until we get to Pluto, and then maybe we could talk asteroids for fun.

I could write a whole separate book about these planets, what they mean, how they interact with each other, and so on. For this book, however, I'm just going to focus on the first triad, which includes your Sun, your Moon, and your Ascendant.

- Ø Your **Sun** sign is probably the one you consider yourself to be. This is likely *the* biggest influence on your personality, and the "foundation" that everything else gets built on top of. That said, if you read the description of your Sun sign and it sounds nothing like you, the rest of your chart could be dominated by different signs.
- Ø The **Moon** sign reflects a more emotional, less conscious part of yourself. It's who you are around your loved ones, and the personality you fall back on when you're filled with emotion. It probably impacts how you love, get angry, and view yourself.
- Ø The **Ascendant** is trickier to pin down, but it's often described as "a mask you wear," or a version of yourself that you adopt when you feel less comfortable. It's probably how you seem to people when you first meet them, or when you're at work with colleagues.

Like the Sun sign, these other two (and all the other planets in the chart) are filtered through different zodiac signs to pick up a variety of characteristics, tendencies, and outlooks. The complete natal chart should encapsulate all the different parts of your personality, but this first triad is a good place to start.

Astrology and Witchcraft

Admittedly, I've spent most of this book focused on the practicalities of witchcraft: what to do, what not to do, things to watch out for, and recollections of things I did, so that you could learn from them.

But magic is more than just actions and producing results. It's also a way of thinking and interacting with the world.

This is where I think astrology is the most applicable in magic. It's a really useful esoteric framework through which you can interpret events, gain a greater understanding of yourself, and anticipate challenges in your life. Of course, you could use religion or any number of secular ideologies for this, too, but personally, I always found it helpful to have a spiritual framework to tap into when trying to analyze esoteric occurrences.

Plus, as with tarot, many people who would otherwise think witchcraft was a bit too far out there for them can get really into astrology. If you have a friend who gives you a hard time about your magic, I recommend giving them a natal chart reading. You'll find that many people come back with a more open mind once you've helped them discover something about themselves.

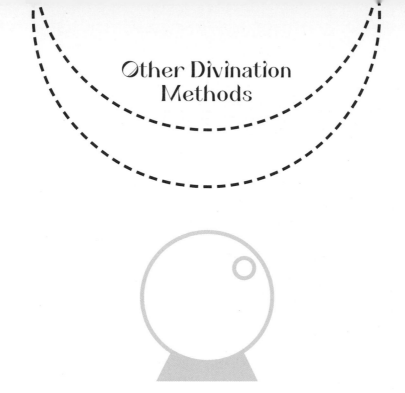

Other Divination Methods

As noted at the beginning of this chapter, there are literally hundreds of divination methods out there, and as such, something out there for everyone. That said, let's go over just some of the most popular types of divination available, in case tarot and astrology didn't appeal to you.

Scrying

Whether you know this term or not, scrying is one of the types of divination most people are familiar with, as this is what you do with a "magic crystal ball."

The word *scry* comes from *descry*, meaning "to catch sight of," and to "scry something" is essentially to *see* something. That is the essence of scrying: You are looking into an object and trying to ascertain meaning from amorphous shapes, or you're staring into something so long that images start popping into your brain.

Scrying isn't just limited to crystal balls, though. You can scry in mirrors, in dimly lit water, in fire, in other crystal shapes, or basically any other light-distorting object.

Pendulum Dowsing

Sorry to all the people out there who like to divine with a pendulum, but this is my least favorite divination practice of the bunch. In this method, you take a pendulum (or any necklace with a heavy pendant on it) and lightly swing it over something to get yes or no answers to your questions. Some people read with a pendulum board that marks out "yes" and "no" for them, but others will read over a sheet of paper, or even their own hand.

There's nothing wrong with dowsing if it works well for you, but for me, there are two potential issues: 1) I need more nuance in my divination than simply "yes" or "no," and 2) I don't trust my own subconscious not to influence how I'm reading something. It's your own hand that has all the control here, and so you really need to trust yourself if you use this method.

Tea Leaf Reading

Tea leaf reading is another option that shows up in pop culture now and then. The quick-and-dirty overview of how to read tea leaves is that you get yourself a cute cup and saucer, drink some loose leaf tea, and then read the leaves left in the cup when you're done drinking. Easy, right?

Unfortunately, it's actually not so easy. For one, drinking loose leaf tea that's not contained in a mesh sieve or other infusion device is not a very pleasant experience. Then, you must leave just the right amount of liquid in your cup after drinking, as you'll be swishing the leaves around and turning the cup over to get a good spread of symbols. If you leave too much liquid, you'll spill tea over your things (and yourself), but if you leave too little, you'll just have a big, unreadable blob of leaves at the bottom of your cup. Even if it all goes well, you still have to discern meaning out of those leaf-blobs.

Personal experience also persuaded me against tea leaf reading. I once purchased a beautiful set of cups and saucers specifically for this type of divination at a local antique mall. Unfortunately, it had six saucers, but only five cups. I spent months looking for a replacement cup to complete the set, to no avail. Then, one time when Rhea and I were visiting Nate in Portland, I saw a lone tea leaf reading cup in Nate's cabinet that matched perfectly with the set. It felt like the stars had finally aligned.

The only issue was that it belonged to Nate's roommate, Joey. He refused to let me buy it from him – although he never used it. Yet, he seemed to have no problem with the concept of using other people's things, considering that he continued to use Rhea's Netflix account on his laptop for five years – without her knowledge. Now, I no longer read tea leaves.

Rune Reading

Rune reading is the act of taking runes, tossing them in patterns, and then analyzing how they fall to gain insight into the future. But first off – what are runes? Technically, runes are just letters (also known as the Norse alphabet or runic alphabet) that were used in Germanic-speaking parts of the world before the Latin alphabet took over. However, when we talk about "rune reading," what we're really referring to are little objects made out of stone, wood, crystal, or clay that are inlaid with these Norse runes. The reader "casts" them on a cloth or on the ground and interprets meaning from the patterns. This form of divination is most popular with those who are Norse pagans.

In a similar vein, I'm also going to mention ogham staves here, because they work in an analogous way. Ogham staves are simply sticks that have been sanded down and carved with the ogham alphabet, or the alphabet used to write Old Irish. As with runes, the reader will divine with them by tossing the staves and then interpreting their meaning from what pattern the sticks fall into. This divination method is most popular with followers of a Celtic pagan path.

Oracle Decks

The spunky younger sister of tarot is the oracle deck. Unlike tarot, oracle decks are unstandardized cards made for the purposes of divination, and most of these decks are quite distinct from each other. They also typically have fewer cards than tarot decks, making them easier to learn for beginners.

In this period of witchcraft revival, oracle decks are having a real moment, as many artists are making their own and selling them online. There are some seriously beautiful decks out there and they can be a great starting point for newbies who want to get into tarot – but their major downside is that, because they're unstandardized, they're a less social divination method. Your friend won't be able to weigh in on their reading as easily, and sometimes that's half the fun of giving another witch a tarot reading.

Closing

Rhea and I started the *Recreational Witchcraft* blog because we believed we had something to add to the conversation: that magic wasn't just one thing, that there wasn't one right way of practicing, and that there wasn't only a single type of person who became a witch. We wanted to make something fun, girly, personal, and unorthodox.

In an ironic twist of fate, it was the fact that so many people resonated with this idea of "recreational magic" that slowly undid our operation. Running our blog morphed from a fun hobby into a full-time (unpaid) job. It helped that we shared this labor between two people, but we were two people going to college full-time, with internships and part-time jobs to boot.

Maintaining *Recreational Witchcraft* was a never-ending to do list. We had to brainstorm new content, which meant constantly searching for inspiration and texting ideas back and forth. Once we settled on an idea we liked, we wrote it out, tested it, and tweaked it. We had to figure out how to photograph it in an aesthetically pleasing and "on brand" way. We planned around the normal calendar year, the seasons, the Wheel of the Year, and astrological events, lest we be overshadowed by another blog or overlook an opportunity to gain new followers. Then, it all needed to be edited, uploaded, QA'd, and scheduled.

Luckily, the platform we used also heavily incentivized users to circulate other blogs' content. That helped lessen the burden, but the tradeoff was that we had an inbox that needed to be attended to regularly. We'd wake up to dozens of questions and comments every day – some were heartfelt and appreciative, but the majority were asking how to adapt spells or make simple modifications. The most emotionally draining questions were those asking about how to leave an abusive relationship, or use magic to perform an abortion, or heal trauma. These messages weighed on us because there was nothing substantive that we could do: magic could help, but it wasn't a substitute for medical or mental health treatment. It was also heartbreaking to realize that, for many of our followers, we may have been the closest thing to support that they had.

On top of everything else, our blog about magic took away time from doing actual magic. At a certain point, we were only trialing spells to see if they were effective enough to post about them. The big rituals fell by the wayside, as did our wild adventures.

The stress and monotony got to Rhea first, for practical as well as emotional reasons. For one, she was the photographer for our blog. New images had to be planned around the right time of day to ensure good lighting, which ate up early evenings and weekends. She could do what I did, but her skills were irreplaceable. She was also getting married, and therefore had bigger personal priorities than making sure we kept our blog running.

If our descent into magic could be best described as a whirlwind romance, then the dissolution of our blog – and our coven and friendship along with it – was more of a slow fade-out.

I could sense Rhea slowly becoming less interested in what we were doing, and I was increasingly picking up more of the burden for planning and scheduling content. It was unambiguous that *something* was wrong, but I didn't want to ask *what*. That would mean dealing with Rhea leaving the blog, and I wanted to avoid that at all costs.

Instead, after weeks of me becoming gradually more irritable and passive-aggressively nudging Rhea to help me, I received a letter in my email inbox from her. It was what I had feared: She said she wasn't interested in the blog any longer. She suggested that we meet in person to discuss it, but it was clear even before I showed up at her house that the outcome was a foregone conclusion.

I would love to write that we spoke honestly and worked through our perspectives productively, but that wouldn't be true. We were both bitter and angry. We both felt let down. We were both right in our own ways.

I tried to keep the blog running for another six months by myself, but it was heavy. I couldn't log in without feeling sad and resentful towards Rhea.

Of course, the obvious answer was for me to quit as well, but I felt an obligation to the people who loved our posts, and I also liked the satisfaction of pulling up our daily analytics and quantifying how good a job I was doing. Sure, my relationship with Halle was a disaster, I still missed Nate, I lost my best friend, and my grades were slipping, *but did you see that 30,000 people engaged with my posts today?* It was addictive, even if it was a trap.

It was around Christmas when I finally gave up. I hadn't gone to Rhea's wedding, Donald Trump had been elected President a couple months previously, and everything around me felt overturned and in disarray. On the blog, I misread something another blogger had written and picked a fight over it, only to realize my stupidity soon after. It finally pushed me over the edge.

I immediately deleted the app from my phone and pushed the blog as far from my daily life as possible. I didn't look at our analytics, I didn't log in at all. I wanted to pretend that it never happened.

It was also too painful to return to witchcraft.

Practicing reminded me of a time and place in my life where I felt loved and connected to those around me – like passing the stalls of fortune tellers at the Renaissance Faire years before and recalling the hope and possibility I once felt. It stung badly. I put all my magic materials in a box in my childhood bedroom and tucked it away.

It took several years for magic to slowly come back into my life. I gave astrology readings at work, then started doing tarot readings for friends. I found other witches by happenstance, even though I had moved myself halfway around the globe. They told me their stories of their time practicing – sometimes very familiar, other times entirely new. I heard tales about working with deities, having sex in trance states, and stumbling upon cities their friends had built in the astral plane. These stories filled me with awe and made me wonder what my life could be like if I traveled again into this secret world.

For me, stories were always the main draw of magic. They continually pull me back in, even if the circumstances of my life are always changing.

This book represents just one turn of the wheel of my journey in witchcraft. I imagine there will be many more rotations over the course of my life, and I will return to these stories for inspiration, nostalgia, and possibilities. I say this not because my experiences are particularly spellbinding or unique, but because magic has the potential to capture our imagination.

I hope that you got something out of all of this, and that someday, you also reminisce over your adventures in witchcraft. I hope you go on to tell other people about your magical successes and failures.

More than anything, I hope that – eventually – we might realize that witchcraft is for everyone.

Recreatio

ft Witcho

onal Recr

Witchcra